The Retailer's Guide to
Loss Prevention and Security

Donald J. Horan, C.P.P.

CRC Press
Boca Raton   New York   London   Tokyo

Publisher:	Robert B. Stern
Editorial Assistant:	Jean Jarboe
Project Editor:	Helen Linna
Marketing Manager:	Greg Daurelle
Direct Marketing Manager:	Bill Boone
Cover design:	Denise Craig
PrePress:	Carlos Esser
Manufacturing:	Sheri Schwartz

Library of Congress Cataloging-in-Publication Data

Horan, Donald J.
    The retailer's guide to loss prevention and security / Donald J. Horan
        p. cm.
    Includes index.
    ISBN 0-8493-8110-2
    1. Retailing-loss prevention. I. Horan, Donald J. II. Title.
HV8079.C65C59 1996
363.2′5.493   96-54326
                                                         CIP

No claim to original U.S. Government works
International Standard Book Number 0-8493-8110-2
Library of Congress Card Number 96-54326
Printed in the United States of America 1 2 3 4 5 6 7 8 9 0
Printed on acid-free paper

Contents

The Author   v
Acknowledgments   vii
Introduction   ix

SECTION I
Elements of Physical Security

Overview   1

1   Locking Hardware   3

2   Alarm Systems   27

3   Electronic Article Surveillance   53

4   Closed Circuit Television   67

5   Guard Force Management   79

SECTION II
Loss Prevention Programs

Overview   89

6   Employee Awareness   91

7   Audit Programs   101

8   Shoplifting Prevention   111

9   Employee Dishonesty   121

10   Sales Audit   133

SECTION III
The Finer Points

Overview   145
11 Investigation and Interview   147
12 Civil Liability   167
13 Robbery Prevention   177
14 Scams, Frauds, and Bouncing Checks   197
15 Civil Recovery and Civil Demand   205
16 Violence in the Workplace   209

SECTION IV
Security Operations

Overview   219
17 Incident Reports   221
18 Apprehension Criteria   227
19 Prosecution Criteria   237
20 Criminal Trespass   245
21 Interaction with Law Enforcement   251
22 Crisis Management   261

Index   271

The Author

Donald J. Horan, President of Loss Control Concepts, Ltd., lends his vast experience in the retail business and as a loss prevention consultant to this book. Designated a Certified Protection Professional by the American Society for Industrial Security, he has directed and managed retail loss prevention programs all over the U.S. for major department stores and specialty chains, and has provided his expertise to a host of client companies during his tenure with the National Loss Prevention Bureau. Most recently, he served as a security training instructor for the Atlanta Committee for the Olympic Games and was the Director of Security for venue retail operations for the 1996 Centennial Olympic Games in Atlanta. Donald Horan's practical experience fills this book with all the tips, strategies, and procedures you need to create an effective loss prevention program.

Acknowledgments

It is appropriate in this section of the book to identify and thank those who were instrumental in the development and production of this work. The material presented here is the culmination of the author's professional association with department store and specialty store retailers, and the talented people whose progressive thinking and tireless energy brought about the transition of loss prevention and security from a cost center to a viable mechanism for profit enhancement.

I owe a great debt of gratitude to the organization at Macy's New York, in whose employ I began my career in retail security. The learning environment there provided the exposure, resources, and mentoring that enhanced those fortunate enough to cross paths with some of the best in the business. Of the dozens of people there that contributed to my personal and professional growth, I would like to thank Dick Johnston, Sam Taylor, Tom Hudson, Ray Loeffler and Katherine "Kay" Wynn for their patience, trust, and guiding hands.

I owe much to subsequent employers as well. The May Company, where I benefited from the drive of Hahne's Chairman Donald Boyle and the wisdom of the sage Phil Smith. And to the memorable B. Altman & Company and its President Jack Schultz, who brought my show back to Broadway. As my professional emphasis moved from department store to specialty store retailing, I had the good fortune to be mentored through this transition by Bob Deevey, a gentleman who embodied the principles of user-friendly loss prevention.

Throughout the work there is mention of the interaction among related disciplines in the retail industry which are supported by the loss prevention function: merchandising, operations, human resources, finance and MIS. Evident among them is the overlap between the security and personnel functions in the retail business, and I am grateful to the human resources executives that shared with me insight into their world, most notably, Ed Scheiblin, Cindy Gibeau, Jim Rolek, Carol Dudgeon, and Al Hagaman.

I have also been privileged to work for and with some of the finest merchants, controllers, and store operators in the industry, among them Michael Becker, William McCarthy, Donald Eugene, Arthur Matura, Frank DePaola, Steven Redshaw, Brian Higgins, Jim Jecker, and especially, David Seim.

The reader will note several chapters in the book that required collaboration with providers of security resources and I am grateful to those who have shared their expertise on the application of security products and services over the years: Robert Thompson, Arthur Rothbaum, David Waxman, Stanley Kirsch, Robert Larkin, Michael McGregor, Homer Moreno, Howard Lass, David Malefsky, and Robert Sprouhl.

I am particularly appreciative of my long-time association with Robert L. Barry, Esq., President of the National Loss Prevention Bureau for his peerless efforts in educating retailers and training loss prevention practitioners.

I am similarly grateful to my colleagues in the industry who have supported this endeavor by critiquing select chapters of the book and my thanks go out to Patrick Ancil, Douglas Wicklander, David Zulawski, Brian Fuller, Jerry Merritt, and John Schmitz.

A personal thanks goes out to Douglas Otis; confidante, tactician, and architect of the "beau geste" stratagem. And a closing note for my brief, but enlightening, association with Bob Kimbrell at Blockbuster Music & Video, without which I would not have realized how badly this book was needed.

Introduction

- *Protect assets from loss.*
- *Secure facilities from trespass.*
- *Investigate criminal activity.*

This has been the purview of loss prevention (LP) programs in the retail business since its inception. And no field of expertise in retailing has had to adapt its methodology more thoroughly, more rapidly, than within the province of loss prevention.

Protecting assets from loss could traditionally be accomplished with the implementation of recommendations that limit exposure of merchandise to theft. The application of physical security measures, a combination of electronic devices and locking hardware, adequately secured facilities from trespass. Staff professionals, trained to investigate losses and interview suspects, detected and resolved incidents of criminal activity; usually in conjunction with law enforcement agencies.

It is the spectrum of these responsibilities that has dramatically changed. Adaptation to the incredibly competitive retail business, its downsizing and restructuring, its specialized market niches, and its reliance on management information systems to drive the business; have all impacted significantly on the conventional practices listed above.

For progressive retailers, the impact of LP recommendations that protect merchandise from theft must be evaluated against the potential of that protection to inhibit sales. The escalating cost and reliability of more sophisticated alarm systems, as well as requirements that locking hardware facilitate security *and* meet prescribed code, each present challenges to providing premises security. And the exposure to liability inherent in conducting in-house investigations, in addition to the reticence of law enforcement agencies to provide resources in assisting those investigations, have rendered proven methods of inquiry obsolete.

What had been the slam-dunk, no-brainer solutions to security problems in the past have run headlong into the charged issues of today: focus group preferences for merchandise presentation, regulatory compliance to local ordinance, and the ramifications of litigation.

It is within the confines of this modern-era arena that loss prevention professionals must fashion their program policies, still accountable to the traditional mission, but bound by new rules of engagement.

Section I

Elements of Physical Security

Overview

Physical security measures are the first line of defense for protecting your assets. From the most sophisticated electronic software to the simple hasp and padlock, physical security systems are task-intensive, and as such require vigilance to be effective.

It is therefore imperative to understand the needs of your business first, in order to properly evaluate the type of security system that will best meet those needs. For a retailer, these needs can be defined in very general terms: merchandise must be accessible to customers and staff without being overly-exposed to loss. The building must be easily accessible to the general public during business hours, offer partial access for employees during nonselling hours, and be secured from unauthorized entry during the closed hours.

The resources available to protect merchandise involve placing barriers between the customer and the product. Glass showcases that require merchandise to be shown have always been effective in preventing theft, and make for an atmosphere where a sales person would sell an item. The costly staffing demands of such a concept, however, has required more and more merchandise to be presented for self-service, and the sales person to act in the less glamorous, but more productive, role of cashier. This made merchandise more vulnerable, but volume sales were enhanced, productivity was increased, overhead was reduced, and floor space was more efficiently used to display the product.

Innovation in fixturing was the next logical progression. Locking devices were fashioned and applied to fixtures in order to protect merchandise displayed on open sell. Lockable plexiglass bins containing accessories-type products appeared, as well as counter top fixtures that held handbags, costume jewelry, and leather goods. When the fixtures themselves were stolen, retailers responded by securing the fixture to the showcase. The war was on, and the arms race had begun.

Determined to maintain a self-service environment, fixturing continued to develop so that customers could touch and feel the product, but not leave with it. Other devices that permitted the removal of stackable merchandise only one item at a time were trendy for a while. Cables and locks were adapted to ready-to-wear fixtures to prevent the garment's complete removal from the rack. Electronic apparatus next appeared, designed to enhance physical security devices by sounding an alarm if the locking mechanisms were tampered with. Soon, hardware enveloped the inventory and all was presumed safe.

In a perfect world, all would be safe. But what renders these systems ineffective brings us back to the needs of the business. In a vacuum, each of these progressive steps of protection had merit. In practice, however, the process required disciplines and maintenance that outstripped the resources. A lock would be broken and not repaired. A key would be lost and not replaced. A battery would die and the alarm would not beep. The level of diligence required to reap the protective rewards of such hardware investments is at times inconsistent with the day-to-day operation of a large retail operation. What was expected was often not inspected, and the protection broke down.

The retailers have to make certain that the security systems put in place are compatible with both the strengths and weaknesses of their operation. Checks and balances have to be considered, and the quality of training, the level of supervision, and management's resolve to commit resources to support security initiatives have to be evaluated.

To introduce by edict task-related security measures into an intense, performance-driven retail environment dedicated to pushing sales up and costs down is delusive. Before a company can rely on any security system, or any set of procedures, standards, and requirements to deliver asset protection, it must first be certain that the desire and discipline necessary to achieve compliance exists in abundant supply.

Designing premises security — protecting the building — differs slightly in that the process to secure a facility is more procedure-driven, rather than task related. However, the same onus on compliance applies. Users have designated entrances and entry times, but again, the needs of the business are often in conflict with the routines of security.

Due to the reactionary nature of the retail business, access to the store is governed more by the frenzied demands of retail preparation, promotion, and competition than by any ironclad schedule. As such, physical security systems must be flexible in order to accommodate the retailer's urgency to respond to trends and opportunities in the market. A rigid security system inevitably leads to rule by exception, and an eventual breakdown of the controls presumed to be in place.

It is therefore incumbent upon the user of the physical security systems described in the foregoing chapters to assess options in the context of operational compatibility, and to recognize that the advantages and limitations of these systems are subject to the priorities of decision makers in the field.

Locking Hardware

1

As suggested in the introduction to this section, applications of locking hardware in a retail setting must conform to the needs of the business to be effective. The diversity of a retail environment suggests varying degrees of locking requirements: areas accessible to the public vs. areas off-limits to customers; perimeter (entrance/exit) considerations vs. interior security (showcases/stockrooms); areas restricted to all but select employees (management staff); and the needs of the home office and security for corporate headquarters vs. the needs of a distribution center/warehouse facility vs. the needs of a branch store in the field. (Figure 1).

Each element of a retail operation presents its own demands for protection, and the astute loss prevention planner must consider the locking hardware applications that control exposure without impeding authorized access and usage. More simply stated, the locking scheme developed has to permit entry to authorized personnel who run the business, and deny access to all others in order to safeguard the assets.

Identifying appropriate locking mechanisms, supervising their installation, establishing accountable key control, and auditing for compliance (to ensure proper care is taken by staff personnel entrusted to secure the premises) are the four components of management's responsibility we will examine in this chapter. As fundamental as this subject matter may be to physical security, its presentation offers a valuable lesson in loss prevention program development, implementation, and management, and provides a model from which the more complex shortage control initiatives can be launched.

Identifying the appropriate locking mechanisms comprises the program development stage. Ideally, loss prevention and operations must collaborate on a system that provides the level of security necessary to protect property yet facilitates normal business operations. It is the nature of the retail business for personnel to have temporary access to various locations. The transitory

MASTERKEYED SECURITY

PADLOCKS

KEY AND CORE CONTROL

MORTISE LOCKSETS

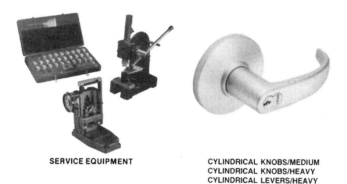
SERVICE EQUIPMENT

CYLINDRICAL KNOBS/MEDIUM
CYLINDRICAL KNOBS/HEAVY
CYLINDRICAL LEVERS/HEAVY

Figure 1 Security hardware. (Courtesy of Best Lock Corporation, Indianapolis, IN.)

nature of management appointments in the retail industry make this a reality of the business which must be provided for when developing locking systems.

For branch stores, perimeter access is required by each member of management charged with opening or closing responsibilities. For this reason, locksets which accommodate multiple users are required; and systems that

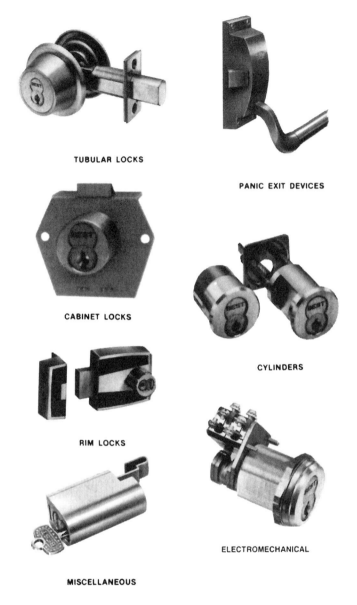

TUBULAR LOCKS

PANIC EXIT DEVICES

CABINET LOCKS

CYLINDERS

RIM LOCKS

ELECTROMECHANICAL

MISCELLANEOUS

Figure 1 (continued).

permit control of the multiple users via interchangeable cores are recommended. (Figure 2)

First, we should review some locksmith terminology: the key is placed
into a chamber, or housing, called a core. Cores are the "figure 8"-shaped
removable entry points for lock cylinders into which the key is inserted. The
core has a preset code of pins that conform to the "cuts" of the operating key

Figure 2   Removable cores. (Courtesy of Best Lock Corporation, Indianapolis, IN.)

and are uniquely "milled" to match up first with the specific keyway, and second, to the individual key codes designated for that keyway. Once the correct key is inserted into the core, turning it aligns the tumblers to rotate the cylinder which deploys or retracts the bolt. (Figures 3–5)

In your house, if you lose your keys or if they are stolen, you must get the locks changed in order ensure unauthorized persons cannot enter your home. That is because your house key operates the lock cylinder. With a commercial locking system, the key does not operate the cylinder, but instead operates the core which acts upon the cylinder. Therefore, entire lock mechanisms do not have to be replaced in the event keys are lost or stolen; only the core has to be changed to render the missing key inoperative. Changing a core requires no special locksmithing skill. A special key, known as a control key, operates a control lug that slides cores in and out of the cylinder, thus making retailers self-sufficient in key control.

The lock mechanism itself need not be a state-of-the-art, pick-proof testimonial to locksmith technology. This is because the locks on the perimeter should be supplemented by an internal alarm system. The most sophisticated, extravagant locking device available can be defeated by a brick through the window, so a locked perimeter is only a first line of defense, not the entire arsenal you need to place between trespassers and your premises.

Commercial grade, heavy-duty locksets with mortise cylinders and extended deadbolts are traditionally prescribed for entrances to retail establishments (Figure 6). For double doors, upper and lower latchsets secure one door in place, while a deadbolt lock is recessed into the door frame and operated with a key from the outside. Unlocking the door from the inside is facilitated by either a thumb-turn knob or interior keyway. The choice between thumb-turn or keyway is not the matter of casual preference it may

Figure 3 Standard mortise cylinder. (Courtesy of Best Lock Corporation, India-napolis, IN.)

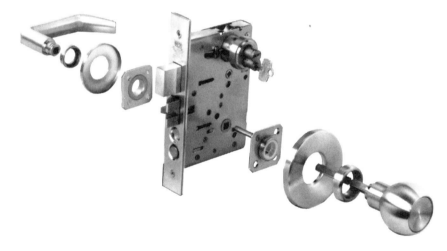

Figure 4 Mortise lockset. (Courtesy of Best Lock Corporation, Indianapolis, IN.)

seem at first glance, but rather a good illustration of how your priorities can become convoluted between operations, security, and local building code.

Originally, the thumb-turn release was employed to lock and unlock customer doors from the inside (Figure 7) so workers who did not have building keys could still see customers out at closing and secure the door behind them. This allowed the manager to tend to other closing duties while an employee handled the task of door monitor. Experience, however, soon taught us that dishonest employees could seize this opportunity to move merchandise out to their cars while the manager was occupied with other matters in the office.

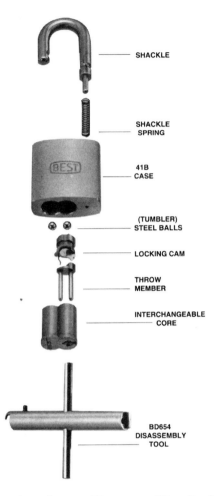

Figure 5   Padlock repair and parts. (Courtesy of Best Lock Corporation, Indianapolis, IN.)

Loss prevention therefore recommended that interior key locks replace the turn-knobs so only trusted employees or "keyholders" would be able to unlock the door after hours. Some fire departments, however, felt key-locked interior doors posed an unnecessary risk of trapping a person inside a locked store during a fire; and that egress must be provided without needing a key to exit. Once the turn-knobs were back in vogue, retailers had to cope with a new exposure, one more problematic than employees surreptitiously carrying merchandise to their cars after hours.

As armed robberies increased, police were reporting the perpetrators of these crimes had begun using the turn-knob to lock the customer doors once

Figure 6   Tubular lock deadbolt. (Courtesy of Best Lock Corporation, Indianapolis, IN.)

Figure 7   Turnknob cylinder. (Courtesy of Best Lock Corporation, Indianapolis, IN.)

they were inside; effectively shutting off the crime from outside interruption. As robbers became more bold — herding employees into back rooms, waiting while the contents of the safe were handed over, and committing assaults — the turn-knob door lock became an ally of the bad guy, and many companies vulnerable to armed robberies heeded police advice and returned to the inside keyway.

Balancing the merits of one approach against another requires a coordinated effort to select hardware that is adaptable to changing priorities, codes, and circumstances.

The quality of the lock and cylinder should be determined from a maintenance perspective as well as security specifications. Paying for quality parts that are functional, durable, and weather-resistant is prudent operationally; you are more likely to encounter security problems from inoperative locks than you are from defeated locks. Metal plates mounted over the exterior locking mechanism protect the lock and bolt from tampering, and give an appearance of heightened security measures to potential intruders.

Avoid overkill when planning locksets for interior use: stockrooms, showcases, offices, etc. Think of the instances where you have seen a heavy-gauge steel lockset mounted on a hollow stockroom door in a plywood door frame in a sheet rock wall. No matter how expensive and strong the lock, the doorjamb would easily shatter with one swift kick, rendering the lock extraneous. Instead, plan interior locksets to be compatible with building construction and able to prevent undetected entry. Interior locksets should be sturdy enough to thwart the opportunist, yet tell-tale in defeat at the hands of a determined intruder to be readily detectable Figures 8–10).

Once locksets are in place, retailers have another opportunity to control access with a keying schedule that restricts areas from unauthorized access. It is impractical to saddle managers and employees with a jailer-ring of keys, so a master-key system is usually employed to allow single keys to open multiple locks (Figure 11a,b). For instance, if a bay of showcases contains three pairs of sliding doors, the locking mechanism for the doors can be keyed alike, on an interior key code to permit the user access to all three showcases with a single key. In this example, the key code could be A-1.

For another set of showcases on the other side of the store, the sliding doors could be secured with locks coded A-2. A-1 keys would operate only A-1 locks; A-2 only A-2. But the manager (or employee designated to have access to both showcase bays) could have an A-Master key, able to open all locks coded in the A series.

In another illustration for a keying scheme for the back of the house, the common entry stockroom door could be designated B-1. Each employee with business in the stockroom would have access to a B-1 key. The manager's office could be keyed B-2, with assistant managers given a key coded B 1/2, permitting entry to both the stockroom and the office with one key.

Figure 8 Cylindrical locks. (Courtesy of Best Lock Corporation, Indianapolis, IN.)

Figure 9 Cylindrical locks (exploded view). (Courtesy of Best Lock Corporation, Indianapolis, IN.)

Within the manager's office could be a lockable cabinet containing records or documents that should be for the store manager's eyes only. This cabinet could be keyed B-3, with the manager having a B Master key allowing entry into the stockroom, the office, and the cabinet.

Interchangeable cores are most useful for key control on perimeter locks: front and back doors. One lesson retailers have learned in the specialty store environment is to keep a spare set of cores on hand at all times in order to "swap out" perimeter cores without delay.

Suppose store #123 has a perimeter keyway coded P123-1. Copies of the P123-1 key are given to management personnel assigned opening and closing duties, and operate the front door and rear emergency exit. Let's further assume that one day this perimeter key is lost by a keyholder outside of the store. The store manager should be equipped to use a "control key," or core-puller, to remove the P123-1 cores and replace them with a back-up set of cores, perhaps coded P123-2. Now the finder of the lost P123-1 key will be unable to use it on the new P123-2 cores to gain unauthorized access.

Figure 10   Series exploded view. (Courtesy of Best Lock Corporation, Indian-apolis, IN.)

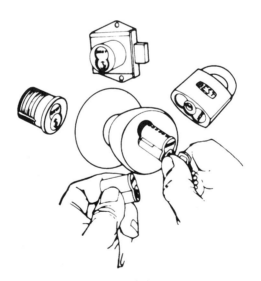

Figure 11(a)   The masterkeyed system employs a standard removable core that is interchangeable with any type, size, or style of lock. Each core contains a pin-tumbler combination: a single control key removes any core and inserts a new core with a new combination. (Courtesy of Best Lock Corporation, Indianapolis, IN.)

A program should be developed which allows the removed P123-1 cores to be sent to the home office or a locksmithing resource to be recombinated, say to P123-3, then returned to the store with new P123-3 operating keys to serve as the back-up to the P123-2 series in use.

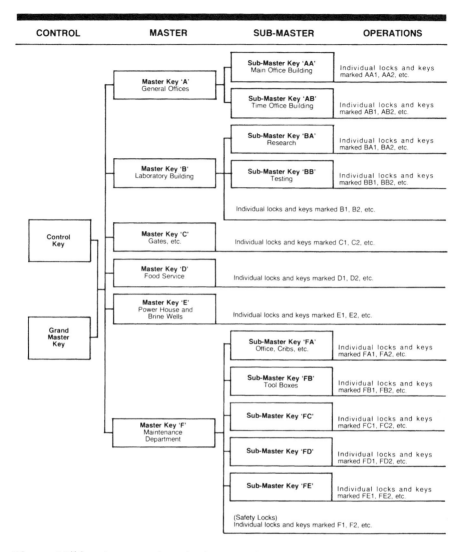

Figure 11(b) The masterkeyed schematic. (Courtesy of Best Lock Corporation, Indianapolis, IN.)

Lost keys, since they are not labeled with the store address, do not pose as great a security threat as would store keys kept by a management person who is separated from the company on less than favorable terms, such as stealing or gross negligence. When dishonest keyholders are found out and terminated, "swapping the cores" should be a standard practice even if their keys are returned.

Having a convenient and relatively low-cost method of changing locks (i.e., changing cores) such as the one described above, makes it less likely store management will procrastinate in taking corrective action to restore integrity in their perimeter security. Should the issue of key control become muddled through turnover or mismanagement, the condition can be corrected in-house with minimal effort and expense.

With the abundance of keying schemes available, retailers are sometimes tempted to overuse the master-keying system. Theoretically, the CEO of a company could have one grand master key that literally opens every lock on company premises. Though available, it is unwise.

If a regional manager in charge of 30 stores orders herself a P master key (for perimeter access to all 30 stores), she has maximized both the convenience and the risks inherent in the system. Should that key become compromised, a new series, one independent of the entire P network, would have to be produced. For this reason, a sub-master keying schedule is more appropriate.

A sub-master for location #123 would be a P123 key, capable of opening the P123-1 cores in use, the P123-2 cores in reserve, and any subsequent recombination (123-3, 123-4, etc.) of the series used in the future. But it could not access the P124 locks of location #124. Sub-masters for all 30 stores could be kept in the regional office so the regional manager would have unfettered access to her stores, while minimizing the exposure of the P series used company-wide.

Companies should carefully plan the keying schedule which will be adopted as they would any other aspect of the business. Forethought at the inception of the program, and flexibility in the program design, will serve to enhance security control and hold down future expense.

Many organizations are moving away from conventional lock and key systems and into electronic access controls. Card access systems control the *users* as opposed to the hardware, and as such offer greater accountability. Card access applications are suited best to the home office and distribution center/warehouse facilities, and can be a cost-effective alternative to the traditional "lobby guard," especially in the off-hours.

In the absence of the "eyes and ears" of the lobby guard, card access programs can regulate hours of entry and record activity for future review. Levels of entry authorization can be established so the system will selectively exclude persons from after-hour entry (daytime clerical personnel, for instance) while permitting access to shift employees (overnight MIS personnel, for example).

A guard no longer "signs" these people in and out; their private passcode or "user number" records their entry and exit times. In addition to relieving man-hour costs for "manning the door," software modifications enable the system to perform time keeping functions for payroll processing as well.

The security elements of such a program afford the same protections as the lock and key systems do, with the maintenance burden shifting from a hardware inventory (assigned keys) to personnel inventory (assigned users). Rather than issuing and collecting keys as needed, and swapping cores when necessary, access cards are issued and user-personnel are "added" and "deleted" from the system.

Depending on the sensitivity of the space protected, and the opportunities to exploit any "unmanned" area for the purpose of trespass, serious consideration should be given to supplementing the card access system with other electronic security support.

Because any entry door accessed by a user can be propped open and left unsecured, surreptitious entry can be gained by an unauthorized person since the lobby guard is no longer present to ensure the perimeter is secure. An electronic "safety net" should be in place whereby a combination of alarms and cameras work to alert management of the breach, and make a record of the person responsible for compromising the integrity of the system. This serves as a deterrent to attempted wrongdoing as well as a safeguard against carelessness. With informed planning and strong procedural controls, card access systems can be engineered to be more cost-effective and provide more vigilance than a guard on post.

To briefly examine an application of electronically controlled entry as a substitute for after-hour guards in a home office or warehouse, we can map out a generic plan that can be readily adapted to most operations. A sample schedule of protection follows:

A card reader is mounted at the door to admit those employees authorized to enter.

- Inserting a valid passcard will disengage an electronic lock allowing entry.
- Inserting a valid passcard will record the time, date, and user ID of the person entering the premises, creating a permanent record for management review.
- Inserting a valid passcard will "shunt" (momentarily turn off) the alarm device mounted on the door.

Forcible entry (no valid passcard) will activate the alarm device mounted on the door which transmits a signal of unauthorized entry to the alarm carrier, and activates a wall-mounted lobby camera/recorder. The alarm carrier will notify management.

Inserting a valid passcard activates an interior wall-mounted lobby camera, recording the entry of the passcard holder and creating a visual record for management review.

The electronic lock re-engages when the door is closed following entry.

Interior motion detectors will electronically sustain the camera's record mode as long as activity/human presence is detected in lobby area.

Failure of door to re-secure (following predetermined interval) transmits trouble signal to alarm carrier. Alarm carrier will notify management.

Assuming a firm wishes to employ a receptionist to greet visitors and announce guests, the electronic controls would be suspended between the hours of 8:30 a.m. and 5:00 p.m., Monday through Friday. Controlled entry would be in force all other times.

The company's next task would be to identify employee access requirements by job description, and issue cards with the appropriate level of entry authorization, for example:

Level One:	8:00 a.m.–6 p.m. Monday through Friday
	Issued to: clerical staff, support personnel, exempt employees on fixed schedules, temps
Level Two:	Level One plus weekends
	Issued to: same as above with weekend shifts
Level Three:	6:00 a.m.–10:00 p.m. 7 days
	Issued to: management and non-exempt employees with executive responsibilities
Level Four:	24 hour/7 days
	Issued to: senior management, MIS technical support, select security personnel
R Level:	restricted to single entry in prescribed window (e.g., 6:00 a.m.–6:30 a.m.)
	Issued to: outside cleaning service, special courier, etc.

For optimum administration of an electronic access system, a separate work station is established and operated by designated employees. Passcards are numbered sequentially beginning with the prefix code of the authorization level, and they are distributed to employees from a controlled location (e.g., human resources/employment office, security).

A dedicated PC at the work station interfaces with the system to add and delete authorized cardholders by their user ID. This PC will also record user entries by day, date, and time; storing the data for management retrieval to create activity logs and user analysis. Regularly scheduled backup on diskette of saved information is recommended. Video records of entry activity produced from extended play (time-lapse) VCRs should be similarly logged and held for a minimum period of 30 days.

Egress from the building can be as effectively controlled. After hours, swiping one's card through an interior card reader releases the electronic lock, shunts the alarm contact, records the user information, and permits a controlled exit in the same fashion entry is achieved. However, in this case, the video record must precede the event.

Unlike entry, when the camera is activated by the external card reader, motion detectors deployed along the approaching corridors to the lobby area should initiate the camera's record mode. Otherwise, the video record may only portray the back of the subject's head as they leave.

Videotaping persons leaving will not only provide a record of the employee exiting the building, but will also depict what was carried out by the employee. Companies with unmanned egress should stipulate by company policy limitations on what employees may carry out with them after hours.

In a less restrictive environment, generic egress may be a more user-friendly option. In this application, one need not insert a passcard to exit. A bypass control is located near the door, and the person leaving merely presses it to release the lock and shunt the alarm. Management still possesses the video record to monitor activity, but a user-specific record of exit times will not be made. Obviously, this application could not do double-duty as time-keeper or payroll manager. In all cases where electronic locking devices are employed, it is essential the system be designed to interface with the fire alarm system. Activation of any points of protection in the fire alarm system (smoke, sprinkler, pull-station, etc.) must automatically disengage the electronic lock in order to permit an unencumbered evacuation in the event of an emergency.

Note: Always review the specifications of additions or modifications to your existing locking hardware schedule with the local fire marshal.

The emphasis here is on local fire codes. Many instances exist where merely meeting federal or state fire code specifications is inadequate; local codes can and do supersede national codes. The local authority is also the issuing body of certificates of occupancy, and therefore your hardware schedule is subject to the criteria of local inspectors. Store planners should routinely schedule preconstruction meetings between the project manager and local inspectors and should solicit recommendations from the local fire marshal on issues of placement of emergency exits and prescribed exit devices.

By definition, exit devices may function to prevent entry, but must allow unobstructed egress in emergency situations. As such, a menu of hardware providing safe egress, yet protection from unauthorized entry, is available. The most common is the "crash-bar" mounted to the exit door that denies entry from the outside, but facilitates a rapid exit (Figure 12). A key-controlled electronic alarm should be considered which would alert store employees if the exit was used in a nonemergency situation, usually denoting an unauthorized exit.

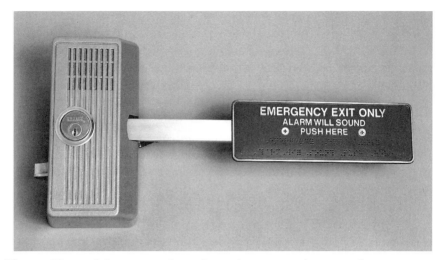

Figure 12 Model 250 exit door alarm. (Courtesy of Best Lock Corporation, Indianapolis, IN.)

Occasionally, renovations and changes to the selling floor create a need for an interior door to operate as an emergency exit. Converting an access door to an emergency exit is best facilitated by mounting a portable "crash-bar" device, equipped with a battery powered alarm to alert store personnel of unauthorized entry (Figure 13).

Exit devices must also conform to the 1994 Americans with Disability Act (ADA) standards for access by handicapped employees and customers.

All of these devices can be incorporated into an automated access control system with camera and alarm interface. What was once considered "Star Wars" security due to the outlay of capital funds to launch an interactive access control system is now a generally accepted and cost-effective alternative to the onerous expense of the lobby guard. An estimate of 14 hours of contract guard service per business day (5 p.m. to 7 a.m.), plus 48 hours of weekend coverage, to provide for after-hour building access control can easily surpass $60K annually. A card access/alarm/camera system can do the same for about one fourth the cost, plus the in-house administrative effort to manage it.

As with so many of the options to physical security, the choices come down to company preferences and the needs of the business. The potential savings offered by access control technology at corporate headquarters or warehouses can help offset the rising costs of store line security equipment.

Because stores are open to the public, companies have less control over their premises than they do in an office or warehouse environment that are populated by employees subordinate to management directives. The balance of this chapter will return to the stores, where devices designed to protect assets exposed to loss from within and from without are discussed.

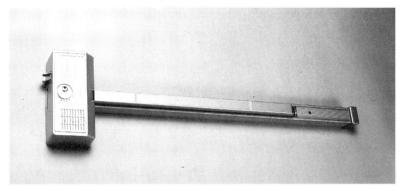

Figure 13 Model 700 exit door alarm. (Courtesy of Best Lock Corporation, Indianapolis, IN.)

With most self-service merchandise presentations, the retailer offers large selections of products for customer examination. Balancing the customer's unfettered browsing with sufficient sales helps to offer assistance and safeguard the merchandise, and is key to both successful customer service and loss prevention. Shoplifters exploit the self-service presentation to access product and move it to a remote location where they attempt to conceal it for the purpose of undetected theft.

Merchants have traditionally identified "hot" products targeted by shoplifters either for its value or for its trendy appeal. Such merchandise is also in great demand by the paying customer, and the retailer feels strongly that these items require prominent, accessible exposure to sell; yet uncontrolled exposure inevitably leads to theft and loss. Loss prevention managers, seeking to protect the merchandise while still enabling its ready sale, have endorsed several fixturing concepts unique to specific merchandise displays.

One example is jewelry, which is displayed in locked showcases for open viewing but separates the customer from the product with glass. This example of the "barrier method" is service-intensive, as a sales person is required to present the merchandise to customers individually, and as such, this method is usually reserved for high-price point goods that can support the labor costs associated with the level of service. Small electronics, cosmetics, and pricey accessories also fall into this category. To maximize selling space, lesser-price point items can be housed in counter-top fixtures, encased in lockable, plexiglass containers that are secured to the showcase.

Over the years, lockable showcases and fixtures have evolved with an emphasis on both aesthetic presentation and product security (Figures 14–17). So, too, have devices that protect ready-to-wear product lines. When skilled shoplifters have been shown to defeat an Electronic Article Surveillance (EAS) system (see Chapter 3), the retailer can employ secondary security with improved lock boxes and cables (Figure 18).

Figure 14 Sliding-door cylinder mounted on glass cabinet. (Courtesy of Best Lock Corporation, Indianapolis, IN.)

Surface Mounted   **Through Bolt Mounted**   **Surface Mounted with retaining pin**

Figure 15 Push-locks for sliding doors. (Courtesy of Best Lock Corporation, Indianapolis, IN.)

To illustrate this application, an $80 sweater may be adequately protected with an EAS tag, but to protect an $800 leather jacket may require the supplementary step of a sheathed cable looped through the jacket and secured to a lockable box mounted on the floor fixture. When properly utilized, a customer can examine the item but cannot remove it from the fixture. The

Figure 16 Cabinet locks. (Courtesy of Best Lock Corporation, Indianapolis, IN.)

Figure 17 Showcase locks with keys. (Courtesy of Protex Corporation, Bohemia, NY.)

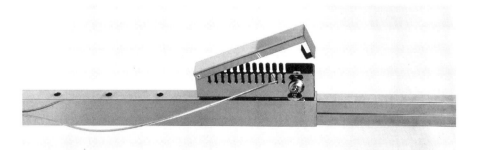

Figure 18 Mini-Merchant Guard. (Courtesy of Protex Corporation, Bohemia, NY.)

Figure 19 Loop alarm with cables that are available in 2',3', 4', and 6' lengths as well as custom lengths. Audio cable is also available. (Courtesy of Protex Corporation, Bohemia, NY.)

cable and lockbox application works with T-stands and 4-ways, and is available in mechanical and electronic models.

The mechanical model requires a salesperson to unlock the cable to allow the customer to try on the item. Shoplifters, equipped with wirecutters to defeat the EAS tag also had success cutting through the sheathed cable. Thus, an electronic lockbox (Figure 19) was then developed to alert employees with an audible alarm should a cable be cut. Determined shoplifters would then pry open the lockbox to disconnect the battery to disable the alarm, and then cut the cable.

Deluxe models were introduced with both tamper and low-battery alarms to protect the lockbox (Figure 20). Locking hardware and shoplifter chicanery does, at times, take on the appearances of a never-ending (and costly) "arms race" (Figure 21). But the protective value is always in preventing losses by making the act of theft cumbersome, and promoting deterrence through heightened detection capability.

The same principals employed to protect ready-to-wear merchandise soon became adaptable to hard goods lines. Cabling, both mechanical and electronic, enabled merchants to better display and protect electronics, preventing the loss of floor models (Figures 22–24).

Locking hardware has evolved to the point where virtually all retail product lines, no matter its size and value, can be protected while still retaining the benefits of open-sell presentation. With all the innovations available in security hardware, significant losses attributable to walk-away theft on the selling floor, can be controlled with informed planning and prudent investment.

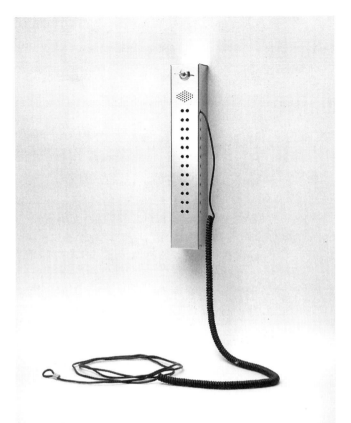

Figure 20 Electronic ProAlert 24 with combination straight/coil loop end cable. (Courtesy of Protex Corporation, Bohemia, NY.)

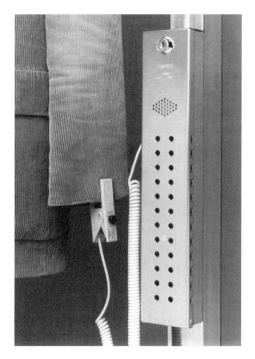

Figure 21 Electronic ProAlert with bi-function ProClip attached to jacket sleeve. (Courtesy of Protex Corporation, Bohemia, NY.)

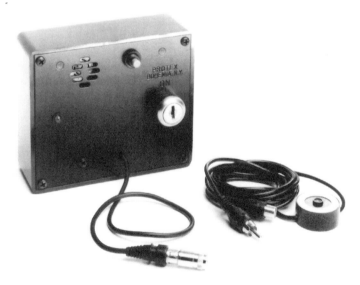

Figure 22 Product display alarm with a pigtail sensor. (Courtesy of Protex Corporation, Bohemia, NY.)

Figure 23 ProLoop with LED connected to boombox (radio) handle; opposite end of cable attached to Protex Electronic ProStrip. (Courtesy of Protex Corporation, Bohemia, NY.)

Figure 24 Computer plug with LED connected to computer notebook with opposite end of cable connected to Protex Electronic ProStrip. (Courtesy of Protex Corporation, Bohemia, NY.)

Alarm Systems

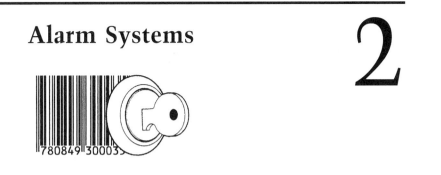

There are two paths for retailers to journey regarding the acquisition and operation of alarm systems for their locations: delegate the project to store planning and construction (or a designated operations executive) and keep it simple, generic, and inconsequential to your overall LP efforts, or enlist an industry expert to customize the system to be a cornerstone of your LP program.

There will be little cost disparity between the choices, only variances in the levels of protection and after-hour supervision of your facilities. The difference between the two rests solely with your understanding of system capabilities with respect to the needs of your business, and the tenacity of your negotiation with the alarm provider.

The first road involves standard alarm application to a fixed site. The needs are very basic: perimeter protection (doors and windows), interior detection (devices that detect motion inside your building after hours), and a means to communicate these events to responsible company personnel for their information and action (the transmission of alarm signals to a monitoring station to initiate subscriber notification).

The equipment package to deliver this protection is elementary: a pair of magnetic contacts on customer doors, fire exits, and roof hatches, in addition to uniformly placed glass break detectors on windows, accomplishes perimeter protection. When your staff arrives in the morning, they turn it off; before leaving at night, they turn it on. If they fail to do either, the alarm company will call somebody (depending on their instructions).

Protecting just the perimeter, however, exposes the retailer to the "sleep-in," the burglar who hides in the store at closing, and emerges when the staff is gone. Since the sleep-in does not violate any perimeter protection to gain access, his presence cannot be detected until he leaves, via a door or window. To detect this type of intruder, strategically placed motion sensors are installed that trigger an alarm based on movement, temperature disparity, or both. They will not blanket every square foot of space, but they will certainly hinder a burglar's ability to move freely throughout the building without eventually being detected.

To facilitate the monitoring of after-hour activity, the system components are integrated with your telephone system, and the alarm status is transmitted over phone lines to a receiving location. To permit subscriber activation and deactivation of the system, a passcode-protected keypad is used so store personnel can turn the alarms on and off. Keypad entries are documented at the monitoring station, so that reports identifying which store personnel entered alarm commands, and the time they were made, can be generated for management review. Do not think of this application as an early warning system, since alarm events signal an unauthorized person has entered your building, or an unauthorized person has been detected inside your building. Alarm events are after the fact notification.

Instead, your response to this condition has to be one designed to cope with a burglary-in-progress situation. As such, your intentions are to respond as rapidly as possible in order to minimize the loss by reducing the burglar's window of opportunity, or in rare cases, effect the apprehension of the perpetrator. Since crimes-in-progress are strictly a matter for law enforcement agencies, the alarm company should, by procedure, dispatch the police to the scene in addition to alerting store management.

This represents the ebb and flow of alarm service. You buy the alarm; they install the alarm. You set the alarm; they monitor the alarm. The alarm goes off; they call you and the police. The alarm doesn't work, so they fix it. They send an invoice, and you pay it. There is a simple, clear delineation of responsibility, which is very advantageous for the alarm company, and a certain level of comfort is accorded the retailer as well, yielding a symbiotic relationship of user and provider. But couched within the ostensibly complete presentation of service above is a host of opportunities for the subscriber, opportunities the customer must know to demand, but which tax the resources of the alarm companies and demand a level of expertise few are willing to showcase.

The reasons are understandable: it is more costly for the provider, in terms of training and manpower allocation, to permit customized monitoring procedures for individual subscribers, and the margin of error (i.e., culpability and liability) widens with each additional function they contractually assume. Hence, a reticence to educate the consumer.

With this inherently adversarial relationship established, we will begin with the process of selecting an alarm provider. Let's use the model of a nationwide 300-unit specialty retailer, divided into 5 regional divisions, each region with 60 stores. Each region is then subdivided into 5 12-store districts. Store sizes range from 3,000 square foot mall locations to 15,000 square foot superstores, with the median facility being a 9,000 square foot free-standing, strip-center tenant.

The needs of this business present few special circumstances; perhaps some stores are located in tougher parts of town than others, but generally the alarm requirements are fairly uniform. The first decision a company needs to make is whether they want one alarm provider to service all locations as a national account, or do they want to allocate the business to competing services by region or even by district. This decision should take into account experience to date with other vendors for services purchased. Are store supplies, window-washing service, carpet cleaners, waste removal, and other operational needs of the store managed centrally through national accounts, or in-the-field with local providers?

If loss prevention services are going to be managed by a Corporate LP Director, a national account affords the best route to consistent standards. If these resources are to be managed at the regional and district operations level, then latitude should be permitted for these individuals to negotiate with local alarm company representatives within the parameters established by the home office. Each company has their preference for either being a large vendor's medium-sized account, or a small vendor's major account. The pros and cons are usually decided between the premium a customer places on product diversity vs. personalized service.

Knowing first the information you want will further reduce the list of potential suitors for your business, be they national or local. The first criteria should be the timeliness of overnight alarm activity being communicated to the proper management personnel of your operation. A standard alarm contract will provide for monthly reports that summarize events by date and zone, with a description of action taken, if any. The company will log alarm activity over a 30-day period, compile the information into a summary report, and mail it out to the designated subscriber representative for their review within 7 days. Add 5 more days, perhaps a week, for that report to reach the office in the field and be examined by this mobile regional or district manager. With this type of reporting structure, it is feasible upper management may not learn until February 14th, alarm activity which occurred at locations on January 2nd, 3rd and 4th, which is clearly an unacceptable window for after-hour activity to go unchallenged by senior management officials.

Rather than dicker about what is an acceptable window for senior management apprisal, limit your search of providers to those who will facilitate next-day reporting. Although next-day faxing of alarm reports is a possible accommodation, it is a poor substitute for an on-line, modem-linked reporting program that allows the subscriber to tie in to a provider's monitoring station for instant access to present status and alarm history data.

National alarm company providers endorse this reporting method for two reasons: it relieves them of the obligation of providing monthly reports, and they sell the software package that permits the computer interface between your executive's PC and their monitoring station. This is not a bad deal, though, when you consider the supervisory advantages this resource affords your mobile, multiple-site manager. District managers can now "dial in" to the central station and observe the overnight alarm activity in their stores: early openings, late closings, and unauthorized entries. Regional directors can likewise review activity in multiple districts, and the corporate LP manager or senior operations executive can survey activity of all locations from the home office.

Prior to this technology, management waited up to 45 days for monthly reports from multiple providers, and reports were poorly detailed and obsolete upon arrival in some cases. As a result, little, if any, action was taken to challenge store management regarding alarm events which had occurred. These reports generally received a cursory review, and were filed for future reference. Future reference usually entailed a future investigation of employee malfeasance, brought to management's attention via an avenue other than these reports. Discovering a pattern of alarm events that indicate employees are returning to the building after hours to commit theft is much more evident the next day than the next month, which prompts the observation: would employees knowledgeable of your next-day detection of their deeds hatch such a plan in the first place?

A properly detailed alarm report offers management a wealth of information not previously available in a remarkably short turn-around time. The applications are considerable when you factor in the potential for site surveillance, employee theft deterrence, and even payroll management. But these benefits are not proffered by the alarm company so easily. Despite the enormous marketing impact value-added alarm monitoring might have on sales, detail and accountability remain great areas of trepidation for alarm companies. Although many sell the implied attributes of an on-line management information system, few actually deliver the end-result in a manner most conducive to the subscriber's needs. This is because central station operations are set up to receive and dispatch alarm notifications with a minimum of fuss and bother for the rows of headset-equipped dispatchers seated at their consoles. Every alarm event prompts an action, and each action prompts a task. If you minimize tasks and minimize staff, you maximize profit, and this idea is completely understandable.

That is why you have to know what you want going in, not after the fact. You have to visualize your after-hour operation, and design the alarm reports to your specifications. The sample screens provided on the ensuing pages will help demonstrate both the reporting capabilities and suggested formats for retail subscribers to maximize their LP investment in alarm systems.

XYZ ALARM COMPANY MAIN MENU

USER: ABC CORPORATION
LOCATION: HOME OFFICE, USA

Log in ....
Password ....

Thank you. Please choose from one of the menu options:

1. 24-hour recap report
2. Event detail by location
3. Work order summary by region
4. Alarm incidents by district summary
5. "Cause not found" summary report
6. Unscheduled early opening report by region
7. Unscheduled late closing report by region
8. Open and close reports by district
9. Current passcode rosters by store
10. Dedicated zone covert monitoring report by store
11. User-initiated zone bypass report by region
12. Billing summary report

SCREEN ONE: 24 Hour Recap Report

The purpose of this report is to summarize the overnight alarm activity company-wide at a glance. A sample screen follows:

24 HOUR RECAP: UNSCHEDULED EVENTS BY DISTRICT

DISTRICT 1: WASHINGTON

STORE	DAY	DATE	TIME	EVENT
702/Adams	Tue	02/21	0800	Early entry (John). OK
704/Madison	Wed	02/22	0143	PR break & reset. CNF. PD disp. OK. (Mary).
705/Monroe	Wed	02/22	0110	Late to close. OK (Scott)
707/Jackson	Wed	02/22	0955	Late to open. OK. (Kelly)

DISTRICT 2: ATLANTA

STORE	DAY	DATE	TIME	EVENT
713/Lee	Wed	02/22	0400	Line trouble. Panel reset 0422. OK (Joe)
715/Davis	Wed	02/22	0235	Glass break. PD Disp. Mgr Tom resp. Bldg. secure 0510.

Scroll down for Districts 3 thru 25.

LEGEND:

PR:	Perimeter zone
IM:	Interior motion
HU:	Hold-up alarm
CNF:	Cause not found
PD:	Police notified/dispatched

This recap report gives management an instant overview of overnight incidents company-wide. This is an expedient alternative to returning calls and reading reports, and it is especially helpful for the multi-unit manager. It allows the district and regional manager to assess the urgency of follow-up measures needed, and helps organize her agenda for the day, so that there are no surprises.

SCREEN TWO: Event Detail By Store

The purpose of this report is to isolate a single store location and review its unscheduled alarm activity over the past 90 days. It is instrumental in determining patterns of unscheduled alarm activity, and accelerates the process to resolve it. A sample screen follows:

EVENT DETAIL BY STORE

Enter store number .... (702)

Scroll down for event details covering last 90 days, beginning with most recent.

Press ESC to end and enter new store location.

STORE	DAY	DATE	TIME	EVENT
702/Adams	Tue	02/21	0800	Early entry (John). OK
	Fri	02/17	0753	Early entry (John). OK
	Tue	02/14	0802	Early entry (John). OK
	Fri	02/10	0758	Early entry (John) OK
	Wed	02/08	0155	IM/Zone 4: break & reset. No subseq. brks. No disp. per Mgr. John. CNF
	Tue	02/07	0744	Early entry (John) OK
	Fri	02/04	0756	Early entry (John) OK
	Mon	01/30	0144	IM/Zone 4: break & reset. PD disp. per John All secure. CNF. Work order req.
	Thu.	01/19	0158	IM/Zone 4: break & reset
			0200	IM/Zone 4: break & reset
			0206	IM/Zone 4: break & reset PD disp. per John
			0244	Early entry (John w/Police). All secure 0315 CNF. Work order req.

Fri	01/13	0154	IM/Zone 4: break & reset
		0158	IM/Zone 4: break & reset PD disp. per Dave
		0236	Early entry (Dave w/Police) All secure 0319 CNF. Work order req.
Thu	01/12	0144	IM/Zone 4: break & reset
		0144	IM/Zone 4: break & reset
		0146	IM/Zone 4: break & reset PD disp per John
		0212	Early entry (John w/Police) All secure 0308 CNF. Work order req.

ESC (we have seen enough).

Screen two allows management to view alarm activity in context. What appeared in the 24 hour recap report (screen one) for store 702 was an early entry by John on 2/21 that could have been dismissed as an isolated incident. Clearly, a pattern of early entries every Tuesday and Friday in February exists, one that warrants follow-up attention. If John is involved in wrongdoing, it took but two weeks to identify, not two months.

It could turn out that Tuesday and Friday are shipping days, and John is coming to work early to get a head start. Maybe he was criticized by his district manager in his January performance review about falling behind, and this is his way of demonstrating initiative. Who knows? But all you have to do to find out is schedule a pre-opening surveillance on Friday the 24th. He'll be there early, and you can too.

Another interesting item is apparent as well. The interior motion device represented as zone 4 shows a steady history of malfunction. Management has been consistently summoned to the store over what amounts to false alarms. Note how the activity has worn down the response:

On 1/12, it took your representative and the police 26 minutes to get to the store. The police remained, conducting a thorough search for 56 minutes. The next event was on 1/13, and response time was 38 minutes; the search lasted 43 minutes. On 1/19, response was also 38 minutes, but the search time dropped to 31 minutes, tantamount to a once-over. Is this indicative of the police getting tired of walking through your store at night? If you look at 1/30, the police were dispatched, but no store representative met them. The police did not enter your store on this occasion, most likely doing only a perimeter check and departing. Did they say something to John on 1/19 about wasting their time? And on 2/8, John told the alarm company not to dispatch the police. Is this store cut off from after hour response because of the false alarm activity? You need to know that. And what has been the resolution of the four work orders that have been noted (and that you are paying for)? To find out, you would move ahead to screen three.

Screen three gives detail on work orders processed by location, grouped by district and region. A sample screen follows:

WORK ORDER SUMMARY BY DISTRICT

Enter District Number.........(1)
Enter Store Number.............(702)

Scroll down for work order history covering last 6 months, beginning with most recent.

Press F2 for YTD work order billing information.
Press ESC to end and enter new store location.

STORE	DAY	DATE	TIME	EVENT
702/Adams	Fri	1/13	1530	ServRep Andy checked zone 4 (CNF 1/12) Adjusted unit. OK
	Mon	01/16	1030	ServRep Andy checked zone 4 (CNF 1/13) Tested sensor. OK. Readjusted sensitivity.
	Fri	01/20	1400	ServRep Tom swapped out unit. Test OK
	Tue	02/01	1230	ServRep Tom reports HVAC duct near unit circulates hot air on timer, probably around 2 a.m. Recommend customer adjust HVAC program or relocate alarm device zone 4.

We've learned a couple of things from that read out. Repairman Andy is not very thorough, and the ensuing alarm event on 2/8 (from screen two) tells no corrective action has been taken. Since we all know what the problem is (do we really?), zone 4 alarm events are being virtually dismissed. Store personnel no longer respond, the police are no longer dispatched, and we no longer request a work order because the service technicians have told us it's our fault. And why was a work order requested on 1/13 not facilitated until 1/16? Does our service contract exclude weekend service calls? Read the fine print!

We can imagine what John has done about this. He's probably called store construction and maintenance, and they've told him they will look into it the HVAC issue. He has probably told his district manager about it, but the alarm company wants $350 to relocate the unit (because we are the ones who agreed to mount it there originally, and they will have to charge to correct this error after the fact), and the DM is thinking about where he'll find $350. And in the meantime, nothing is done. The alarm malfunctions from time to time, and we live with it until somebody does something about it. The store should have four motion detectors protecting the interior, and since we are no longer responding to zone 4, we have effectively eliminated 25% of alarm coverage because of inertia.

Without screen three, how quickly would this situation come to senior management's attention in your company? Since we can see the ripple-effect of unresolved alarm incidents, the store director may want to see a by-region summary of alarm events in order to determine if service problems are isolated to one region, one district, or are commonplace throughout the company.

Screen four permits a corporate executive an at-a-glance summary of company-wide incident activity, as well as the regional manager an overview of district events. Alarm incidents are the unscheduled events as described in the screen one 24 hour recap. A sample screen follows:

ALARM INCIDENTS BY REGION (90 DAYS)

Enter Region Number............(1)
Press Esc to end and enter new region number

DISTRICT	#INC	% TOT	CNFs	PD DISP	FINES	$YTD
01/Wash.	22	27	8	14	6	$225
02/Atlanta	16	20	4	5	1	$ 25
03/Tampa	6	8	1	2	0	$ 0
04/Miami	28	34	9	17	3	$150
05/Charlotte	11	14	2	8	0	$ 0
REG. TOT	83		24	46	10	$400

Press F2 for District detail by-store
Enter district number.

Noting that district four accounts for a third of region one alarm incidents, the regional can then summon detail for that district, formatted by store. And if two stores are found to account for a significant percentage of district events:

Press F3 for detail by store
Enter store number.

This function will then default to screen two information for the store locations entered. One report prompts another report, with user-friendly cross-checking features.Of all the alarm incidents that are cataloged by location, three types of events are useful for senior management tracking:

CNF: because they are nuisance calls that undermine confidence in the system and occasionally result in store personnel being rousted to the store after hours for no reason. They also represent the potential for strained relations with local police that lead to fines and/or service disruption.

LATE-TO-OPEN: excessive incidents of this nature may be symptomatic of poor standards and disciplines, with at least some pre-opening tasks being performed below expectations.

LATE-TO-CLOSE: excessive incidents of this nature indicate after-hour activity in the building that should be challenged, if not for reasons of loss prevention, then certainly for reasons of payroll management.

To expedite senior management's capacity to monitor these events, separate screens (five thrrough seven, for instance) can be formatted to summarize these events only, cutting through all data to isolate and display specific incident types of particular interest to management, such as the three itemized above.

Screen eight is particularly useful to field management: the opening and closing report by day and by store. It is formatted for use in two ways. First, the regional and/or district manager can call up a specific date and view the open and close times by location for that date. Second, a specific location can be entered to view a 90 day history of open and close times for that store. A sample screen follows:

OPEN AND CLOSE REPORTS BY REGION

Enter Region Number ....(1)
All Districts...........Y/N
Enter Date for Review.............mm/dd/yr

STORE	DAY/DATE	NORM OPEN	ACT. OPEN	USER	NORM CLOSE	ACT. CLOSE	USER
701	Wed. 03/01	0900	0901	John	2300	2254	Paul
702	Wed. 03/01	0900	0856	George	2300	2258	Ringo
703	Wed 03/01	0900	0847	Mary	2300	2308	Alice

^scroll down

760	Wed 0301	0900	0902	Jan	2300	2247	Dean

Region complete. Press ESC to enter new Region.
Press F2 to view location history.
F2 (enter)
Enter location number ....(760)

STORE	DAY/DATE	NORM OPEN	ACT. OPEN	USER	NORM CLOSE	ACT. CLOSE	USER
760	Wed. 03/01	0900	0855	Jan	2300	2251	Dean
760	Tue. 02/28	0900	0846	Scott	2300	2308	Jan
760	Mon. 02/27	0900	0858	Scott	2300	2248	Dean

760	Sun. 02/26	1100	1103	Cathy	1900	1907	Cathy
760	Sat. 02/25	0900	0859	Jan	2300	2243	Dean
760	Fri. 02/24	0900	0836	Jan	2300	2246	Dean
760	Thu 02/23	0900	0844	Cathy	2300	2303	Scott
760	Wed 02/22	0900	0901	Jan	2300	2238	Dean
760	Tue 02/21	0900	0850	Scott	2300	2259	Jan
760	Mon 02/20	0800*	0756	Scott	0000*	2341	Dean

*denotes exception: President's Day Holiday hours schedule in effect

| 760 | Sun 02/19 | 1100 | 1058 | Cathy | 1900 | 2008 | Cathy |
| 760 | Sat 02/18 | 0900 | 0906 | Jan | 2300 | 2344 | Dean |

^scroll down to continue

Press ESC to enter new store location

Overall, this is an unremarkable open and close history, both for the region on the date in question, and the specific location examined over a 12-day period. But there are still observations the astute regional manager can make at store 760. Note the schedule of store manager Jan. It is what retailers might consider a self-serving work week. Apparently, Jan is scheduled to open Saturdays, is off on Sunday and Monday, and works the closing shift on Tuesday. This places the store manager absent from the store by design from 6 p.m. Saturday through noon on Tuesday. It could be indicative of depth and strength at the assistant level, or cushy-schedule tactics on the manager's part. Note too that Cathy draws open-to-close manager duty each Sunday, affording Jan, Dean, and Scott Sundays off. If Cathy is up to the task, fine. If Sunday revenues are consistently below comparable sales to last year, maybe she is not. Also, Dean is either the most proficient closing manager of the four, or he is cutting corners to get out early. Either way, it might be interesting to see if his payroll record reflects his scheduled departure time or the actual time he leaves. And what happened at closing on Sunday the 19th? Maybe Cathy and the staff stayed late to set up for the next day's sale. Maybe she was chatting on the phone waiting for her ride to show up.

You might want to run the closing report for 2/19 to see how many stores in the region stayed late on Sunday to prepare for Monday's sale, and get a snapshot of what might have been unplanned payroll costs attributable to the holiday promotion. These are little things the system can do besides protect the store after hours from burglary.

And while we are on the subject of open and close reports, companies that prescribe pre-opening bank deposits of the previous days' sales should be cognizant of the dual open and close report. The initial entry into the building by the opening manager should be followed shortly by an entry that re-arms the system when the manager leaves to go the bank. That event should then be followed sometime later by an entry that disarms the system when the manager returns from the bank.

This secondary arming and disarming of the system serves three purposes: (1) it protects the building from unauthorized entry during the period the store is unoccupied in the time it-takes to get back and forth from the bank; (2) a report of this secondary arming and disarming of the system would allow management to observe that daily deposits do take place as prescribed; (3) in the event the manager does not return from the bank within a reasonable period of time, the alarm company can notify a district or regional executive that something is amiss. It may even be comforting for the manager to know somebody will know if he is waylaid on the way to the bank with the deposit.

Screen eight can be easily adapted to this function:

Enter F3:   provides secondary arm & disarm times for all stores by region on a given day. This way the regional/district manager can see at a glance when deposits were made with a date-specific inquiry.

Enter F4:   provides secondary arm & disarm times history for a specific location to view deposit activity in context of a thirty day period.

Enter F5:   exception report listing all stores and dates for which NO secondary arm & disarm times were recorded, indicating perhaps, that deposits were NOT made as required.

Capabilities such as the ones described for screen eight will not be found in promotional literature furnished by alarm companies pitching your account. As stated, these customized features are not generally encouraged by providers due to the onerous attention to detail they require at the central monitoring station.

Screen nine is a case in point. Passcode file maintenance is an on going task for both the subscriber and the provider. Retailers have to cope with many administrative tasks due to the turnover rate indigenous to the retail industry. Loss prevention generates its share of tasks in this respect as well, given the proliferation of access controls required for security: keys to the building, combinations to the safe, password-protected POS transactions, and alarm-user passcodes; all should be changed when key store personnel resign, get transferred, get promoted, get fired.

In an organization such as the national, 300-store chain we are using as a model, turnover and reassignment of personnel is prolific, and management must be especially diligent to ensure security is not compromised because of it. Alarm user passcodes are Personal Identification Numbers (PINs) that identify which employee has entered authorized commands into the alarm control keypad. These authorized commands, depending upon the user's authorization level, arm and disarm the system, change the hours of operation the system is in use, add and delete users, and permit entire zones of protection to be bypassed.

Accountability for these commands, via user identification, is essential for management to determine the appropriateness of such commands, and deter dishonest employees from compromising the protection to facilitate theft. If passcodes are poorly protected, unauthorized persons will have access to command functions within the system thought to be secure, permitting them an opportunity to circumvent the protection. The chart below suggests user authorization levels by job description:

LEVEL	TITLE	AUTHORIZED COMMANDS
1	Asst. Mgr.	Arm & Disarm system. Test function.
2	First Asst.	Level 1 plus add & delete level one users. Restricted zone bypass
3	Store Mgr.	Level 2 plus add & delete level two users. Unrestricted zone bypass, change open & close schedule.
4	District Mgr.	Level 3 plus add & delete level three users. Obtain activity reports for designated district via modem-link to provider central station.
5	Regional Mgr.	Level 4 plus add & delete level four users. Obtain activity reports for designated region via modem-link to provider central station.
6	Corp. Exec(s).	Level 5 plus add & delete level five users. Obtain activity reports company-wide via modem-link to provider central station.

Screen nine should be designed for verifying user passcode rosters by store are current and complete. District and regional managers, effecting transfers, promotions and separations, can follow-up electronically to ensure their instructions to add or delete personnel were carried out. They can also determine that authorization levels correspond with job responsibilities.

Levels 4, 5 and 6 should also function remotely, so that the executive's physical presence at a specific store keypad is not required in order to enter commands. Due to the in transit nature of multiple-site management, communicating alarm commands for individual locations at this level should be facilitated with the central station directly, via the on-line software program.

A point of contention that will arise in establishing passcode rosters and user designations with most providers is the alarm company's preference for using "man numbers" instead of "name identification" as the "user" on its reports. If this point is not addressed up front when negotiating report formats with the provider, your "screen eight", as it appears on the preceding pages will *not* list Jan, Dean, Scott and Cathy as the users for store 760. The report instead will read man number 1, 2, 3 and 4 as the users. The reader would then have to cross-reference man numbers to names by location in order to establish *who* actually came and went.

On the surface, this may not seem to be a significant issue. But designing the system to be user-friendly is essential for companies that place a premium on the time field executives spend on administrative tasks. The "man number" cross-reference creates *another* roster to be updated due to turnover, and impedes the at-a-glance benefit of the customized report. The end-result may be that your supervisory field executive becomes less diligent in pursuing avenues of inquiry that would normally be made if the system functioned in a more benevolent fashion, or a budding investigation is compromised because the investigator has to *ask* store number 760 for the identity of man number four.

If the provider remains unwilling, or portends to be unable, to modify its reports to accommodate this format, invite your MIS department head to illustrate how modern POS systems generate a name ID on sales audit reports generated from a numeric ID entered by the employee ringing the sale at the register. Really insist upon this feature.

Screen ten is reserved for covert monitoring of a select zone. Few subscribers recognize that the supervisory function of an alarm system need not be limited to merely after-hour events. Alarm systems can perform "intelligence gathering" services during store hours as well. Too often, store managers enter the building and disarm the entire system. The reality is normal business operation requires only the zones monitoring customer entrances and interior motion to be disarmed. Just as the fire alarm system continues to monitor water flow and smoke detectors day and night, so too should the burglar alarm system continue to monitor zones covering fire exits, roof hatches, and delivery doors.

Zones which are not normally deactivated are referred to as dedicated *zones,* designated for "day-burg" monitoring. A good example is the zone assigned to the hold-up alarm. Day or night, when the hold-up alarm is pulled, the central station receives the signal, even when the system status reads "unarmed". That is because dedicated zones are exempt from the opening and closing (arm & disarm) function controlling other points of protection, like the perimeter and interior motion. Zones carrying the hold-up alarm and fire protection devices are never disarmed because the emergencies they monitor can happen at anytime.

Retailers should give careful thought to expanding day-burg coverage to other areas of protection: fire exits and roof hatches, for example. Is there a good reason store management should *not* be alerted to someone using these access ways to the building during the day? The alarm company would call during business hours to tell you they received a signal for the dedicated zone

covering your smoke detectors. Should it not be part of the protection program that they call and inform you someone just entered your roof hatch?
That constitutes an unusual event worthy of management notification.

Now if the landlord has told you he will have workers doing duct work
on the HVAC system all morning, the store manager can "shunt" or bypass
that dedicated roof hatch zone for the duration of the maintenance activity.
This will preclude unnecessary alarm activity and the ensuing notifications
at the central station. Once the work is completed, the manager can "restore"
the zone. As a safeguard, should the manager for some reason neglect to
restore the zone, the bypass will be evident to the closing manager (who will
be unable to arm the system at night without restoring the zone).

Another useful application of expanded day-burg monitoring would be
a program that "supervises" the delivery door. The delivery door, or back
door, is a prevalent source of consternation to LP policy makers because it
is a remote and uncontrolled exit from the building. It is used to take out
the trash. It is used to take in deliveries. Employees go in and out to sneak
a smoke. It is propped open in the summer to get a breeze in the back office.
Not surprisingly, it is often cited as the primary route dishonest employees
use to move merchandise out of the building, be it in the trash or simply
deposited in the back alley for subsequent retrieval. Your alarm system can
be used as an electronic eye on that door; all comings and goings being
reported on screen ten.

Procedurally, you must first establish rules governing the use of this exit:
trash must be taken out daily prior to noon. The door may not be propped
open (buy a fan). Do not use this exit to slip out for a cigarette. You probably
have similar regulations already, but little monitoring capability to ensure
compliance.

By placing the delivery door on a day-burg monitoring mode, you compel
the store manager to bypass it each time the door is used. That should be
once for trash, once (twice?) for deliveries, and that's it. Each access is preceded by a bypass, recorded for your review on screen ten, with the time,
date, duration and user of the delivery door.

Screen ten can be reviewed by region, with each store showing similar
activity: the morning bypass for trash removal, the afternoon bypass for
delivery. But the bypass noted from noon till 5 P.M. will tell you somebody
had the door propped open all day; just as the 8 P.M. exit and re-entry will
arouse your suspicion.

The check and balance in the event the user fails to identify himself by
neglecting to enter his passcode for a bypass, is the alarm company receiving
the signal as an alarm event, prompting them to call the store and advise the
manager of the breach. By definition, that incident would appear the next
day on your screen one and two reports of unscheduled alarm activity.

Similar to the invaluable information you're accessing on screen eight, alarm providers reviewing your specifications for screen ten will resist such constant demands on their monitoring facility. Do not settle for the alarm company's preferred mode of operation: that you disarm all zones during business hours and make their job easier. Find a hungry salesman willing to over-promise, but don't let him under-deliver. You are in the driver's seat only once: when they are pitching the account for your business.

Something we touched on earlier, authorization to bypass points of protection, is a feature that permits the system to adapt to needs of the business that supercede the normal opening and closing schedule of each zone. We've seen the example of how utilizing the bypass command affords management the luxury of keeping multiple zones on day-burg monitoring. Bypass commands allows the system to be partially activated for monitoring, while *shunting* other points of protection that cannot be alarmed due to special circumstances. For instance, suppose a location was undergoing renovation, and trades people worked overnight on the construction project. Normally, a member of management would be requested to supervise the crew, or a contract guard would be brought in to control access to the building. In addition to these measures, the perimeter zones of the alarm system could be armed for monitoring by bypassing the interior zones (which cannot be armed due to the after-hour traffic). You can then supplement the effectiveness of your management representative or contract guard electronically, with the alarm company poised to notify you of any perimeter breach (i.e., an unscrupulous laborer passing merchandise out a fire exit). This application is helpful anytime personnel are engaged in authorized after-hour projects: carpet cleaning, inventory, maintenance, etc. However, management must be able to verify bypass activity is not capriciously practiced by store management.

Screen eleven can be formatted to report a history by location of bypass activity: what zone was bypassed, for how long, by whom, and for what reason. At a glance, the regional manager can obtain the present bypass status of each store.

Remember our manager John at store 702 way back on screen two? He had the dilemma of the malfunctioning motion device attributed to the HVAC blower. The last event was received on 2/8, the incident where neither store management nor the police were dispatched. Our work order summary on screen three never referenced the alarm company relocating that device, and the regional doesn't recall authorizing a company maintenance request to reprogram the HVAC schedule. Yet, no further false alarms have been noted since 2/8 for that pesky zone 4 motion detector. Did it just fix itself? Did the problem just go away? Of course not. Call up screen eleven and you'll note that John bypassed zone 4 on 2/9 pending resolution of his conundrum.

Now everybody gets a good night sleep, but this is hardly the remedy senior management would prescribe. Screen eleven keeps you in the loop.

Screen twelve is reserved for billing inquiries. As with all services purchased contracts, cost control is essential to realize the ROI on the expense. Most retailers prefer flat-rate arrangements that can be planned as a fixed expense. Alarm providers generate revenue from four sources:

- Equipment purchase (be it sale or lease)
- Monitoring fees
- Service and Maintenance contracts
- Field work orders

Most recognized alarm companies engage in little subterfuge regarding equipment purchase and monitoring fees. They understand it is a competitive marketplace, and any price-gouging maneuvers will be easily detected in the bidding process. Service and maintenance contracts deserve a wary eye, but are generic in spirit: equipment failure due to malfunction will be the responsibility of the provider; equipment failure due to damage or abuse will be the responsibility of the subscriber.

Make sure, if you are inclined to accept service and maintenance agreements, that you make two requests of the provider as part of the deal: (1) that the provider include at no charge a walk-test of each point of protection twice a year, to be performed on site by a service technician at each location; and (2) that an orientation and training session be held for the management staff at each location upon installation, and that the class be repeated each year on the anniversary of the installation, at no charge.

A word on alarm testing — alarm companies frequently cite the subscriber's failure to test the equipment on a regular basis as the primary cause when a system fails to perform. Most keypad consoles contain a test command that runs a "diagnostic" on each zone of protection to verify the system is "receiving" the individual devices located throughout the building. The authorized user enters the test command, followed by the corresponding zone; a green light signals the panel "reads" the zone OK. Some test modes run the entire schedule of protection automatically without individual zone entries.

This function, albeit a nice feature, merely indicates that the panel reads the device. It does not indicate that the device is performing up to specs. To illustrate, the test command would read an interior motion device as OK in the test mode even if an unscrupulous person turned the device toward the ceiling (or placed a bag over it, for that matter). The panel would read it, the green light would flash OK, but the device has been compromised by tampering and rendered ineffective nonetheless.

A real alarm test requires the system to be challenged by someone attempting to defeat it. Interior motion devices have varying ranges of detection. It is important for the person conducting alarm tests to operate on the very fringes of that range to determine if the unit is functioning at optimum levels. If you walk over and wave your hand in front of the motion sensor, it will detect your presence. But if you slink along the far wall, and maneuver around the device with the stealth of a burglar, then you will find out whether the unit's sensitivity requires adjustment. You will not learn that from the green OK light on the panel.

All tests should be pre-arranged with the central station so that an operator can be on an open phone line with you, informing you which signals were received in which sequence: "*You have just tripped zone four. Now you have opened the west fire exit; I'm reading motion in zone two, and that was the back door that just tripped.*" That's an alarm test. If you have ever tested a hold-up button on an open line with the alarm company and they tell you they read the signal as water-flow, riser two, then you become a believer in alarm tests.

Field work orders, or "extras," represent an area of concern for retailers working on a fixed budget. This factor comes into play after installation when it is determined that equipment allocation is inadequate or placement is inappropriate. Embellishments to the system, after the fact, are eventualities that alarm companies depend on to recoup some of the giveaways they have endured in the negotiations to close the deal.

Establish a fall back position with the provider that enables you to revisit certain locations for modification. For example, suppose you agree on a three-tiered equipment schedule for three distinct store designs: a standard package for the 3,000 square foot mall store, the 9,000 square foot free-standing location, and the 15,000 square foot superstore. You later realize that due to configuration or store layout anomalies, you need the tier 3 package in a tier 2 location. Identifying the upgrade expense early-on, while you are still negotiating a company-wide deal the vendor wants badly, will prevent excessive pricing down the road, when the vendor is trying to recover his eroding margin from all the concessions you have finagled.

Screen twelve can be the balance sheet that tracks alarm expense throughout the fiscal year, alerting you to potential cost overruns due to unplanned expense in field work orders, the inevitable hike in monitoring fees associated with equipment enhancement, and fines for false alarms incurred from municipal agencies.

Format a standard expense control document, posting the planned budget amount against the actual expense incurred, tracking monthly variances year-to-date for the four primary alarm system cost centers: equipment, monitoring, service contracts, and field work orders. Tally the totals against last years costs to determine the ROI for any capital investment made for the interactive software package and new equipment that was required to convert stores onto your new and improved proactive alarm system.

Now that your interest has been piqued by the capabilities of such a system, the question most retailers will have is, how do I get there from where I am now? That is, few retail operations have the luxury of building a 300-unit division from the ground up; optimum conditions for uniform standards of provider and protection.

More likely, a 300-store division is the byproduct of successful growth and acquisition from a core market to a national chain. The resultant alarm system situation is apt to resemble a hodgepodge of systems, equipment and vendors, tagging along through your expansion or inherent with assumption of assets (liabilities?) from acquired companies. If the indoctrination on the multiple applications of alarm system technology presented so far in this chapter seemed a bit futuristic, the process to convert your 300 stores so that you can exploit the advantages described will bring you right back down to earth.

We will examine a conversion program identifying as many of the potential obstacles as we can anticipate. We will assume that the existing alarm system resources are a mixed-bag of owned and leased equipment; some with, some without service agreements; a potpourri of vendors employing both generic systems which can be adapted by a national provider, and obsolete systems that are ill-suited for upgrade.

Assuming you establish that the proactive alarm technology discussed has tangible benefits to improving field operations and offers a significant improvement in loss prevention capability for your organization, the first step is to assess whether or not this approach will be cost effective for your company. This is best determined by getting a clear handle on your existing alarm expense in order to establish how much you are spending now, for presumably substandard protection and service. Knowing what you can have, and then evaluating what you do have, and factoring in the cost will be the best indicator of whether or not this project should go forward.

If you discover that corporate management of alarm services has been negligent through the years; that contracts have been continually renewed by virtue of anniversary clauses; that the interminable cost for leased equipment has gone on for so long that the system has paid for itself time and time again; that increases have been passed along unchallenged; that service contracts are in effect and repair calls are routinely billed and paid anyway despite these maintenance agreements; that monitoring costs for similar facilities have a disparity of more than 25% from the same provider; that the monitoring fees of competing providers vary by as much as 100% from low to high; and/or that false alarm fines are paid with regularity; you will quickly come to the conclusion that you will save significant expense dollars by stepping up to a consolidated alarm operation, and this time managing it.

On the other hand, if your experience to date is that corporate management of alarm systems has been diligent; that you are not carrying the baggage for bygone sweetheart-deals made in the field; that previous ownership of an acquired chain did not enter into punitive contractual agreements you inherited; that fee structures have ceilings; that contracts are renewed only after careful review by informed executives; that new markets were awarded based on a competitive bid process; that invoices for services not covered in the service agreement are challenged; that over-billing and fines incurred due to provider negligence are routinely charged back; then you will quickly come to the conclusion that there is little opportunity for savings, that the merits alone of an upgraded system will have to justify the investment.

Once you have researched your entire alarm expense history, you are in the position to project an estimate of present cost. For the purposes of developing an action plan for our model company, we will assume a conservative figure of $90.00 per month being allocated per location under present circumstances. This figure includes all the projected costs of equipment leases, repair to equipment owned, service contracts, aggregate monitoring and reporting fees, and unplanned service costs based on past performance. As an item considered by many one of the "costs of doing business," this may be the first time you recognize annual alarm expense is planned at $324,000. Its actual performance against forecast could exceed that figure due to unforeseen events in the field, but you are on the hook for at least that amount if all goes well.

As with any undertaking of this magnitude, one of expressed ambitions of the project should be to rein-in costs. Therefore, you should set an expense reduction goal, or project margin, that produces a quantitative savings that embellishes the rather subjective estimates regarding reductions to inventory shrink and administrative cost that are routinely offered as justification for LP investment. In this case, a project margin that exceeds 15% of planned expense would be acceptable, as it would represent an annual savings of approximately $50,000; a virtual windfall for companies unaccustomed to give-backs from the loss prevention expense centers. Working with hard numbers, your revised forecast is about $270,000, amounting to $75 per location monthly.

The next step is to shop your account among national providers eager to add your 300 units to their client list. This eagerness can and does translate into cost concessions in exchange for the regular monthly income your account represents to the alarm company's coffers, as well as the prestige accorded the provider for landing the deal. Understand that major alarm companies have made a significant capital investment in national alarm monitoring stations, and like hotels, their P and L's are dictated by occupancy rate: they require maximum utilization of their facilities to recoup their investment. Any account exceeding $250,000 annually is worth vying for in the alarm system industry.

Shopping your account will be a little tricky. News of a 300-store division out for bid spreads quickly in the alarm industry, and your current provider(s) will get wind of it. This results in touch-base calls from your present carrier, perhaps the first unsolicited service contact you have had with them in years. The service representative will try to persuade you from pursuing other vendors, offering to review your present contract agreements and perhaps negotiate a new arrangement, elevating your account to a "preferred customer" status. In the course of these discussions, the ramifications of escaping your current contractual obligations will be implied, either subtlely or heavy-handedly. It may not be in your best interest to tip your hand prematurely in this situation.

Some companies use alarm consultants to solicit bids in a manner that keeps the end-user anonymous, at least in the early stages until preliminary bids are evaluated. This approach may be useful for the executive who wishes to elude the implorings of your present provider. Then, only the vendors in the running meet with the potential client. For the uninitiated, retention of the consultant through the deal brokering process may be advantageous. Once a bona fide provider is elected, then the substantive negotiations are initiated.

The first task is defining a schedule of protection, or equipment package, for each location. As described earlier, standard devices for perimeter protection and interior motion detection are prescribed for the basic package. For most entrances, magnetic contacts on the doors are prescribed. Recessed contacts are best since they make tampering more difficult, and because they are less exposed, the potential for inadvertent damage is lessened (damage you pay to repair). Glass break detectors need to be evenly spaced, but not at the extreme range of the unit is specifications. Adding a few more units to create overlap ensures more dependable coverage.

Likewise, motion detection devices should overlap to compensate for sensitivity adjustments and the degradation of the unit over time. A ceiling-mounted unit projecting a 360° field of protection covers more space than a wall mounted unit projecting a cone-shaped field. Dual-tec devices detect both motion and temperature variance (detecting the body heat of an intruder) and is therefore more selective before activating, resulting in fewer false alarms.

Enhancements such as hold-up alarms, proximity alarms for the safe, sirens, and strobe lights designed to scare off intruders, are nonessential features in routine applications, but need not be dismissed out-of-hand.

The key elements involve the alarm panel and keypad, the central communications link to the monitoring station. Some providers will insist that only their brand-specific panels be used, in order to best facilitate customized operation. The upside is that it may contain unique programming features compatible with the central station. Although this may or may not be true, the downside is that the user becomes restricted to a single-provider, as this brand-specific panel will not communicate with a competitor's system, should you choose to switch over down the road. A safer route is a generic panel designed to interface with multiple systems technology. This way, your options remain open should your chosen provider fall short of expectations.

In keeping with the communications-link to the central station, make sure your telephone line resources are adequate to provide a dedicated line for alarm communication, especially given the day-burg zone monitoring advantages we have incorporated. Shared phone lines with faxes, point of sale (POS) and PC modems are not advisable. Also, get a status on the telephone junction box from which lines are run in to the building. Newer and renovated malls and shopping centers have buried cable; older locations may still have exposed boxes subject to sabotage. If your phone lines are cut by an enterprising burglar, standard alarm panels will be unable to communicate alarm events to the central station. Local alarms (i.e., horns, sirens, strobe lights) will activate in an alarm condition, but the transmission of that alarm to summon response will not occur.

Cellular telephone technology is available as a phone line backup system, and some panels allow for a pulse-signal communication with central station to detect phone line trouble, but these advanced system applications are costly. If you own a jewelry store, get it; if you own a shoe store, forget it.

Once you have established your schedule of protection, you usually have two options in procuring the equipment: buy it or lease it. Buying it involves a substantial up front investment of capital expenditure that retailers would much prefer allocated to areas of the business that generate revenue: expansion, renovation, fixtures, etc.

Leasing the equipment hardly facilitates the project margin, adding fixed monthly expense cost to the operating budget of each location. By the time you pay the equipment lease, the monitoring and reporting charges, the service and maintenance contracts, plus prorating the installation cost, you will be back up to $90 a month per store. You have improved the protection, improved your ability to supervise your locations, and are in a better position to detect and interdict some methods of employee theft, but you have not generated the expense savings that defines a successful conversion program.

A third alternative, offered only by the most progressive providers, involves the alarm company giving you the equipment to use. This is not to imply there is a free lunch here. Alarm company profits do not emanate from the sale of equipment; their primary source of revenue and margin come from the monitoring fees generated from equipment sales. That, coupled with service agreements and a decent return on installation jobs (that are frequently subcontracted), is the core market of their industry.

This arrangement certainly tightens the bond between user and provider, and the advantages may inhibit your leverage to exact pricing concessions for other services, but the premise is sound. After all, do you really want to own alarm equipment? Is this the kind of fixed asset you need to be spending capital allocation to acquire? And although leasing the equipment spreads the cost out over 60 months, do you want to carry that operating expense so you can own a five year-old alarm system at the end of the lease for $1? In five years, technology could be such that your owned system is obsolete.

If they will give it to you, take it. The provider, of course, will still own the system; and should relations sour down the road due to, say, nonpayment of disputed invoices, they could come take it out and you would be hard pressed to stop it. But chances are if the relationship is that far gone, you are shopping for a new provider anyway.

The next step in the conversion program is to extricate your company from existing contracts with your current providers destined to be replaced by your new supplier. Have corporate legal develop an action plan to give notice, and then formally discontinue service with your incumbent vendors. This may not be a slam-dunk process for most companies, especially those who failed to specify 30-day discontinuation clauses in the original contracts. What is worse is that some renewal clauses call for graduated extensions, for three, sometimes five years after renewal, which is not good.

Also, some companies may not be able to even locate original contracts. This is often the case when contracts were negotiated in the field and new market locations merely added on via verbal communications with the local representative. That results in multiple locations being grandfathered into master agreements, the language of which may not favorable to the subscriber.

In addition, expect volatile disputes over who owns what, and punitive sanctions for early termination of existing leases on equipment. Next, discord over the condition of equipment claimed by the ousted provider as unsaleable may arise. In consideration of these developments, an alarm consultant may be valuable to supplement the efforts of your corporate legal counsel in vacating the terms of your existing contracts. There are "failure-to-perform" justifications for releasing your company of its obligations to an alarm provider that an outside expert would be better able to exploit.

Designate a region for conversion, and commit only those stores to the new provider. You will want to evaluate their work in a test environment before handing over your entire company. Send out registered letters to your current suppliers informing them of service discontinuation in 30 days. Some may not even respond within the established time frame, forfeiting their opportunity to contest your action. Others may stamp their feet initially, but the prospect of losing more stores in other regions may temper their response and they may accept a negotiated settlement for a nominal amount.

Monitor progress carefully, emphasizing the performance of the on-line reporting software to perform as advertised, especially in the areas you have customized to meet the needs of your business. Each occasion the system fails to measure up should delay the commitment of another region until the provider delivers.

Your last preparatory task to kick off the conversion program involves assigning an opening and closing schedule to each location. The needs of your business will be the overriding factor in establishing this schedule, but try to be as well defined in this area as possible.

The opening schedule is the earliest time an authorized passcode user can disarm the alarm system. A general rule for programming allows 90 minutes prior to the time the store opens to the public as an adequate window for the opening staff to complete their pre-opening tasks. Entry into the building prior to this time is reported as an unscheduled early opening, appearing for your review on screen six. You can arrange for only personnel with level 3 authorization passcodes and above to be recognized as a valid level for unscheduled openings. Persons without level 3 authorization would require pre-approval with the alarm company by an approved user.

Also arrange for late opening notification from the alarm company in the event the station does not receive an opening signal 30 minutes prior to scheduled opening time for business. The alarm company would then notify senior management that no one has reported for the opening assignment at a given location. This allows management to rally the troops and get the store open for business.

The closing schedule should allow 90 minutes from the close of business hours to complete closing responsibilities and leave the building. Should the alarm company not receive a closing signal within 90 minutes of closing time, they are to call the store and obtain an extended closing authorization from a level 3 user or higher in order for staff to remain in the store. Extended closing authorizations would appear on screen seven for your review.

In the event the alarm company does not receive a closing signal and cannot reach personnel at the store, they are to assume the staff left without setting the alarm, and summon response back to the building from the after-hour call list. This feature is comforting to the assigned closing manager as well, as at least he will know he will not have to spend the whole night tied up on the safe room floor after a robbery waiting for the opening manager to discover him the next morning.

As with all special instructions, the alarm company will seek to protect its interests, specifically the obligations of the central station to perform customized responsibilities for your account. Ensure the differences between unauthorized and unscheduled openings are detailed. Alarm companies accept the burden of reporting unauthorized entries. These are events where a valid passcode is not received. By rejecting an invalid passcode, the system will not disarm and the user is violating perimeter and interior points of protection. Alarm companies routinely treat this event as a break-in. But most monitoring stations will not initiate action when a valid passcode is received to disarm, even if that command is received at 4 a.m. with an opening schedule of 7 a.m. This early entry outside the parameters of the opening schedule must be treated as an unscheduled entry as described earlier, with appropriate notification to management.

Unless you specifically instruct this distinction be made, they will not offer it, and incidents of valid passcode users circumventing the opening schedule will proliferate. Remember, only by tracking unscheduled entry beyond the scope of established schedule will enable you to monitor re-entries after closing. Without it, valid passcode users can close for the night and return one hour later and gain entry. With instructions in force as outlined above, a post-closing re-entry is treated as an unscheduled early opening, and reported. Employees will understand once the building is secured, it is secured for real.

Once your conversion is successfully completed, follow through on your obligation to train your senior field management personnel, and insist this new supervisory resource at their disposal is utilized effectively. Use the novel exception reports that are provided to catch somebody early, so the merits of deterring employee theft can be quickly realized in shortage reduction.

Electronic Article Surveillance

3

Shoplifting has long been the most visible of the factors that contribute to inventory shortage. Long before the realization set in of the damage done by dishonest employees, shoplifting was the ever-present reminder of shrink. Not that the occasional internal theft went completely unnoticed, but the theft of merchandise by customers was the most frequently discussed issue in retail shortage meetings. It is what store employees wanted to talk about most, and it seemed that was what upper management wanted to talk about too.

Attributing shrink primarily to shoplifting allowed retailers to blame a faceless third party for their losses. Workers were not made to feel uncomfortable, as happens in blunt discussions of employee theft; and the financial group was spared some accountability for bookkeeping errors which contributed its own share to the mix. Laying the problem at the feet of the shoplifter seemed a painless and pragmatic approach to programs designed to reduce shortage.

Retail security personnel knew better. The gradual erosion of the social restraints over the past three decades that kept criminal activity restricted to an underclass of crooks and swindlers certainly impacted the rise in shoplifting occurrences, as persons engaged in such activity no longer seemed burdened with the stigma of being a social outcast. But all along, loss prevention professionals were aware that the same element was infiltrating the ranks of loyal employees, and that the employee population was a microcosm of society as a whole, susceptible to the same deterioration of moral values. But, the time had not yet arrived for a diversified shortage program, and shoplifting was as good a bandwagon as any.

The emphasis of the era remained on shoplifting. Resources were marshaled toward this end: catch the crooks and lower the shortage. Security departments were staffed with uniformed agents to provide a visible deterrent, and undercover detectives to apprehend those not deterred. Upper management sat enthralled as security executives presented apprehension analysis, massaging the statistics to equate body counts to progress in the war on shortage (sound familiar?). Appeals were made for more troops, more radios, more hardware, more equipment. Lookouts, coops, and perches dotted the landscape of big department stores with one-way mirrors, as detectives on catwalks scurried east and west for the best vantage point from which to make the case.

Still, the shortage numbers went up, almost in direct proportion to the burgeoning costs of a payroll-driven security program. The retailer was losing on both ends: high shrink and high expense, but in the haberdasherer's heyday it was tolerable as long as shoplifters were being caught and prosecuted to the fullest extent of the law.

The tolerance waned with the onset of tougher economic times, and the necessity to vary the loss prevention approach to shortage programs became apparent. But first, this appetite for shoplifter apprehensions had to be sated before loss prevention programs could move on to ripe areas of opportunity: internal theft and inventory control.

The challenge had become how to exploit better opportunities amidst a culture that measured success in arrests. Senior management listened attentively as LP executives laid out plans to make in-roads internally that would more than offset any increase in shoplifting losses resulting from a demilitarized security department; sort of a "retail-ization" of the shortage program. Still, the skeptics needed assurances that the store would not be given away to shoplifters whose exploits seemed to grow bolder each year. Something needed to be done to check their advance before attention could be turned inward, and payroll dollars were drying up fast. A better way to protect open sell merchandise, other than physically guarding it, had to be found.

If only there was a way to electronically guard the merchandise, something that could take the men out of the loop. The demand was so great there had to be, and in the true entrepreneurial spirit that made this country great, an industry was born: electronic article surveillance (EAS).

The technology of EAS has been available since Marconi invented the wireless: a transmitter and a receiver. An electronic device could be attached to each piece of merchandise, or article, which would "watch over it" until it was purchased, replacing the need for manpower surveillance of the merchandise. This electronic device would transmit a signal to a receiver at the store exits, sounding an alarm as the article it was attached to was being removed from the store. Since the device would be removed from the article at the point of sale, it could be safely presumed that the alarm indicated merchandise was leaving the store for which payment had not been received — unless, of course, if the clerk somehow forgot to remove the tag, and then the alarm did not mean that at all. Well, that part will need some work, but we've got the technology. All we need now is a vendor.

Several companies jockeyed for position in this cottage industry to meet the demand of retailers to safeguard their merchandise and bring some relief to the payroll lines. Soon, a provider emerged that became as synonymous with EAS as Kleenex had become with tissues. The Sensormatic Corporation of Deerfield Beach, Florida, successfully marketed a transmitter in the form of a magnetic strip sheathed in plastic tags that could be attached to assorted apparel (Figure 25). Receivers were boxed in pedestals, stationed like silent sentries at the exits (Figures 26–28), that generated a field through which the passing of the magnetic strip would transmit the alarm, alerting any employee of a shoplifting in progress — unless, of course, if the clerk forgot to remove the tag, then the alarm did not mean that at all. That part will also need some work, but we've got the technology. All we need now is the training.

In short order, white, plastic tags dangling from the sleeves of jackets, dresses, sweaters, robes, and the legs of pants inundated the selling floor, becoming as recognizable as hangers to merchandise presentation (Figure 40). The tags came in a variety of sizes and shapes, as competing providers patented their innovations. The loss prevention community became awash in EAS brochures, and expense appropriations (tied to payroll reduction formulas) were forthcoming with regularity.

The birth pangs of the revolution were enormous. Shoplifters, ill-prepared (at first) to cope with this technology, were apprehended by uniformed security personnel at the exits at an "alarming" rate. The success ratio of legitimate "hits" emboldened security personnel to throw caution to the wind and equate the EAS alarm with a larceny in progress.

As the legal community eventually awoke to this inherent defect in apprehension practices, this trend led to the inexorable spate of dismissed criminal cases. Even in cases where the merchandise exiting the building was clearly unpaid for, the incompleteness of the observation of theft by the complainant was sufficient for the acquittal of all but the most destitute defendants. The courts were initially uninformed about this new-fangled shoplifter detector, and were unaware of the presumption of guilt deduced in the private sector with respect to EAS alarms and the subsequent recovery of unpaid for merchandise at the door. As such, they were unprepared to convict based solely on the inferences of an EAS alarm without supporting testimony describing the act of the theft witnessed by store security. Few shoplifters filed suit following the dismissal of their cases, most were relieved to have just gotten away with one. The litigation explosion of the 1980s, however, was just around the corner.

Figure 25 Standard application of an EAS tag to a garment. Tag is removed at the point of sale. (Courtesy of Sensormatic Electronics, Deerfield Beach, FL.)

Retailers, reveling in the windfall of recovered merchandise, did little to rein-in their aggressive door monitors. The sanctions resulting from the dismissed criminal cases of known shoplifters were minimal, but a more ominous trend was building: real customers, who had made legitimate purchases, were being accosted in a hostile manner by agents of the company predisposed to treating them as shoplifters. Several factors were contributing to this phenomenon: one that would soon find its way into the civil courts for remedy.

Over time, retailers began to learn certain facts of life about their beloved EAS system. The first was that the field generated by the receiver pedestals had a tendency to expand, as excessive pedestrian traffic caused the detection "bubble" to swell beyond the specified range initially planned. As the traffic

Figure 26 Entranceway detector pedestal. The array of available styles are unobtrusive to store decor and can protect openings of varying widths — from double doors to mall entrances to overhead bay doors. (Courtesy of Sensormatic Electronics, Deerfield Beach, FL.)

dissipated, the field would condense and regain its normal parameters, much like the water level in a tub would recede when the bather got out. This unexpected development resulted in the field of detection, during periods of heavy customer traffic, expanding to the point where it came into contact with tagged merchandise on display racks too close to the door, causing false alarms. Until this operational deficiency became identified and corrected, door guards responding to the false alarms would routinely stop patrons and search their bags for stolen merchandise.

Another contributor to the false alarm epidemic was defective systems being pumped into the marketplace by vendors foregoing quality control to meet the ever-growing demand for product. This was especially evident from suppliers of "knock-offs," vendors trying to undercut the established providers with substandard equipment and tags at bargain-basement prices to attract the business of cash-strapped retailers. The net effect of this troublesome development was "ghosting," alarms that would activate for no apparent reason.

More factors came to light as the false alarm issues progressed from operational nuisance to industry crisis. The boom in the consumer electronics

Figure 27 Entranceway detector pedestal. (Courtesy of Sensormatic Electronics, Deerfield Beach, FL.)

industry began to fill the airwaves with a myriad of transmissions and signals for pagers, mobile radios, and cell phones. It seemed anything that used to be plugged in was now portable, emitting or receiving over one frequency or another. The sheer density of electronic signals in a busy downtown area would randomly interrupt the magnetic field of the EAS system, causing an alarm event. Customers carrying beepers, car-alarm deactivators, even pacemakers, were subject to the impromptu bag check of a security employee suspecting them of theft.

Unscrupulous store detectives, seeking to make quota or pad their statistics, exacerbated the problem. Operating under a misguided belief that the EAS alarm justified the brief detention and cursory search of a customer that had aroused their suspicion, security personnel would activate the EAS alarm themselves, using a tag secreted on their person to manufacture the opportunity to stop and question suspects, and check their bags.

Figure 28 Entranceway detector pedestal. (Courtesy of Sensormatic Electronics, Deerfield Beach, FL.)

Even in situations where none of the aforementioned factors came into play, we still had the clerks at the register forgetting to remove the tag at the point of sale. Clearly, the training was lagging behind the implementation, and all the letters of apology and baskets of fruit sent to customers who complained was not going to stem the tide of ruinous litigious action if controls were not put in place and policies enacted for EAS systems.

And with all this said, one irrevocable fact remained: inventory losses went down. Considerable improvement in shrink results was quickly realized in most retail operations where EAS was introduced. That EAS made a significant impact in preventing shoplifting was indisputable, and substantial dollar savings were evident over comparable inventory periods. We have the technology; all we need now is to fix it.

With vendor support from the leading providers, retailers rolled out aggressive training and support systems for EAS. Clerks were trained ad nauseam to remove tags and check garments over meticulously. Second generation systems were produced, and were better able to screen out interference. Electronic shielding became available to prevent the fluctuating field from enveloping nearby merchandise.

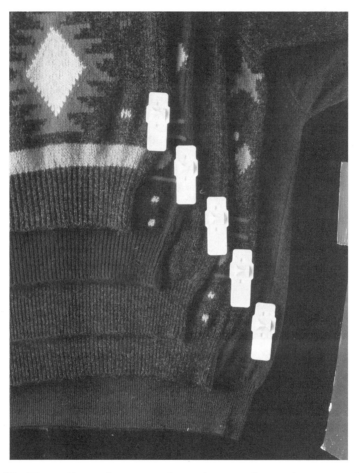

Figure 29 The uniform placement of tags does not detract from merchandise presentation (Courtesy of Sensormatic Electronics, Deerfield Beach, FL.)

Security personnel were replaced with inventory control representatives, who offered customer service and apologies for inconvenience caused by alarms at the door. Polite responses replaced the innuendo of theft during customer approaches, and over time, EAS tags became a part of the normal shopping experience. Soon, the door monitors became superfluous, and sales associates handled the alarms themselves with tact and confidence.

Quality control returned as the industry policed itself, and tagging innovations that permitted hard goods and other nonapparel items to be tagged became available (Figures 30 and 31). Today, sophisticated electronic tags interface with camera systems and alarms that alert the retailer someone is tampering with a tag (Figure 32). There's even an "ink tag" (Figure 33) which leaks an indelible dye onto the product when forcibly removed, making the item useless to a shoplifter, sort of like the mutually-assured-destruction idea.

Figure 30 The self-adherent magnetic tag allows protection of a variety of products which were not adaptable to the tag-and-pin application shown in Figure 26. (Courtesy of Sensormatic Electronics, Deerfield Beach, FL.)

This is not to suggest that EAS put shoplifters out of business. Once their initial perplexity wore off, they soon went about their business of defeating the system. Common tools, such as pliers and cutters, were standard issue for shoplifters who would forcibly remove tags prior to stealing the merchandise. But those not so well equipped were deterred, all to the benefit of the retailer. And apprehended shoplifters who used pliers or cutters to defeat the tag, faced the added criminal charge of possession of burglary tools.

Shoplifters who were successful in removing the tags had to contend with disposing of the tag as well. As clever as they were in concealing defeated tags in racks, bins and the pockets of adjacent garments, the tags were eventually discovered and the event documented. Loss prevention personnel used the reports of found defeated tags to identify target areas in the store where shoplifting activity was prevalent, and channeled their surveillance resources to those places. Shoplifters soon realized that it took longer to effect a theft because of the added time it took to remove the tags, so their "haul" was generally less than it would have been otherwise, and they were cognizant they were leaving visible evidence of the crime behind. The pros refined their skill sets to compensate; the amateurs were effectively stopped.

Nearly 20 years after its widespread introduction as a retail loss prevention mainstay, EAS is still a viable LP tool. Refinements in both tags and systems has enabled it to retain its effectiveness as a deterrent to shoplifting. Rather than being the driving force in shrink reduction as it once had been, EAS is used today as a component of a more diversified shortage program.

Figure 31 A magnetic tag is "demagnetized" at the point of sale, allowing the cashier to swipe the tag instead of removing it, thereby speeding up the checkout process. (Courtesy of Sensormatic Electronics, Deerfield Beach, FL.)

This is because EAS addresses only a single element of inventory losses: shoplifting. It has little impact on losses attributed to employee theft and inventory control. Even its usefulness in preventing shoplifting is more or less restricted to the amateur opportunist who is unable to defeat the tag.

Since few retailers can attribute their inventory losses to this narrowly defined group of amateur shoplifters, sole reliance on EAS to resolve chronic shortage problems is unwise. The ancillary benefits, however, do sustain LP awareness among employees, and for that reason EAS should be included in the retailer's arsenal against shortage.

With amateur shoplifters deterred, and professionals slowed down, EAS does its part to free up management's attention and resources for duty against other shortage causing factors. Employees involved with EAS, those tasked with tagging goods or auditing merchandise for tagging compliance, are fulfilling the employee's role in shortage prevention. Defeated tags found in the store help ward off complacency, and serve as reminders to remain vigilant. Knowing shoplifters will attempt to remove tags before concealing merchandise has helped employees refine their timing and tact for approaching shoplifters on the selling floor, and gives them confidence to act.

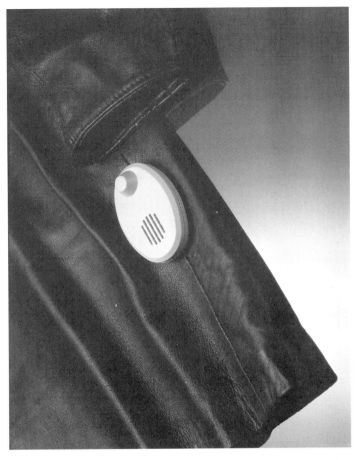

Figure 32 An advanced electronic tag sends out an audible alarm alerting store personnel of tampering or attempts at unauthorized removal. (Courtesy of Sensormatic Electronics, Deerfield Beach, FL.)

Investment in EAS is a considerable undertaking for most companies, and management in the field has to be diligent in both the implementation and maintenance of the system to fully derive its benefits. As much as a well managed EAS operation sustains employee awareness in loss prevention, a neglected, malfunctioning system will erode the employee's confidence in it and undermine the credibility of management's commitment to shrink reduction.

It is unfortunate when the very device companies acquire to demonstrate their resolve to improve shortage performance is inoperative and left in a state of disrepair. Employees figure management does not care, and can easily rationalize lessening their own efforts. Maintenance requests for EAS service should receive prompt attention, and a system to recycle tags put in place to assure replenishment. Managing the EAS program requires ongoing training,

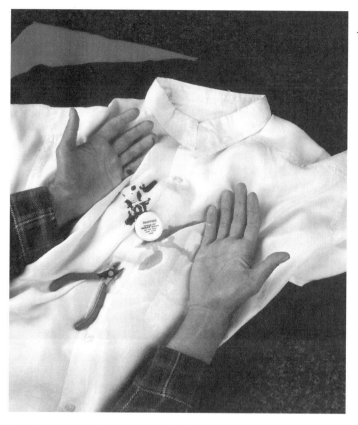

Figure 33 The advanced "ink tags" leaks an indelible dye onto the garment when forcibly removed by means other than the approved detacher, depriving the shoplifter of the item's value. (Courtesy of Sensormatic Electronics, Deerfield Beach, FL.)

an aggressive maintenance plan, and accountability in the field for compliance to EAS standards.

The future for EAS in retail loss prevention appears promising. The next generation of systems will result from leaders in the EAS industry collaborating with individual product manufacturers to design tags that can be imbedded into the finished product. In the retail music business, work has already begun with the music labels to incorporate a generic EAS tag into compact discs and cassettes as part of the manufacturing process.

This technology, known as "source tagging," hopes to deliver goods to the retailer with a universal EAS tag built-in to the product, alleviating the expense involved with maintaining an inventory of tags, as well as the labor costs associated with tagging and untagging the merchandise (Figure 34). Products that are source tagged would be "deactivated" with a magnetic wand or pad at the POS, neutralizing the signal.

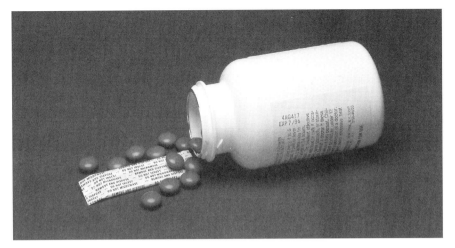

Figure 34 "Source tagging", an application where the manufacturer places the tag within the product contents offers the maximum protection from tag tampering by would-be shoplifters by placing the tag outside of their reach. (Courtesy of Sensormatic Electronics, Deerfield Beach, FL.)

In addition to the anticipated expense savings, source tagging would inhibit even the professional shoplifter's ability to identify and remove EAS tags from products they wish to steal. The ensuing impact of taking the professional shoplifters out of the loop would bring about a renaissance of the contribution EAS can make to shortage reduction.

Closed Circuit Television

4

Application of CCTV in the private sector has grown considerably in the past two decades. Always a mainstay of physical security in banks, casinos, jewelry stores, and other establishments that handle large quantities of cash or precious merchandise, cameras were used to discourage misdeeds by employees and customers alike. They were most often employed in fixed positions, with an agent of the company assigned to observe activity at a row of monitors while engaged in other clerical duties. Some were hooked up to recording devices, which relieved the agent from dedicated surveillance, as events could be retrieved and reviewed at later times.

In time, this application became a prudent security measure for protecting office buildings and large facilities from unauthorized trespass, without having to resort to a foot patrol of the premises. Also, as armed robberies began to branch out from the usual target of banks, jewelry stores, and liquor shops into gas stations and convenience stores, merchants employed cameras as both a deterrent and a means to identify the hold-up men.

Retailers used cameras primarily for surveillance of employee activity. Although some units were discreetly placed on the selling floor, they were seldom monitored and rarely recorded. They served silently in a deterrent capacity. Mobile camera systems were used by security personnel to surveil cash registers where leads on cash theft or illicit product discounting had been furnished. Covert installations monitoring the receiving dock and stockrooms were also useful to security personnel conducting investigations of shipment discrepancies.

In its early utilization, cameras served the investigator by enabling him to observe activity that would be interrupted by his physical presence. Innovative camera placement brought loss prevention investigative resources into places thought safe from scrutiny, and substantive information was gained and observations made that facilitated many apprehensions of employees involved in theft. Generally, the investigator would observe conduct on the monitor that he could act on, be it the concealment of cash or the removal of merchandise, to culminate in an apprehension. The evidence of the case was more his observation of the event, than it was any physical evidence provided through the CCTV system. Recordings of a theft on tape, introduced in court, were rare, as the system capabilities early on did not lend themselves to the user-friendly applications we see today. Taped images were in first-generation time lapse technology. Movement was blurred and advanced at irregular intervals, making the discernment of the recorded actions difficult for the viewer.

Today, CCTV technology has made dramatic strides in meeting the needs of any consumer who wishes to monitor activity at the workplace (or the home for that matter). No longer must hours be spent observing the monitor or reviewing taped images. Systems have become computerized, with programmable hours of operation and automated retrieval and play back. Video recorders have greater time lapse capacity and options, as well as the ability to record multiple camera shots simultaneously.

Retailers who have not availed themselves of this technology to enhance their loss prevention and security resources may wish to revisit this area in light of the advances that have been made with respect to adapting the system to specific needs. Customized applications, integrated with existing access control, POS, and alarm systems, can be introduced into a retail environment with minimal fuss at reasonable cost. The following pages will detail some of the more proactive systems available, and will demonstrate the control improvements such applications may deliver.

CCTV applications function best when operated in tandem with other resources. To expect the mere presence of live cameras to single-handedly resolve chronic inventory losses overestimates the technology and underutilizes the more primary LP formulas: employee awareness and training, customer service, watchful supervision, and compliance auditing. Successfully managing these components of the shortage program lays the foundation for introducing CCTV into the efficient, accountable environment such an investment needs in order to deliver a sustained impact.

We should first define the benefits that can be derived from CCTV, and then structure a system best suited to meet those ends. The primary advantage for a retailer is enhanced control: control of the premises, the employees, and the merchandise. Electronic surveillance improves supervision, especially in its capacity to create a permanent record of events — one that can be retrieved for training or investigative purposes. Cameras that monitor building access, and those situated to provide a deterrent to armed robbery, allow the employer to demonstrate a commitment to worker safety, and to offset the intrusive nature of surveillance in a positive way. Even a modest investment in CCTV can illustrate to store employees that the company recognizes the enormity of the asset protection tasks asked of its workers, and will match those efforts with equipment and support.

To realize these benefits, the ideal system would incorporate the following elements:

- Provide both deterrence and surveillance capability
- Function independently of operators at a manned console
- Separate routine activity from unusual events
- Store events efficiently for future review

Of all the uses for which a camera system may be employed, shoplifting prevention is perhaps the most labor-intensive. As opposed to applications to detect internal dishonesty, effective shoplifting reduction is most often achieved at the time of the theft, when the incident can be prevented or the shoplifter apprehended. This requires live monitoring by an authorized employee who can initiate a response to observed events (Figure 35).

Unless the company employs in-house loss prevention specialists to operate a CCTV system designed to monitor customer activity, the system must allow employees engaged in other activities to operate the controls. This is especially true for stores with self-service merchandise displays and minimum staffing allowances. Shoplifters seeking to conduct their activity in remote areas of the selling floor may not get the attention required to prevent the theft because the store staff is occupied with other duties. However, a half dozen strategically placed cameras feeding back to a monitor at the POS station will allow the cashier on duty to observe the preliminary stages of a theft in time to alert another employee, who can effect the approach and deter the loss. Fixed cameras (Figure 36) can be monitored simultaneously on a "split screen", or assigned "channels" which the operator can switch to. These channels can be programmed to automatically rotate on a preset schedule and sequence to permit at-a-glance viewing of multiple locations by a stationary sales person. Should the employee determine a subject on the screen warrants scrutiny, she can lock-in to that camera shot; then resume the scan mode once the subject's intentions have been determined.

More sophisticated systems permit camera angles to pan or tilt, in order to "follow" a person moving throughout the store. This is often seen in conjunction with a "dome," opaque housings which obscure the camera location from the view of the subject (Figure 37). Fewer of these cameras may be needed to properly cover the selling floor, but they require more hands-on control. Empty housings, placebo domes situated around the selling floor, (Figure 38) creates a kind of "shell game" for the shoplifter to figure

Figure 35 CCTV monitoring station, bringing the observation capabilities of a single loss prevention agent to a multitude of areas simultaneously. (Courtesy of Sensormatic Electronics, Deerfield Beach, FL.)

out which units contain a functioning camera from those that do not, and provides a modicum of deterrence at minimal cost.

The control unit can be a keyboard or "joystick" which the operator uses to trail a suspect and maintain uninterrupted surveillance (an essential element if an apprehension is contemplated). For close-in observation, many of these units are fitted with zoom lenses. When used in conjunction with a video recorder, evidence equal to eyewitness testimony is produced; an invaluable record should a prosecution ensue from the apprehension.

Recent advances in utilizing CCTV for shoplifting prevention now permit the system to interact with other electronic safeguards, particularly Electronic Article Surveillance (EAS) systems. An electronic inventory tag "signals" the integrated CCTV unit that it has been "compromised" by unauthorized

Figure 36 Simulated camera housing. (Courtesy of Sensormatic Electronics, Deerfield Beach, FL.)

removal. In effect, when a shoplifter attempts to remove the EAS tag to defeat that system at the door, he inadvertently "summons" the camera system to come over and have a look. An audible alarm at the console alerts the operator to the event.

It is in this area of system integration that CCTV has relieved itself of the burdensome payroll costs formerly associated with it. Automated recording features enabled the monitoring station to go unattended; however, the system remained on continuous record, capturing hours, sometimes days and weeks, of routine activity. This collection of unremarkable history lent itself to the maintenance of an unwieldy videotape library, the value of which became suspect. CCTV technology has since developed software enhancements that permit cameras and recorders to interface with other electronic security systems that feature programmable, event-specific, recordings. For example, after-hours entry into the home office building were monitored by lobby guards with sign-in logs. In time, many companies replaced the cost of these night watchmen with access control devices which recorded the ID number of persons coming and going. Fixed cameras provided a video record of the events, which could be retained for future reference.

In order to determine if the night shift computer operator removed a company-owned PC from the premises, the investigator would peruse the egress log to note the times the subject left the building in the days following the reported theft. Those times would then be listed, and the corresponding

Figure 37   The domed housing for movable or stationary cameras conceals the camera's viewing angle from would-be wrong-doers, depriving them of the freedom to operate freely outside of the camera's vantage point. (Courtesy of Sensormatic Electronics, Deerfield Beach, FL.)

videotape would be reviewed to observe the subject's departure. This was an involved process for the investigator, since the tapes contained countless hours of recorded "dead time," which are periods of zero activity in the lobby. Further, due to the fact that the recorder did not capture events in "real time" so that storage capacity of a single tape could be expanded and the frequency with which tapes had to be changed reduced, the event was recorded in "time lapse" photography.

Time lapse is a series of "snapshots" — still frames put in motion to create an almost animated reproduction of the event. Depending on the programmed "shutter speed" of the recorder, i.e., 8 hours for real time (necessitating tapes be changed three times a day), or up to 168 hours for a one

Figure 38 Simulated mirrored camera dome. (Courtesy of Sensormatic Electronics, Deerfield Beach, FL.)

week documentary, the subject could elude detection by having the good fortune to exit between frames.

The challenge for the CCTV industry was to develop a system that integrated the camera system with the access control system, in order to flush out sustained periods of inactivity from the videotaped record. This would preserve tape time for actual events, and enable the system to function closer to real time, improving the playback imaging while still limiting the number of prerequisite tape changes.

Programming the cameras to interface with the access control system resulted in the recorder capturing only the activity designated as noteworthy. When an employee inserted his access control ID card to either enter or exit, that action prompted the recorder to activate, and a video record was made of this isolated event. The unit would then deactivate once the entrance was secure, conserving precious tape space for the next event.

In a computerized integrated system, our investigator could now enter the employees IDs and get a readout of all times the worker exited, rather than culling through egress printouts. Those events could then be entered into the CCTV system for automated cueing, and the video record for the requested events would be displayed. With periodic dead times edited from the tape, the playback is enhanced because the time lapse can be programmed closer to real time; 8 hours of event-only recording may be equivalent to 96 hours of dedicated, time-lapse recording.

Bringing this technology to the store level has more obvious advantages. Having a camera on the "back door" to record employees taking out trash and receiving shipments has always been a useful application of CCTV in a retail operation. But the incessant recording of dead time, coupled with little indication of when the door was in use, made playback a tedious hit or miss proposition. Integrating the camera with the burglar alarm device on the door made for expeditious review: the recorder would now capture only the moments the door was opened, and the ensuing activity until it was closed.

On a larger scale, imagine the control enhancements a retailer would enjoy by tying in a camera system to the loading dock operation at the distribution center. Operational audits generally highlight control of these bay doors as one of the more pronounced LP exposures in the industry. Cameras positioned to monitor the shipping process would improve supervision, quality control, and productivity, and would make the restrictions on building access more enforceable.

Returning to store level system integration, burglar alarm and CCTV interfacing enables the retailer to acquire a videotaped record of many of the alarm exceptions detailed in chapter two. For instance, a camera system lying dormant after-hours could be activated by an intruder breaching zones of protection during a burglary. In addition to notifying the alarm company of a break-in, the alarm device would also notify the CCTV system to initiate the record function of cameras situated on the selling floor.

Another area of opportunity is presented at the POS station. Cameras monitoring events at the register have long served a useful deterrent to employee theft. As with other applications of dedicated surveillance, a manager would have to identify a suspicious transaction on sales audit reports, then retrieve the event manually on the recorder for play back. A programmable system integrated with designated POS functions can deliver event-specific re-enactments of transactions management may want to review.

Certain register transactions create "exceptions" in the sales audit process. These exception events, e.g., voids, refunds, exchanges, no sales, price discounts, etc., are flagged on exception reports when the clerk initiates a transaction of this type. A CCTV system which is integrated with the POS can be prompted by the same transaction events that trigger exception reporting, to activate the camera's recorder and preserve the transaction for future reference. This would enable the store manager to verify the circumstances of the $200 void or the 50% discount he notices on the sales audit exception report. Such accountability would go a long way to deter fraudulent POS transactions retail employees sometimes engage in. POS integration is especially useful in CCTV application that records a sequence of programmed camera shots, because the POS exception can override the sequence program, signaling the recorder to "stay put" until the POS transaction is complete.

Let's examine multiple system integration as it applies to a standard CCTV package for a typical retail location. The equipment package for a model specialty store may include the following components:

- Position 1: domed camera to monitor north quadrant selling floor.
- Position 2: domed camera to monitor south quadrant selling floor.
- Position 3: domed camera to monitor east quadrant selling floor.
- Position 4: domed camera to monitor west quadrant selling floor.
- Position 5: fixed camera to monitor primary POS station.
- Position 6: fixed camera to monitor secondary POS station.
- Position 7: fixed camera to monitor rear area delivery door.
- Position 8: fixed camera to monitor office safe area.
- Programmable time lapse VCR secured in manager's office.
- 19" TV monitor for office playback.
- 8 position sequential switcher (to rotate camera positions on screen).
- Keypad control unit for domed camera units operated from office.
- 13" TV monitor located at primary POS station (for cashier use: a 19" monitor suspended from the ceiling in front of the POS station permits cashier viewing as well as notifies customers a live CCTV system is in use).
- 8 position sequential switcher at primary POS station: the 8-position switcher at the primary POS station should have camera position #8 (the office safe area) locked out to prevent customer observation of the safe room area.
- Keypad control unit for domed camera units at primary POS station
- 31 blank VHS cassettes for one month's daily storage in tape library.

A CCTV package such as this would be a formidable asset to the store's LP efforts, even if it were to function independently of other security systems. But integrating it with other systems quantifies the subject matter to be recorded by enabling the user to select priority events for taping, rather than rely on random sequencing, and makes the time invested in supervisory play back considerably more productive.

The nerve center of an integrated CCTV system is the programmable VCR. Depending on the level of compatibility with related systems, the VCR can be programmed to override its random sequencing operation, and direct its recording function exclusively to a priority event. As discussed, these priority events can be initiated by electronic interface with burglar alarm, POS, and access control systems. In doing so, the user is assured of capturing activity that is more germane to the issues of loss prevention than of routine store operation, and the speed and accuracy with which unusual events can be addressed is greatly enhanced.

Without system integration, your store manager could be sitting at his desk completing schedules oblivious to the fraudulent refund being transacted at the POS station, which is sequencing through his monitor on camera position #6. With an integrated CCTV and POS system, the transaction function at the POS which initiates a refund would prioritize this event on the monitor, and alert him with an audible alarm to view the monitor.

Without system integration, your store manager could be doing a lunch relief at the register, and be oblivious to the employee on break in the back office opening the delivery door and passing out merchandise to a waiting accomplice, which is sequencing through his monitor on camera position #7. With an integrated CCTV and burglar alarm system, the breach of the perimeter door could prioritize this event on the POS station monitor, and alert him with an audible alarm to view the monitor. Without system integration, your manager could be in the back counting down the safe after closing, and be oblivious to the fact that the closing clerk who was supposed to be vacuuming the selling floor, has instead brought a box of merchandise to his car. With an integrated CCTV and access control system, the employee's unscheduled exit would be noted, and the manager alerted to view his monitor.

System integration does not necessarily have to be automated to achieve similar levels of protection; it is simply preferable to the manual process of cross-referencing individual reports generated from independent systems to the video record. Synchronizing the time/date generators of the POS, burglar alarm, and access control systems with the CCTV recorder still enables the manager to reconstruct unusual events after the fact, and provides evidence to act on, even if gathered from separate sources.

Despite the advances in technology and capabilities of security systems, they are still operated by people who are prone to occasional lapses; either deliberate or unintentional. Many a fruitful investigation that relied on systems and equipment has been thwarted by the oversight of a well meaning individual, or the sabotage of a cunning adversary. To minimize exposure to these eventualities, the integrity of CCTV systems needs to be tested regularly. Equipment and recorded tapes have to be secured to prevent tampering, and checks and balances established to ensure tapes are recycled on a rigid schedule.

Senior management must emphasize with the field that the tools to investigate impropriety have been furnished, and that store line management is expected to be diligent in its pursuit of suspect activity. Once the novelty of integrated security systems wears off, complacency sometimes sets in; the guard is lowered and the enterprising employee creates opportunity. The home office should be periodically challenging the productivity of its LP investments, making certain that stores utilize the resources provided in innovative ways.

After a given period of orientation, the Home Office should be able to realize a substantial drop-off in cash over and shorts, void transactions and refunds, shipping discrepancies, and unscheduled alarm events. These factors can serve as a barometer of operational aberrations, and they should be reduced in direct proportion to the deterrent impact achieved by the introduction of a CCTV system. However, many of these events were the result of illicit activity; the cessation of those events derived from deterrence should be reflected in the overall reduction of the total number of exceptions reported over time. Stores unable to meet revised shrink goals, or which fail to perform favorably against previous exception history after the introduction of a CCTV system, warrant close scrutiny to ensure the resources allocated are properly deployed and managed.

Designing integrated security systems takes much forethought and planning to accomplish. Identifying a progressive provider willing to customize their equipment to your operation requires the oversight of an informed company executive, one who is able to sift through the glitter of a vendor's sales pitch and come away with a product that meets the retailer's demands.

As previously stated, the integral component of a flexible CCTV system is the VCR and its programmable features. Close attention to its capacity for multiple-imaging recording (capturing several camera shots at once), yet capable of uninterrupted individual camera play back, is essential. Too often, play backs include picture-switching through the programmed sequence of camera shots, and the continuity of an observation of theft is disrupted, compromising its evidentiary value.

Lastly, procurers of CCTV systems for use in the workplace need to be cognizant of legislative initiatives that limit covert surveillance in private places, and that require prerequisite notice be given to those who could be potentially observed by electronic surveillance devices. Although legislation has yet to be enacted on a federal level, such matters may be governed by local ordinance, and inquiry into statutory regulation at the state level is advisable.

Even in the absence of statutory restriction, users of CCTV and other surveillance equipment must insure that the use of such devices is reasonable and justifiable in order to insulate themselves from invasion of privacy charges. It may be legal to place cameras in employee locker rooms for legitimate investigative purposes, but it may also be deemed unreasonable and injurious to an employee's privacy.

Companies should set internal policies for limiting surveillance operations because of the volatility of privacy in the workplace issues. Policy should require some level of upper management approval prior to initiating electronic surveillance in the field to safeguard the company from overzealous applications that could be construed as abusive to privacy. Where circumstances permit, employees should be notified in general terms that the company uses surveillance equipment.

CCTV is a legitimate tool for retailers to protect their assets and improve the controls in their operation. It is, however, coming under the scrutiny of lawmakers and privacy advocates more and more, and users need to stay abreast of developments in this area to ensure both the employer and the employee are protected when electronic surveillance systems are in use.

Guard Force Management

5

One resource retailers must often consider in providing a physical security presence in stores is the use of outside guard service. Contract guards are frequently utilized in a deterrent capacity, i.e., their uniformed presence alone is expected to prevent shoplifting activity. These are not employees of the company, but rather personnel contracted out from a guard company to perform a specified set of duties.

The retailer should make very clear with the provider the scope of these duties. Since neither party should make presumptions in this area, this chapter will assist the retailer in establishing the parameters of service which the vendor can provide and the retailer should expect.

Prior to contracting guard service, companies should examine their shortage program and identify which elements of it are ineffective to the point of requiring outside assistance. Rarely are contract guards effective against employee dishonesty and inventory control issues in a store setting, so the presumption must be that external theft is beyond the store's ability to control to the degree that outside assistance is warranted. This is often the case in urban areas experiencing high property crime rates, where two factors come into play: (1) police response is slow due to more pressing criminal activity that occupies their attention, and (2) unless some sort of uniformed authority is in evidence, shoplifters will target a store due to a reduced perception of risk. The latter point is underscored for merchants with highly desirable goods, in demand on the street for either prestige or ready resale value.

Retailers should examine whether their operation is properly staffed to create an employee presence that can deter shoplifting. Light coverage is an invitation to theft, and perhaps the expense of guard coverage would be more productive if invested in staff hours. Also, capital purchases for camera or

EAS systems may have a greater long-term effect on reducing shoplifting than the quick-fix of a guard at the door.

More often than not, however, it is an issue of employee intimidation that prompts retailers to opt for guards. Regardless of the staffing level, or camera and EAS resources dedicated to a particular location, if the staff is afraid to approach and deter shoplifters, they will not. Street toughs are effective in eroding an employee's resolve to prevent shoplifting. They are known to ridicule, harass, and even threaten store employees who appear too diligent. Management must respond swiftly to these events, to protect its assets and to demonstrate support for employees trying to do their jobs well.

There are several areas of opportunity the retailer should try to exploit when making an investment in uniformed guard coverage. The first area is that the company use this resource to express its commitment to store employees that preventing theft is a worthwhile cause; one that justifies the expense allocation that is sure to effect the prevention and loss performance of a location that introduces guard coverage into its expense structure. The second area is that providing uniformed guard coverage in no way alleviates the employees from their responsibility to prevent theft. On-site guards are there to assist employees in their role of primary asset protectors.

Guards will not fill a void in loss prevention caused by employees turning their attention elsewhere; they can only serve to supplement the efforts of the staff. Store management has to understand that security is not delegated to the guard; the guard serves as an extra set of eyes to observe and report activity to management for action.

Third, the guard is useful in demonstrating to store personnel that employee safety is an ongoing concern of upper management, and that employees going about the business of asset protection do so more aggressively, and with greater confidence, if trained security personnel are ready to protect employees engaged in a loss prevention-related encounter with a customer.

Once an environment exists where retailers can realize these benefits of guard coverage and get mileage out of the investment that puts the shortage program back on track, genuine improvement in shrink results can be expected. That expectation of improved results needs to be communicated to the contract guard agencies competing for your business. Choosing a guard company involves a selection process where the client company sets a criteria and the service company demonstrates its ability to meet it. Knowing how guard companies operate, where their margin is derived from, and what their expense structure can and cannot accommodate, is essential in determining whether a long term arrangement can be mutually rewarding for both client and provider.

Contract guard agencies live and die with a billable hours schedule. Unlike retailers, guard companies do not carry an "inventory" of product from which they draw upon to meet customer demands. The job is sold, then the workers are hired, trained, and deployed. This is because providers cannot carry guards on their payroll without a client to bill them to. Oftentimes, vendor representatives are in the predicament of committing resources they do not actually have, and they then must scramble to fill the order.

Typical scenarios involve the sales person "pitching" a 40-hour schedule to a retail location. The rationale is for the guard to come on duty at 3 p.m. (for when the kids get out of school) and leave with the staff (walking them to their cars) at 11 p.m., one hour after the store closes at 10 p.m. This enables the guard company to hire and assign one census unit to the job site, Monday through Friday. When the subject of weekend coverage is discussed, the vendor representative would suggest an 8, 10, or 12-hour block, "because weekend traffic patterns are busier." This formula works very well for the vendor, but is it the best arrangement for the client? Is the "after school rush" that troublesome?

Would not a 5 p.m. start time, to supplement floor coverage during the approaching employee meal hours, provide adequate guard coverage during the nighttime hours, the period employees feel most apprehensive about? This would cut the base schedule by 10 hours, and the guard agency is then tasked with finding another 10 hours in the work week for their guard to make his 40 hours. It is the balancing act between the quirks of customer shifts, and the desire to deliver full time work to its guards, that has saddled the contract guard industry with its "meat-market" label. In order to attract and sustain a core force of guards, the company may have to route these people to several locations a week. In the relatively low-paying guard positions, these individuals seek to complete their 40-hour schedules as early in the week as possible, then move up to the time-and-a-half overtime rate that accompanies extra shifts, in order to make a living. This is how the guard industry is able to accommodate the flex shifts desired by many of the clients.

In the example above, if the client opted for the straight 40-hour week, the weekend shifts would be filled by other guards short-scheduled during the week trying to get in their 40-plus hours. If the 30-hour schedule was adopted, the weekday guard would be working a sixth or seventh day at your location to make his full week.

In the guard industry, overtime opportunities are plentiful, because jobs are sold prior to the staff being assembled. That interim is filled by supervisory personnel or guards in good favor to whom overtime shifts are allotted. This allows the guard company to initially staff an account with experienced, quality officers, which seems to dissipate over time as the new recruits are processed and placed.

Competitive bidding in hourly rates among companies further stretches the caliber of guard they can provide. No vendor says "we are gonna send you the first knuckle head we find who will work for this pay." In reality though, no matter how much the vendor cherishes your account, your hard-ball negotiating on cost limits his ability to match an individual with suitable skills to the needs of your business. If you squeeze the vendor on rate, they have little recourse but to send you a minimum-waged, unproven guard, in order to sustain their margin.

The choice comes down to the customer's willingness to pay. If you can exceed the market rate, then you are in a position to demand a higher level of service. Since the guard is a visible representation to the employees of the company's commitment to shortage reduction, substandard guards actually do a disservice to the program. Keep in mind that guard pay rates average 55% of the billable rate. The remainder must support the guard company overhead: administrative costs, equipment and uniform expense (some of which are shared by the guard), payroll taxes, workers compensation, benefits (if any), and usurious premiums for liability insurance. A worthwhile net profit must also be yielded from this mix. Holding the vendor to a stringent low-ball rate leaves little room for customer accommodation.

Be wary of the rock-bottom rate guard companies. These enterprises have further tarnished the guard industry by undercutting legitimate bids by estab-lished companies, then pocketing the overhead expense of workers compen-sation, payroll taxes, and insurance premiums until the string finally runs out. Then they close up shop, lay low for a few months, and then reopen under another license and another name.

Assuming the vendor and client can reach an agreeable rate, one that permits latitude to customize a security plan for meeting the needs of the business, the retailer should exact several stipulations in the service contract. In consultation with your legal and insurance carrier representatives, deter-mine first the limits of liability insurance coverage you can insist the guard company carry for your account. Realize that your company will in no way be insulated from litigation brought about by the actions of a contract guard while employed on your premises. But knowing that a policy is in effect to at least share the liability offers some comfort. Also, the degree of difficulty the agency has in obtaining increased coverage is an indication of how well established this company is and its standing within the insurance community, as well as providing an insight into its cash flow.

The next consideration, where the fee arrangement allows customer dic-tates, is to establish hiring standards for guards assigned to your account. Most states are moving toward regulation of the private guard industry, and criminal background checks, inclusive of fingerprint checks, are becoming mandatory. In addition, some state-prescribed training for security officers, usually an 8-hour course on the powers of citizen's arrest, use of force, first aid, and emergency response, must be completed before a guard can become certified under the statutes of participating states. Armed guards undergo a more extensive background check and training curriculum.

Still, this is no guarantee the guard sent to your location is not a sociopath. The guard company is required to submit an applicant's fingerprints for a criminal background check. It is unclear how quickly the state is required to check them and report back. In the interim, the guard company has fulfilled its obligation, and the guard may work until the agency is notified otherwise.

To ensure the guard assigned to your store is both capable and trustworthy, insist on officers who have a work history with the service company. Request that you be able to contact other clients for whom this guard has done work to verify his competence. You will probably have to allow for some new hires where this step is impractical, but stipulate a reasonable limit on guards new to the company. Guard companies also do background checks independent of state requirements. Ask the parameters of these checks and require they at least meet the standards you practice in hiring employees.

Failure by the client to monitor the due diligence of a guard company's staffing process has resulted in the frequent disappointments experienced in the private sector with some providers of guard service. Unchecked, guard companies will take short cuts to meet growing demand with shriveled supply. Guard agencies that follow a mantra of "anywhere, anytime, any job" compel their workers to take on extra shifts, and they rush new recruits through the hiring process. It is not unheard of to find a guard arriving for midnight shift in an industrial park who is beginning the third tour of a 24-hour day. He is unwashed, his uniform is unkempt, and he is fully prepared to nap through his shift. This image has haunted the contract guard industry since the Brink's job, but the lure of the overtime rate, coupled with the guard company's zeal to meet even unreasonable demands of their clients, feeds the stigma.

It is tempting to turn a blind eye to the service providers that play fast and loose with the unfair labor practices that are occasionally observed: the double shifts, the missed meals, the docking of pay. But dismal working conditions produce dismal workers, and to expect enthusiasm and integrity from dissatisfied employees is unrealistic. Your store manager should interview each new guard assigned to his store, and determine if this individual's attitude is consistent with goals of the program.

Set ground rules with your vendor that no guard may report for duty in your building that is coming off a full shift elsewhere. Specify grooming and uniform standards that cannot be compromised. Acknowledge that you will provide orientation about the store operation, and that only a small cadre of guards that are "post certified" be assigned to your account. Approve all future substitutions, and establish a minimum number of visits to the store by the guard company's field supervisors. The generic training mandated by some states may be sufficient for a security officer to guard a warehouse or patrol a parking lot, but it is inadequate to equip a guard for duty in your store with your customers.

Work with the vendor to outline a specific post assignment for the guard. This is welcomed by most guard companies as it is often customer vagueness in this regard that leads to misunderstandings of expectations and results. Ideally, your store manager should be able to direct and supervise the guard's activity. As such, the guard should check in with the store manager and receive his duties for the day, as would any other employee in the store. This helps develop a teamwork relationship between the guard and the store staff which allows the guard to have a role in the operation and to be able to make a defined contribution.

When the guard comes on duty, the manager should have prepared a number of duties for the guard to perform. One task may be to inspect the selling floor, racks, and bins for evidence of theft (tickets, wrappers, EAS tags) that may have occurred prior to the guard's arrival. Another may be to begin a series of cash drops, escorting the clerks from the register to the office. Having the guard present when employees receive product at the delivery door could be another assignment.

Interaction between the guard and staff employees is the most difficult to manage. You want the employees to bring incidents and suspicious people to the guard's attention. You want your employees to feel the guard is some-one who will protect them and the merchandise from harm. You want the employees to respect the guard, both the job he is there to do and the skills he demonstrates to do it. Likewise, the guard wants acceptance from the employee population and to be assimilated into the group dynamic. He is neither employee nor customer, but feels a kinship with the workers. Most idle chatter between the guard and employees is harmless shop talk. However, the store manager must prevent these impromptu sessions from compromising the guard's effectiveness. In essence, the manager sets one of two tones: the guard is a store employee, who will gravitate toward other employees for camaraderie; or the guard is to keep a professional distance that the manager can use to enhance supervision. Familiarity with the guard may make employees more comfortable around him and lends itself to including the guard in discussions relevant to the store operation the guard may find useful. Employees may even confide LP issues in a guard they feel has earned their trust, rather than bringing the matter up formally with store management. But on the whole, these remote benefits of permitting a cozy relationship between guard and employees should be discouraged.

A shrewd manager learns to utilize the guard as an extension of his eyes and ears. The manager should remind the guard that his presence can serve to deter employee theft as well as shoplifting. Discreet surveillance of employee activity (personal phone calls, friends at the register, brief exits from the building, etc.) should be within the guards purview to observe and report. An adversarial relationship between guard and employee is not productive; but an understanding that the guard's responsibilities include reporting irregularities in employee conduct, checking employee's bags at closing, and challenging suspicious transactions by bringing them to the manager's attention for review, moves the guard from co-worker status to something different. He is not a boss, but he is not a buddy, either. The ideal guard is a sentry — there if you need him and unobtrusive when you do not. He can relate to employees and have cordial interactions with them, but they must account for his whereabouts and activity if they try something underhanded.

For a contract guard to grasp these nuances of his job description takes patient counseling from the store manager. Oftentimes, the guard is given direction by the store manager that is contrary to orders issued by the guard company. This is especially evident in the area of apprehensions, where the manager wants action but the guard's employer wants restraint. For instance, the guard will report that he observed a customer place merchandise in a bag and leave the store. The guard will supply date, time, description of items taken, even the tag number of the getaway car. The exasperated manager will shriek at the guard *"why didn't you do something?"* In fact, the guard did as his employer, the guard company, instructed him: observe and report. The manager will berate the guard for taking no action; the guard company will tell him he did the right thing. The manager loses confidence in the guard; that perception is communicated subliminally to other employees, and the guard becomes ineffective at this location.

These situations can be preempted by demanding that guards receive "incident training" from the guard company that is pertinent to your operation. Do you want guards to detain customers suspected of theft? If so, the guard company must provide training that prevents bad stops. Do you want guards approaching customers on Electronic Article Surveillance (EAS) alarms? If so, the guard company must train the guard in the prescribed approach. Once the parameters of the guard's authority in these events is established, they must be communicated to the store manager so that the expectations of the guard's role do not exceed the authority he has been given.

Another aspect of deploying uniformed security officers is whether your needs are for armed or unarmed guards. Armed guards are a drastic step, but one that companies do consider, especially in the wake of frequent robberies. If armed guards are deemed necessary, it must be established from the outset that the primary role of this extreme measure is deterrence. As such, the guard should be positioned visibly at the entrance, where persons casing the establishment for the purpose of robbery notice that an armed guard is on duty, hopefully prompting them to move on to a more vulnerable target. To diminish the deterrent effect by having the guard conceal his weapon or be otherwise unidentifiable to a criminal assessing the risk can lead to a robbery attempt that may have been otherwise averted by the guard's presence. Armed robbers, armed guards, unarmed employees, and unsuspecting customers is a formula for disaster.

Since a store shoot-out is the last thing the retailer wants, posted instructions for the armed guard must clearly specify that no retaliatory action may be taken in a robbery except to protect life. Robbers, undeterred by armed guards, are a determined lot, willing to shoot and kill to escape. The odds of an armed guard foiling a robbery without casualties pale in comparison to the likelihood of calamity. Asking an armed guard to draw his weapon during any criminal event where only merchandise is at risk is irresponsible.

For nonretail settings, those instances where guards are used in the home office or a warehouse/distribution center, a dual role is established. By day, the guard functions in the capacity of receptionist; greeting visitors, checking identification, monitoring CCTV, and managing various control logs for deliveries and property leaving the building. During off-hours, the guard becomes more of a night watchman, tasked with premises security and managing the alarm system. Guards assigned these positions are generally responsible, helpful individuals with strong people skills. They should be well trained in aspects of emergency procedures, especially CPR, power failure, and fire control, with the training to direct emergency response units throughout the building and the knowledge of locations for sprinkler shut-off valves and electrical panels. Persons who manage the visitor area should be cognizant of any external threats to the company or employees, and should be alerted in situations where any employee is harassed or stalked as part of the company effort to address the concerns of violence in the workplace.

In a warehouse/distribution environment, guards need to be aware of company rules and regulations governing access and egress to the building, employee handbags and satchels, restricted areas off limits to visitors, and the protocols of admitting drivers to the work area. Violations of policy should be reported to the appropriate supervisor. Guards can also be trained to manage key control, to handle the inventory of trailer seals, to provide escorts of valuable shipments to and from the security cage, to participate in safety inspections, to operate the camera system, and to track shipping discrepancies reported from the field.

As with all assignments given to contract guards, management needs to implement a system that measures productivity. An established schedule of tasks submitted for review enables the client to quantify the administrative contribution guards make to the operation. The idleness of the standing post must be replaced with purposeful activity to keep guards motivated and accountable. Mere "busywork" is no substitute for a challenging work environment.

Post assignments drawn up for guards should be designed in a way to help assimilate regularly assigned guards into the company culture. This inclusion process helps guards develop a vested interest on the client's behalf, and shapes their loyalties from the guard company to your own. Acknowledging a guard's performance with regular job reviews submitted to the guard company can lead to recognition and merit increases for the guard, an effort that can be reflected positively in the guard's attitude and motivation.

To further these two keys for guard performance, consideration should be given in allowing the guard to participate in employee award programs that recognize significant achievement. A cash bonus, or other such perk awarded to employees for outstanding service or contribution to loss prevention, would pay lasting dividends from a guard in enthusiasm and dedication, two factors cited most often as lacking in contract guards.

In conclusion, employing contract guards to strengthen your physical security presence depends on identifying specific areas of opportunity that guards can help exploit. Whether it is to improve plant security, provide administrative support and security presence in a warehouse, or give store management the necessary comfort level to deal aggressively with shoplifters, it is incumbent upon the user of outside guards to define their role, supervise their activity, and foster vendor accountability. This is best accomplished with a program that brings the guard into the mainstream of the operation, and creates the environment for job satisfaction.

Section II

Loss Prevention Programs

Overview

The formative principles of modern loss prevention have developed through the decades in tandem with the considerable evolution in the retail industry. Formulas were proven, tactics borne out, procedures fine tuned, and visionaries ordained. The end-result was generally the semi-autonomous, specialized division of loss prevention.

The focus of this type of organization centered on the detection and investigation of theft activity, and departmental resources were marshaled to that end. Structured for a quasi-police function, regimented in its policies, and not particularly adept at adapting to changes in the workplace, alternative strategies for LP became necessary with the convulsive change and dramatic downsizing that typified the retail industry in the late 1980s.

Gradually, lessons were learned in the areas of merchandise handling and presentation that dawned the era of operational standards, which started the age of the audit, which spawned the entity of inventory control.

While security was out catching the crooks, the auditors were compiling compliance check lists, and the controllers were monitoring inventory transactions. Each rolled along at its own pace, the cop, the clipboard, and the bean counter, with its own agenda, working to justify its own methodology, that was often at odds with retail reality.

Many of the gains made by this triumvirate of LP warriors were offset by fractious personalities and turf feuds. Eventually the onset of restrictive economic times, coupled with the redundancy of its own nature, caused this system to collapse under its own weight.

The aftermath became a hodgepodge of programs, short-lived and inconclusive, as the retail industry itself became divided among the struggling department store, the emerging discount chains, and the specialty stores ensconced in their own market niches. For loss prevention, a hybrid program to service the needs of all three became the Golden Fleece.

Today's retailer has embraced the spectrum of technological advances in management information systems, and has emerged a stream-lined, bottom-lined, number-driven executive. LP programs have followed suit.

No longer structured solely to catch shoplifters in the haberdashery, LP disciplines were integrated into the mainstream of business practices. Resources are deployed to monitor, not spy. LP management is more diversified, able to forge partnerships with merchandising, operations, human resources, and finance. Freed of the cloak and dagger, LP personnel are cast in a softer light, as trainer, arbiter, and problem solver.

It is in this context that LP programs are presented in Section Two. Proactive involvement in recruiting, hiring, and training, and working toward improving morale, reducing turnover, and providing a safe work environment are the tools LP employs to establish and sustain employee awareness of inventory shortage.

Sound audit programs that educate, not assassinate, are implemented to detect weaknesses in operational controls. Profit opportunity and positive feedback motivate store line management to comply with standards and procedures, rather than intimidation and onerous regulation.

Successful LP programs contribute comprehensive benefits to the retailer's bottom line. Reduced inventory shortage is, in essence, reduced expense. Couple shortage reduction and cost control, and LP becomes a major player in the profit picture. As a trade-off to downsizing its structure, LP draws more of its resources from in-house assets, modifying the primary functions of other divisions to serve double-duty in a support role to LP. This approach with human resources, sales audit, MIS, and distribution departments has enabled LP to tap resident expertise and create an atmosphere of shared accountability in shrink performance.

The programs that work best are the ones that close the loop of retail shrink and provide for procedural integrity from distribution and receiving through check-out at the point of sale. Each step along the way is an opportunity for loss that can be turned around and exploited for gain.

Employee Awareness

6

Many of the most successful loss prevention programs flow from the central issue of employee awareness. This is because so many LP techniques are designed to alert employees to conditions and events around them. For example, the assumption inherent in the application of security devices is that, once alerted, caring employees will become involved and take action to safeguard the company's assets. No amount of electronic hardware will prevent losses if employees are not trained and motivated to respond effectively to LP situations.

Management has a good opportunity to educate employees in LP awareness during the new hire orientation process and the formal job-specific training that follows. Each segment of the job description should be presented in a way that demonstrates that employee integrity and diligence contributes to reduced losses. Companies should be innovative in tying in the LP implications of most job-related tasks to shortage performance, whether it be for store clerks, warehouse workers, or supervisors. No subject should be mentioned without its relationship to shrink being illustrated.

Most organizations provide employees with a fundamental appreciation for the important role workers play in reducing shortage. Where the message becomes muddled, however, is when trainees assume their positions in the store line operation, and the lessons fade as they become overwhelmed with the priorities of their new responsibilities. When new employees are indoctrinated into a retail organization, the company goes to great lengths to present the organization in its most favorable light. This reassures the trainee that the company is right for them, attempts to instill pride in their work, and illustrates that they can contribute to the company's success while enhancing their own business skills and careers.

These positives are challenged immediately when the employee encounters other workers and evaluates whether the experiences of their co-workers is consistent with the expectations they have formulated based on the orientation process. They are often assigned to entry-level tasks, and receive on-the-job-training from more experienced employees. In addition to the requisite job experience the senior worker imparts to the trainee, the opinions and perceptions of both the company and the store operation are impressed upon the new employee by the mentor. The insights and views shared will either reinforce, or undo, the careful molding process the company initiated during orientation. Management must take care to exercise some form of spin control of this situation.

Care in selecting the appropriate senior worker to indoctrinate trainees is essential if the positive messages from orientation are to be sustained from theory to practice. This is especially true if the lessons of loss prevention, which involve attitude and commitment, are to be retained. A jaded employee, privately cynical of the company and the store operation, may be adequate to train the new employee on register operation and stock keeping, but this is hardly the person who can communicate the spirit of a shortage program effectively.

Store managers should frequently interact with new workers, ensuring that they are clear on procedures and keeping shortage matters fresh in their minds with LP-related observations and anecdotes. Supervisors should also ask new employees if they have observed any practices they may feel contribute to exposures that need to be addressed. Over time, the trainee should become curious about the way things work and about how the company is able to keep track of its cash and product. Managers should demonstrate the checks and balances the company has, pointing out such things as the POS exception report, compliance audits, cash over and short reports, and shipping discrepancy logs, to the new employee to highlight controls that management has implemented.

Employee awareness cannot begin and end with new hires. In short order, they become seasoned employees, the strongest asset to effective loss prevention. Corporate should sponsor a menu of LP awareness programs that keep workers educated and motivated to fulfill their shortage reduction responsibilities. Topical issues, replete with videos, posters, handouts, etc., should be furnished on a regular basis to drive home the messages of awareness and accountability through training. A strong foundation for employee awareness would be a program rolled out quarterly to emphasize the four primary areas of LP concerns:

First Quarter: *Inventory Control*

This phase would seek to educate the employee on the quality-control aspects for processing internal paperwork correctly. The link between paperwork error and shrink would be emphasized in the context of price changes, interstore transfers, and manifest checking. In-store audit reviews would serve as a backdrop to measure procedural compliance, and would provide a forum for training in anticipated or recent policy changes. Guidelines for the upcoming inventory-taking process, and the vital role a good physical inventory plays in the shortage performance would be presented, along with a countdown of inventory preparation tasks to be completed.

Second Quarter: *Employee Theft*

The second quarter includes frank discussion of the harm dishonest employees do to the company and to themselves. A video presentation designed to escalate the perceived risk associated with such activity can be shown illustrating the consequences for those found involved in theft from the company.

To promote deterrence, persuasive reminders that the company acknowledges employee theft as a major contributor to shrink can be presented that describes the resources the company employs to detect and respond to employee dishonesty. Tangible evidence of the company's arsenal, both the technological advances in POS exception reporting as well as security devices and outside resources available, should be shown as effective and expanding as the company promotes a zero tolerance policy for criminal behavior. This is an opportune segment to reissue the company's rules and regulations brochures. Policies enacted to control access to the building, personal property in the workplace, bag checks, employee discounts, and authorization levels for select POS transactions can be emphasized in the context of shrinking opportunity through accountability.

Third Quarter: *Risk Management*

This segment focuses on loss prevention issues that seek to control the losses associated with liability and safety in the workplace. Topics of safety inspections, workers compensation, product liability, emergency procedures, and incident reporting can be covered in a way to illustrate the impact of general liability to a company's earnings. More sensitive subjects, those dealing with violence in the workplace, sexual harassment, and labor relations issues can be addressed to field management in this portion of the employee awareness program.

Fourth Quarter: *External Theft*

With the holiday shopping season approaching, a review of shoplifting prevention procedures is appropriate. Professional videos which simulate shoplifting techniques is beneficial, along with policy reminders on the apprehension and prosecution criteria of the company.

Especially pertinent to the holidays is a refresher on the scams and con games that surface during the peak shopping season. Short-change artists, impostors, bad check passers, refunders, and credit card fraud proliferates with the holiday rush, and retailers are the prime targets. Also appropriate in this segment would be a review on armed robbery prevention, and procedures to be enacted in the event a store is held-up.

Another subject indigenous to retail loss prevention awareness programs is the subject of employee rewards, i.e., the payment of cash for information or action which leads to the identification of a dishonest employee or to the recovery of product from a shoplifter. Proponents of such programs contend that cash bonuses motivate employees to go above and beyond the call of duty in preventing theft. The cash inducement serves as a means to recognize and reward employees for getting involved, and serves to set this example for other workers.

Opponents of such programs believe that loss prevention is part and parcel to the employee's job description, and to single out performance of the expected for meritorious recognition is tantamount to relieving the employee of the routine duties of loss prevention. These two points of view need not be mutually exclusive. A strong foundation that LP is everybody's job does not necessarily preclude acknowledging swift thinking and decisive action on the selling floor. Where programs that reward employees for shoplifting prevention bog down is when a "bounty-hunter" mentality pervades the work force, and your employees are actually deriving secondary income from catching crooks.

Shoplifting prevention that is apprehension-driven and fueled by cash rewards inevitably leads to street chases and employee assaults, and for these reasons a reward program can undermine the good intentions of recognition and motivation. Aside from sending the wrong message that apprehension is more desirable than prevention, the potential for bad stops and false arrests escalates when amateur detectives, store associates, become aggressively involved in making arrests — arrests that may be motivated more by the cash reward than the safeguarding of company assets.

This mixed message can be mitigated easily with employee awards that recognize employee prevention of theft. Naturally, parameters must be set that exclude an employee from award consideration for performing the customer service-related tasks of their job description. The company is still entitled to, and must insist upon, diligence in approaching customers and monitoring their activities. But the active interdiction of a theft in progress, one that prevents the loss and recovers the merchandise, is as beneficial to some companies as a properly effected apprehension may be, and as such, is deserving of award consideration.

This needs to be distinguished from the cashier who responds to the EAS alarm and ends up recovering unpaid-for product from a customer as a result of the approach. Sales associates are trained in this approach, and handling alarm events is inclusive in the employee job description. The company has already invested in the EAS system and the employees to manage it; and as such, no award consideration should be forthcoming.

Defining exactly what form this employee award should take is a matter of company policy and prudent formula. A cash benefit, one that is substantial enough to energize the employee, but is reasonable enough to ensure that the prevented loss exceeds the monetary payout, is one possibility. Other perks besides cash can also be beneficial. Some companies give an employee discounted product, paid time off, preferential parking, or a certificate of achievement to acknowledge their initiative and involvement. But a comprehensive award program cannot be restricted to only matters of shoplifting — to do so de-emphasizes other aspects of retail shrink that must be kept foremost in employee's minds. Granted, shoplifting is the most visible element of shortage to them, but LP professionals agree that an award program must be directed toward lead information on employee theft. Getting an employee to come forward and "turn in" a co-worker for theft needs to be a highly-publicized element of the award program; one that demonstrates reciprocal loyalty between company and employee. Once the employee understands that they can share in the benefits of a crime-free workplace, those not actively involved in theft activity see little reason to remain silent.

Creating a positive climate for employees to come forward requires persuasive argument that plays down the stigma of "ratting out" co-workers. One of the subtle operatives that plays well to honest associates is to exploit the latent envy many honest employees feel toward their dishonest counterparts. In human nature, employees that are deterred from theft by the fear of consequences are nonetheless jealous of those they know steal and get away with it. This group secretly hopes the dishonest workers get caught, in order to vindicate their belief that crime does not pay.

When dishonest employees go undetected and flaunt the proceeds of their ill-gotten gains, the honest worker becomes resentful. Their disdain of employee theft may be due to the harm this activity does to the company on the surface, but an underlying factor is they are covetous of the illicit rewards they know to be undeserved.

Just as the fear of consequences deters honest employees from participating in theft, so too do those fears surface when grappling with the notion of reporting dishonest workers to management. The consequences of being ostracized, and perhaps concerns over retribution, result in many employees waiting silently for management to act. Most of all, uncertainty over whether management is capable of handling such a report in a way that effectively removes the thief from the workplace and insulates the tipster, causes the hesitance management must overcome.

The ingredients for proactive participation are certainly present: honest employees are resentful of dishonest employees who go undetected because they are jealous of the "easy money" that enhances the lifestyle of the dishonest employee over the hard-working associate who is playing by the rules. They harbor a subliminal ill-will for these people, and require little more than a clean, risk-free method that permits them an avenue to facilitate the downfall of the wrongdoer. If, in the process, they can profit by it, all the better.

The Internal Revenue Service has been most successful in fostering the class warfare between taxpayers who grudgingly pay, and those that evade their fair share. Some honest taxpayers are more jealous of tax evaders, whom they secretly admire for having the courage they lack themselves to defy the government, than they are offended by it. The IRS plays on this conflicted sentiment to encourage people to report tax evaders out of a sense of civic duty, but are, in reality, giving them the opportunity to level the playing field between the haves and the have-nots. They endow the informant with the noble qualities of "good citizenship" to help rationalize active involvement, and have demonstrated a proven track record for handling tips in strict confidence that keeps the tipster anonymous.

Retailers can take a page out of this book in developing an employee award program that espouses the same principles. Targeting employees who are chagrined by the dishonest employee's supplemental income, yet who are fearful to indulge themselves, the program can replace the "civic duty" aspect with the lofty accolades accorded the "loyal employee." A cash enticement that seals the deal is a strong motivator to move people off the fence, and serves notice to the dishonest employee that others may seek to profit from their crimes. Management's obligation to establish a structure for the confidential reporting of lead information is essential to the process. Many companies use confidential toll-free hotlines to initiate communication with informants. Caution must be exercised to insure this method does not degenerate into a vehicle for vendetta and smear campaigns. This is especially true for programs that solicit anonymous information. Award policies should stipulate that management has no duty to pursue anonymous leads, but may follow up the information provided by nameless sources at their own discretion. Should such an investigation prove fruitful, the company should think twice before accommodating an award request from an employee who comes forward after the fact to claim a reward.

This caveat is important for the company to retain the moral high ground when encouraging employees to report the misconduct of co-workers or management. The company should distinguish between the employee willing to give their name and involve themselves to a fact-finding investigation for the good of the company, from the potential rabble-rouser who merely wishes to watch management spin their wheels or sully the reputation of another employee.

Supervisors and investigators must build a reputation for competence and integrity when handling matters reported in confidence. Any employee who reports their suspicions and gives their name should be discreetly spoken with, on the record. The investigator should assure the employee that each has a mutual interest in resolving the tipster's concerns, and that any investigation of their claim will be managed professionally. Employees who have taken the step to come forward will not be dissuaded by legitimate inquiry; but witch hunts will undermine the success of such a program in short order.

Regardless of the outcome of their tips, informants should be kept abreast of developments and cultivated for future leads. For many, this is their first exposure to the investigatory process, and the impression they are left with will ultimately determine whether they remain an ally to your cause or revert to a more passive role.

The award program should also be flexible to extol contributions other than theft detection. Recognizing effort in shortage reduction sustains employee involvement in the overall program and acknowledges performance that translates into savings on the bottom line. Employees who offer novel suggestions, innovative procedural enhancements, or win contests aimed at elevating shortage awareness should be cited for their achievement. This is especially evident when tapping into internal resources from other departments. Although the concept of monetary rewards for persons who contribute their specialized skills to shortage reduction may again cross the line between what is expected of an employee and what constitutes going above and beyond, some form of tangible acknowledgment stimulates participation. For example, if a nondescript MIS programmer, tasked with making modifications to POS reports to facilitate detection of malfeasance at the register, produces a system enhancement that far exceeds expectations, and the added refinements are due solely to that employee's initiative, inclusion in the employee award program should be considered.

Whether or not store managers and their assistants should be eligible to participate in award programs is another aspect open for debate. For companies whose bonus structure for store management includes shrink performance, perhaps their involvement should be limited to recommending their store employees for consideration. This boosts the manager's prestige in the eyes of their workers as well as permitting them an active role in the program. But in cases where the managers are compensated more or less through a fixed income, supplementing their initiative in loss prevention may be appropriate.

It is the store managers whom we expect to police the standards of conduct we depend upon to control losses. Many of the supervisory tasks related to the checks and balances that serve to deter employee theft are mundane, yet essential to the process. Store managers who demonstrate initiative in solving shortage problems that are clearly beyond the call of duty, including actions such as exceeding expectations in pursuing leads, cultivating police relations, periodically conducting off-hour surveillance of the store on their own time that pays off in a major way, should be recognized for exemplary commitment.

The true essence of employee awareness is not derived from a gimmicky reward program. It is the by-product of careful hiring, formal training, and a work environment conducive to the employee's willingness to contribute to the company's success. Sustaining that commitment is predicated upon the reciprocal relationship that goes beyond the standard work-for-pay employment agreement.

Corporate cultures that stress loss prevention in daily dialog with employees are better able to maintain diligence and awareness among workers to look out for the interests of the company. LP events happen every day within a multi-store operation, and provide ample examples of how shoplifters steal, employees embezzle, and careless work habits lead to loss. Publicizing incident reports, apprehensions, and known losses helps to focus attention on shared concerns and systemic problems that impact shrink.

Management must be clear by word and deed that shortage awareness is not mere corporate rhetoric. Employees who hear the same themes of customer service and personal integrity become disenchanted with the message once they realize management provides little else to the cause but talk. In the "town hall" meetings companies frequently have to elicit operational feedback from employees, close attention should be paid to their sentiments on shrink.

If store managers are vocal about their inability to provide the proper level of customer service required to deter shoplifting due to shrinking staffs, management cannot nod their collective heads and fail to address the issue in one of two ways: (1) challenge the store manager to deliver an ROI in shortage reduction and/or increased revenue to offset the additional payroll sought, or (2) revise the shrink forecast for that location and reevaluate its viability.

Showing the stores that the company means business often involves sharing insights into the business. In prudent measures, showing store managers how sales performance and profitability permits growth and prosperity can include the negative impact of shortage in real dollars that inhibits such opportunity. Confiding the impact of poor shrink in terms store managers can appreciate — such as delay in capital investment for certain projects, reconsidering system upgrades that were planned, and the inability to corner the market for a specific product line hinging on whether the company proves capable of protecting it — all register with store line executives managing the margin. When the occasion arises and an announcement is forthcoming concerning a store closing, a mention of its shrink performance as contributing to the location's demise would not be inappropriate.

Trial attorneys are trained to never ask a witness a question that the attorney does not already know the answer to. Retailers should exercise similar caution in open forums concerning shortage problems. The answers they get will invariably point to company deficiencies in systems, equipment, or manpower. Where management's investment in these areas has been consistent with the need, the company can question the employee resolve to work harder at the problem. In cases where legitimate LP needs have gone without, such as EAS maintenance, camera equipment, and adequate staffing, management will not find their answers from the people on the front line.

Audit Programs

780849 30003

Conducting on-site reviews of retail locations for procedural compliance is the primary role for upper management in loss prevention. Once the shortage program has been defined and implemented, an audit program serves as the corporate "watchdog" to verify and sustain compliance in the field. Without this component, stores will inevitably replace the tenets of shrink reduction with priorities-du-jour, and the safeguards thought to be in place will erode.

Companies need to maximize the impact of the audit function so that it serves both as a training mechanism in the finer points of shortage control, as well as the "report card" for measuring locations to prescribed operational standards. By definition, audit programs assume a certain degree of policy deficiencies exist; otherwise, the concept would exist merely to reward, not to correct. The purpose of the audit is to determine how significant the deviations from standard are; and whether a general sense can be had that the spirit, if not the letter, of the program is followed.

An operational audit is only as effective as the policies they seek to verify. Without stringent procedures that define company standards, the audit becomes a subjective analysis of whether the home-spun controls fashioned location-to-location are sufficient. Where disseminated guidelines on company policy exist, the audit can be an objective review on compliance to company-established controls. The latter makes for a far more strengthened audit, one that measures a store's ability to implement and manage corporate mandates. Since LP requirements initiated by management go to the issue of expense control (shrink is a planned expense to be managed), profit-minded companies have a vested interest in ascertaining how well stores conform.

Another factor is that audits also bring to light the matter of accountability to shortage performance. There are people responsible for insuring specific procedures are put in place and followed. These are executive-level individuals granted only marginal leeway in policy implementation. Programs issued from corporate rarely call for optional participation. The audit, therefore, can measure how well management personnel respond and adhere to standards set forth by the company. If policy states X and a store manager does Y, that store manager can be called into account for his failure to perform. For Corporate to do less undermines the return management anticipates from the procedural regulations it issues, and relinquishes the nonparticipant from accountability.

Audit programs should be based on the premise: people do what we inspect, not what we expect. Although companies may wish to believe that their field management personnel are committed and thorough in the execution of procedural instruction, experience teaches that the occasional oversight can be costly; and left unchecked, evolves into a pattern of failed protection.

An audit of a field operation for loss prevention controls should encompass five elements: (1) the physical security of the location; (2) an audit of the cash control procedures; (3) procedural review; (4) the utilization of the POS exception report to challenge unusual register transactions; and (5) overall merchandise standards on the selling floor and in the stockroom. The physical security segment should address issues of alarm testing, password protection, a review of after-hour alarm activity, key control, and the operational integrity of both EAS and camera systems (where available).

The auditor wants to ensure that (1) management and staff are trained on the proper maintenance of security systems, (2) that accountability for after-hour access to the building is uncompromised with respect to keys and alarm codes, and (3) that investments in security hardware (i.e., cameras, EAS) are effectively utilized.

Persons assigned the audit function, whether they are corporate representatives or senior executives in store line, need to prepare for an audit assignment much the way an investigator prepares for an investigation. For a physical security inspection of a specific location, the auditor should be familiar with the management turnover activity at the store in order to assess whether perimeter locks, safe combinations, and alarm codes remain safeguarded. A review of alarm activity prior to the audit will help the auditor determine that testing and maintenance schedules are in effect, and that prescribed passcode authorization levels conform to company standard.

Auditors who discover deficiencies in the physical security standards of a location are certain to find compliance problems in the internal operation as well. These will likely be manifested in the cash control policies, as the auditor examines the store safe and financial logs. The following areas of concern should be inspected closely for compliance, and the supporting documentation should be presented for audit or review:

Over and Short Log

Evidence that register imbalances are recorded daily by terminal number and clerk ID. Cash discrepancies from register end-of-day reports are plotted over 30-day periods. Documentation that management has addressed occasions of cash shortages with clerks should be evident in employee files.

> **Red Flag**: Over and shorts that "wash out," (e.g., $10 short on Monday/$10 over on Tuesday) indicating employee "borrowing." Shortage patterns of dates, times, or clerk IDs, indicate unchecked accountability.

Daily Deposits

Validated or "franked" deposit slip receipts received from the bank are filed with end-of-day paperwork in order to verify that amounts deposited match daily totals, and that deposit schedule conforms to company policy.

> **Red Flag**: Deviation from the prescribed schedule (e.g., no deposit Tuesday and Wednesday/three deposits on Thursday), indicate that deposits are "floated" (to perhaps enable a manager to pay back monies "borrowed"). Unvalidated slips (an unfranked carbon) denote only the date the deposit slip was made out **not** the date the deposit was actually made.

Petty Cash

Whether separate funds exist or miscellaneous expenses are managed via "paid-outs" from the cash drawer, the auditor should be satisfied with the legitimacy of both the expense itself and the supporting documentation filed to verify external purchases. Documentation should be presented that demonstrates the fund is balanced daily and confirmed among persons with access.

> **Red Flag**: "Homemade" receipts, excessive item-specific purchasing, and no "chain-of-custody" documentation among managers for petty cash fund accountability between shifts.

Change Fund

As with petty cash accounts, daily balancing between shifts/managers-on-duty should be documented to establish accountability.

> **Red Flag**: Absence of documentation establishing accountability.

Gift Certificates/Promotional ("Cash Back") Coupons

Reserve of stock of gift certificates and negotiable coupons are secured and accounted for daily. Documentation that verifies the on-hand gift certificates together with those sold balance to the store inventory. Redemption practices that "void" redeemed gift certificates are followed, preventing "recycling" of redeemed certificates back into inventory.

> **Red Flag:** Stores with gift certificate redemption rates which exceed gift certificates sold, inadequate documentation to balance on-hand with sales to match opening inventory, and a coupon redemption rate significantly higher than comparable stores norm.

These are the key areas of cash defalcation uncovered most often in LP investigations of employee theft. The auditor should be aware of these symptoms and accept little at face value. The "red flags" noted above each demonstrate how an employee may attempt to conceal thefts. For instance, a $32.00 receipt from the U.S. Post Office in the petty cash or paid-out log for a roll of stamps may appear legitimate, but a manager working in concert with a post office employee may have access to valid supporting documentation for postage which is then substituted for cash in the petty cash fund. Picking receipts up off the floor from office supply stores is another avenue of receipt-for-cash substitution for those engaged in the systematic depletion of the petty cash fund.

Services purchased, such as window-washing, floor mat cleaning, minor landscaping, snow removal, etc., which are not invoiced directly to the company, but managed locally at each store, is another opportunity for considerable cash embezzlement. Unscrupulous managers cut deals with providers who routinely overbill for such services, then split the overcharges. Even the occasional guard coverage for special events, contracted and paid at the store level, has been a source of such fraud.

Negotiable coupons and gift certificates are prime targets for cash substitution because they are accessible and explainable. All company-generated tender should be serialized and accounted for as inventory items. Sloppiness in this area should be seen by the auditor as an opportunity to defraud, and evidence of noncompliance should be treated as a serious exposure.

Procedural review is an essential element to the audit because it creates a training exercise for store line personnel that goes to enhanced accountability. The auditor should "pop quiz" employees about the methods they use to complete tasks, and then review with the employee the applicable procedures governing specific topics. The auditor should take care to explain the controls that these procedures afford the company, and emphasize the loss prevention benefits gained by consistent compliance.

This process enables the auditor to determine levels of employee awareness to shortage-causing factors, to determine the effectiveness of the training they have received, and to evaluate the contribution they make to the overall

LP effort (i.e., are the employees here an asset or a liability to shrink?). Further, the employee who acknowledges their understanding of the auditor's remarks, or agrees the auditor's discussion has enlightened them to aspects of the program they have not considered, tacitly accepts accountability for future performance in these areas.

For example, an auditor may ask the employee assigned to the shipping/receiving function to "walk-through" a typical receiving operation. The auditor can then observe the employee's grasp of procedures regarding manifest checking, discrepancy reporting, merchandise handling, inventory balancing, and product preparation (proper pricing, EAS tags, etc.) for the selling floor. The auditor can then point out violations he has found with respect to these policies, and ask the employee to suggest methods which may reduce such instances in the future.

The auditor can also take valuable feedback on company procedures back to corporate for assessment. Occasionally, policies are enacted which hamper store line operation or result in laborious procedures that can be streamlined without compromising the controls sought in the policy. Such interaction is constructive in demonstrating that management is attentive to recommendations from the field and that the company is flexible in matters that achieve a desired LP goal.

Another area of procedural review for the auditor to discuss with the staff is adherence to company rules and regulations, especially those governing employee purchases, personal property brought into the building, and the employee's responsibility to insure the integrity of transactions rung on the register. For the auditor to establish employee accountability in such matters early in the visit helps set the stage for subsequent conversations that follow the auditor's examination of POS exception reports that "flag" unusual register transactions.

This type of dialog is effective in sharing most audit findings in the area of POS exception reporting with the staff. Hearing first from the employees about their interpretation of the written rule as it applies to the specific register transactions the auditor may find questionable enables the auditor to define whether violations uncovered are incidents of deliberate negligence by people who know better, or misperceptions that can be remedied with additional training.

The auditor can best prepare for this segment of the audit by analyzing the POS exception activity for a specific location prior to his arrival. As detailed in Chapter 10, the corporate sales audit department should be able to furnish POS exception trends and deviations from company norms that are evident in a particular store. For instance, if a store shows a high volume of refund transactions to comparable store percentages, the auditor would want to verify that documentation for these transactions is complete and filed on-site for his review. The auditor should examine the paperwork for proper authorization and query the staff about the frequency of returns, noting the explanations provided. If the auditor cannot be satisfied that reasonable factors contribute to the high activity, or that insufficient documentation is presented due to poor record keeping, then the auditor may conclude noncompliance to return procedures may be responsible for the high percentage of returns.

Discussion on POS exception activity and other register procedures (gift certificate redemption, interim cash drops, over and shorts, voids, discounts, etc.) will give the auditor insight into the audit results, enabling him to determine whether the trends detected in sales audit reports are problem areas for additional investigative follow-up, or mere anomalies in an otherwise well-run operation. The key element in the POS exception reporting review is for the auditor to determine how efficiently the store manager uses the information in his reports to challenge unusual transactions or patterns with employees. This is an essential accountability tool, and should the auditor find himself pointing out concerns to the store manager for which the store manager has not initiated an inquiry on his own, it is demonstrative of questionable register activity going unchecked.

Each "void" should have the supporting documentation and authorization which legitimizes the transaction. "No Sale" transactions should be explained with reasonable justification. Each refund should have complete customer identification, reason for return, and second party verification that merchandise was indeed taken back before cash was paid out. Each discounted price reported should have a corresponding price change authorization. Some effort to reconcile gift certificate sales with gift certificate redemption should be evident to the auditor.

End-of-day paperwork that allows the auditor to reconstruct a complete business day indicates strong procedural controls and the watchful eye of a concerned supervisor. Incomplete sales media files compromise the daily check-and-balance that detects employee dishonesty early and lays the foundation for investigative inquiry. The auditor's assessment of this managerial function should be weighed heavily in the final audit result, as no manager can be inattentive in this area and produce the desired shortage results.

Inspections that rate compliance to LP merchandising standards are more of a black-and-white issue for the auditor, less open to interpretation and store "custom." Product which is to be displayed in locked showcases cannot be found accessible to customers in open-sell fixtures, unless a conscious decision to operate outside of established policy was made. Merchandise which is scheduled for EAS tags, found on display without them, is more indicative of short-cuts and inattentive stock keeping, than it is a systemic problem in receiving and processing goods.

Stockrooms, which serve as the central staging, processing, and storage areas for product, equipment, and supplies, should be organized in such a way that facilitates the operation yet affords inventory accountability. Companies should have written guidelines for stockroom organization, as without them, it becomes a potpourri of incoming product, outgoing transfers, damaged merchandise, and customer holds and returns, intermingled with broken fixtures, old promotional signage, employee coats, and cleaning supplies. This is a ripe environment for an employee to "stash" merchandise he intends to steal, or set up a shipment to be slipped out the back door. With published organizational standards for stockrooms at his disposal, the auditor can exert his will with the store manager to effect a protective environment for reserve stock.

An audit program which inspects these five elements of store operations — physical security, cash control, procedural compliance, POS exception activity, and merchandise standards — can effectively measure a store's performance to shortage program requirements. More comprehensive audits that include safety inspections, emergency readiness, and adherence to mandated labor practices can be designed to provide management with the assurances stores are in compliance with general standards and operating guidelines set forth by the company.

However, for an audit program in the field to address the issues of inventory shortage, it must be balanced with an audit program at the warehouse/distribution center. Store-side compliance to shortage programs is essential to protecting merchandise and having it accounted for in the physical inventory. But retailers often live with aberrations in the book stock, and it is this figure, the "ledger" of owned product, that the physical stock is compared to (less sales) that produces the inventory shortage figure.

Having a clean book stock figure requires integrity in the paperwork transactions between the company's buying operation, the various merchandise suppliers, and the accurate accounting for receipts at the distribution center. An audit program which does not address the indigenous potential for a flawed book stock number fails to close the loop for precise inventory reconciliation. In companies that operate distribution centers that receive and process merchandise from suppliers; and then ship predetermined quantities to stores, simple keypunch errors can create distorted shortage results by location.

The paper flow process, be it hard copy or electronic, that facilitates the ordering and receiving system servicing the inventory needs of multiple store locations must be the subject of intense audit scrutiny. To better illustrate the shortage factors involved with the paper flow in a distribution operation, we can look at a model process using generic terms and definitions:

Purchase Order (PO): Buyer-generated to place order with vendor

Packing Slip: Vendor-generated to accompany shipment

Key Rec: Distribution center (DC)-generated to acknowledge receipt of shipment

Receiver: DC-generated from PO to create tickets (bar-codes, pricing, SKUs)

Manifest: DC-generated to record shipments distributed to stores

Invoice: Vendor-generated to bill retailer for goods shipped

Purchase Journal: Company-generated to monitor buyer transactions

Let's suppose the buyer for the Accessories division ordered 1200 pieces of a new product line from an established vendor. The buyer would forward a copy of the purchase order (PO) to the supplier authorizing the order. The buyer would also forward a copy of the PO to the Finance division, which would reduce the open-to-buy in the Accessories account by the amount due the vendor from the PO.

The vendor would ship the goods to the buyer's distribution facility with a packing slip that references the PO number and lists 1000 pieces shipped with 200 more on back-order due to heavy demand. The DC issues a key rec for the amount received, referencing the PO number and forwarding a copy of the packing slip with the key rec number to Accounting, to be held in anticipation of the vendor invoice. The DC may also provide the buyer with a copy of the receiver, so that the buyer can verify the bar-code information regarding stock keeping unit number (SKU) assigned, pricing, style, season, color, etc., which will appear on the price ticket they generate for the goods, and be recorded at the point of sale (POS) in stores. The buyer should note the number of price tickets printed, as it will indicate the number of pieces received. This information may also appear on electronic manifests generated to verify quantities shipped to each location.

Once the vendor's invoice is received in Accounting, the bill should be matched up to the PO and the packing slip to verify quantities ordered were received, and the cost is correct. The invoice is then forwarded to Accounts Payable and the vendor is paid. The complete transaction is then posted to the buyer's purchase journal for buyer review. In this instance, exposure exists that the vendor may have generated his invoice from the PO which called for 1200 pieces. Since only 1000 were shipped, accounting would have to adjust the invoice to properly reflect the packing slip and key rec information. If the packing slip was not properly routed to accounting, or someone there was not diligent in matching-up the invoice to the packing slip, the vendor could be overpaid for this shipment.

The result is a paper shortage in the book stock. The company believes it "owns" 1200 pieces because it processed payment for 1200 and closed out the PO as complete. A physical inventory would yield only 1000 units present and accounted for in the stores, and a 200 piece shortage could be erroneously attributed to theft six months down the road when inventory results are published. Safeguards against such an occurrence exist when the buyer checks her purchase journal. From the key rec, receiver, or shipping manifests, she is aware only 1000 pieces were received. Should Accounts Payable have erroneously paid the invoice in full, the PO number in her journal would be "closed." When the invoice is posted to the account, she can verify that only partial payment was made, and that the PO number is still "open" in anticipation of receiving the balance of the order. Bottom-line profitability is ample motive for buyers, DC managers, and store executives to insure integrity in the book stock. Still, an audit function that verifies counts, paper work flow, and accounting practices needs to be in place for an organization to instill discipline in this process.

Just as the DC must be watchful that product received equals the vendor totals on the packing slip before issuing a key rec, so too must stores be certain that the manifest listing quantities shipped from the DC equal the amounts received at the store. Once a shipment is received as complete, the store "owns" that product in their location book stock. Companies that practice and maintain "separate store stocks" in their inventory allocation need to furnish individual stores with "journals" they can reference to insure shipments received (and shipments transferred out) have been properly posted to the store ledger. Many aberrations that appear in the first "flashes" of inventory results are later rectified through a reconciliation process that traces these paper transactions. Inventory Control personnel uncover numerous instances where the paper trail was compromised in their efforts to resolve substantial shortage anomalies. Companies that experience dramatic "swings" in the shortage results from the first flash reported to the final number booked should design an audit program that examines this paper trail to strengthen the checks and balances among the buying line, store line, the distribution center, and accounting.

The audit process should test quality-control in receipt verification, insure adjustments are reflected in the information passed along to accounting, and check that the buyer is vigilant in reconciling purchase journal entries with purchase orders issued. The reverse-scenario, that of verifying that credits for goods returned to the vendor are reflected in adjustments to the book stock, also represents an area of opportunity for paper trail auditing. An audit program is a tool for management to measure compliance to standards and respond to operational deficiencies. Timely response to shortage-related issues uncovered in the audit process serves to amplify the presence of senior management in the field as a key player in the shortage program. Strident disapproval by upper management of substandard audit findings tends to correct chronic exposures and foster a willingness to conform. For these benefits to not be short-lived, recognition of improved performance noted in follow-up reviews must be forthcoming as well.

Shoplifting Prevention

8

Protecting merchandise from theft is the culmination of the investment made in physical security measures and employee training and awareness. The physical safeguards employed — locking hardware, EAS, CCTV, etc. — represents the passive protection shoplifters must be prepared to overcome in order to successfully remove product from the store. A proactive employee population, attentive to customers for service purposes, yet savvy enough to respond appropriately to customer malfeasance, provides the active resistance necessary for the physical protections to be most effective.

The two types of shoplifters most often encountered are the opportunist and the professional. The opportunist comes in two forms: the person who would have purchased an item except for the incredible ease with which a theft opportunity is presented; and the person who enters your store for the express purpose of seeking vulnerabilities to exploit. Rationalization is the primary motivator of the opportunist whose intention to purchase is subverted by the impulse to steal. This rationalization usually comes about by virtue of a perceived wrong that can be made right by theft: a customer becomes so disdainful of your operation that they steal in order to get even. The process that justifies theft is more often than not brought about by customer service levels that are so poor that the person feels the store is getting what they deserve. The customer rationalizes: *"I'd buy this item if I could only find someone to wait on me. My time is valuable, and I shouldn't have to stand around looking high and low to pay an overpaid salesman for overpriced merchandise. If they don't care, why should I?"*

Or, the customer has a recollection to a time when they felt they were not properly accommodated or compensated in a situation where they felt they sustained a loss: *"it wasn't my fault the damn thing broke two days after I got it home; if they won't give me another one, I'll take one."* Or, the customer perceives that an unfair penalty was assessed for their poor decision, and tries to offset the loss: *"Damn! I should have bought that last week when it was on*

111

sale for $9.99. Now it's $14.99. I would've paid the $9.99, but it's not worth $14.99. If they're *going to be so greedy, I'm just taking it."*

Some of these motivating rationalizations are beyond the retailer's ability to control; others are not. Positive shopping experiences build customer loyalty and corporate profits. Creating a benevolent shopping environment where the customer's perception of your operation is quality, value, and service not only serve as the foundation for successful retailing, but eliminates the atmosphere of contempt that fosters these rationalizations. In the big picture of inventory shortage, this type of opportunist poses little threat to a store's operating profits. These episodes are infrequent, having little impact on the shrink reserve built-in to a location's earnings forecast. The other opportunists though, the ones who test your prevention measures and staff awareness, are numerous enough to warrant vigilance. These players do not intend to buy, but they do not intend to get caught, either. They will probe a store's compliance to procedure, evaluate an employee's level of concern, and look for weaknesses. In another reality, they would make effective auditors. They seek or create opportunities to shoplift. For many of them it is a contest of wills: they are the something-for-nothing gang. The more benevolent of this crowd scour a store for likely targets: they pack their own groceries hoping to slip unwanted product from a previous customer that is laying around the checkout into their bag. They leave merchandise surreptitiously in the bottom rung or basket of their shopping cart hoping to pass through the checkout without the clerk spotting it. They switch prices when the mark-up can be easily peeled off or obfuscated. Their alibi if detected is the innocent mistake; the payoff if undetected is free merchandise.

The more malevolent of the opportunists creates situations that compromise your safeguards: they will try on six coats hoping the clerk will fail to re-secure just one of them to the fixture. They'll rummage through a carousel looking for the one piece that may not be tagged with an EAS device. They'll move back and forth between sampling merchandise in locked showcases, waiting for the clerk to leave one showcase unlocked that can be compromised later. They'll look for discarded receipts on the floor; receipts that can be matched up to merchandise later and presented for refund. They'll spy unattended registers for a quick till-tap, or unlocked stockrooms for a quick hit behind-the-scenes. (If detected in the stockroom, he will claim to be looking for the restroom. Guaranteed.)

The wherewithal to frustrate this opportunist is at your disposal: rigid compliance to merchandise protection standards. He seeks only the opportunity provided when the store fails to adhere to its own policies. He carries no pliers to remove EAS tags, no cutters to defeat cables, no picks to compromise your locks. He relies on employee carelessness, affording the worker the chance to be lazy. He capitalizes on employee indifference to your profitability and success to create the opportunity for him. He is frequently more successful than you imagine.

Take a reality check: is your store line operation so downsized and staff so streamlined that the level of attentive customer service and follow-up required to maintain compliance is compromised? If so, this is the environment in which the opportunist flourishes. They lie in wait for the flustered clerk, waiting on several customers at once, answering the phone, ringing on the register, to lose track of which showcase was left open. Does this frenzied pace tire the employee, replacing diligence with indifference, and permitting the employee to rationalize: "*if they were so concerned about stuff getting stolen, they'd hire more people?*" Keeping your employees motivated to protect your merchandise will defeat the opportunist by definition.

The term professional is often used to describe a person whose purpose for entering your store is to shoplift. The moniker suggests their skill level to be beyond your capacity to detect and deter. This is not so, for although they are of single purpose, the absence of their intent to buy, the pattern of their activity, and the methods they employ to circumvent your protective measures all contribute to their detection by the discerning employee. Rather than consider this type of shoplifter a professional, consider him as bold and determined. The boldness emanates from a reliance on employees to be either indifferent to, or intimidated by, his actions; the determination is resultant from the need for the income derived from his activity.

Many retailers have encountered the shoplifter who shuns customer service, attempts to disguise his purpose and actions, and ultimately shoplifts despite a wary eye from employees. The store staff suspected what he was up to, attempted to discreetly monitor the subject, but failed to make an observation of theft itself, and were hesitant to stop him as he exited. Once he's gone, they examine the racks and discover the empty hangers, product wrappers, or defeated EAS tags left behind in silent testimony to the loss. This is hardly a professional caper: his intent was rightly assessed and his actions were subsequently discovered. He succeeded not by virtue of a flawless plan and skillful execution, but rather by his boldness and determination in the face of suspicion. His confidence is rooted in the belief that the employee is reluctant to confront, that retail etiquette precludes behavior by employees which would be deemed offensive by customers, and that his status in your store is that of a customer until proven otherwise, with all the rights and privileges accorded patrons.

Therefore, when he is approached and asked if he needs assistance by a clerk offering service, he can decline that offer in such a way that the employee feels uncomfortable remaining close by the subject, for fear that the subject will chastise the clerk for "hovering." Once chastened by a gruff customer, the employee has few options but to back off, lest a confrontation ensue whereby the customer accuses the employee of unfair scrutiny: *"you're watching me because you think I'm going to steal!"*

The flaw in this type of straight-up customer service approach is that it is anticipated by the shoplifter, who is prepared to manipulate the situation to his advantage by deterring the employee from surveillance. Informing the employee that their assistance is neither needed nor welcomed places the onus for remaining present in an unprovocative manner on the clerk, and only that presence will prevent the theft. Therefore, standard customer service techniques are ineffective with the bold and determined shoplifter.

Instead, a more aggressive posture needs to be taken in order to drop the pretenses of this "dance with wolves." Once you determine a customer is no longer a customer, but a shoplifter waiting for his chance, a more appropriate response, aimed at diminishing his boldness and determination, is required. Making that determination, however, is more art than science, and sales people have to be shrewd and knowledgeable of shoplifting tactics in order to make informed judgments.

Knowing the circumstances shoplifters prefer will enable employees to evaluate whether or not the subject's actions are consistent with establishing the preferred setting for theft. Ideally, the shoplifter wishes to be positioned in a manner that inhibits casual observation. Therefore, be mindful of the areas of the store where obstructions exist and discreet surveillance is difficult. If he heads to those areas, score one point for location. Recall the subject's dress and possessions when he came in. If you did not observe him enter, a walk-by to note these details is appropriate. Should the subject be wearing clothing (e.g., overcoat, baggy pants, shirt outside, etc.), or carrying a shopping bag, tote bag, backpack, etc., that would facilitate the concealment of product, score one point for means. If his clothing is inconsistent with the weather (e.g., a raincoat on a sunny day), add another point.

Awareness of the merchandise most often pilfered, i.e., concealable items, desirable brands (hot-selling labels), high-end retail with a potential for resale on the street, enables you to score a point for selection, should the subject focus on coveted inventory. Next, evaluate your resources. Subtract two points for a visible, functional camera monitoring the subject's area. Subtract one point for a "dummy" camera, mirror, or other passive device utilized as a deterrent. Add a point if no such resource is deployed. Subtract a point for EAS protection of the product at risk; add a point in the absence of EAS. The most important factor for determining customer from shoplifter is history from previous encounters with the subject. If he has been watched before, suspected before, or has been seen in the company of others who have been previously scrutinized, add two points. If he has purchased merchandise or has engaged in legitimate consumer-related conversation with the staff on prior visits, subtract a point. If he is unknown to the staff, add one point.

This abstract assessment of customers and their potential for wrongdoing is a benign exercise in awareness for the staff at the least, and the prompt for action if the tally reaches +6. That action is not approaching the customer and asking if you may be of service. A customer service approach would be appropriate to deter the opportunist, but as discussed, this tact is expected by the professional, and he is prepared to decline assistance in such a way that makes your observation of his actions more difficult. You do not fire the first volley of contact with the bold and determined shoplifter. You reserve your one free shot of unchallenged contact for a more appropriate time. This way, you are free to maintain a presence longer before being "shooed-away" by his decline for service. While maintaining your low-profile presence, consider the steps the shoplifter will have to complete in order to shoplift. Will he have to position himself in such a way as to obstruct view from camera or mirror? Will he have to defeat devices such as cables or locks? Will he have to remove and dispose of EAS tags? If so, you can delay your approach until one or more of these steps has been initiated.

You may want to turn up the heat a bit prior to the onset of the theft. For instance, some protective devices make an audible sound when tampered with or defeated: the beep of an alarm cable, the snap of an EAS tag. Shoplifters depend on background noise to offset this problem. It may be unsettling to the professional to overhear an employee in close proximity call to another worker: *"hey Joe, turn the music down; I can't hear myself think back here!"* This abrupt change in the store environment can unnerve a shoplifter, or at least cause a brief, faint smile from the more bold and determined shoplifter aware of your ploy. You have compromised his cover, and perhaps by code alerted another employee of your suspicion. He has "added a point" to his assessment of his adversary, which is step one in diminishing his resolve.

So far, there has been no formal approach…and no opportunity for the subject to object to your presence. He is going to have to come to you if he is to be rid of your presence as desired. An old trick is to bring you a selection and ask if you might have it "in the back" in another size or color. Here we separate customer service from asset protection. If you determine this person to be a likely shoplifter, he is not entitled to your customer service efforts in the strict sense of the term. A legitimate customer making this request would be gladly accommodated, but a shoplifter is attempting to get distance between you and your merchandise. This is a wonderful opportunity for the employee to turn this encounter to his advantage:

SL: *"Do you have this jacket in a 42? Maybe in the stockroom?"*

EMP: *"Oh no, I'm sorry. Everything in this style is out on the floor. Although, I could have sworn we had a 42 this morning. Let me look. Gee, I hope nobody stole it!"*

This tongue-in-cheek banter demonstrates to the shoplifter you are not naive to theft in your store. In his attempt to remove you from the area, he has instead received a subtle reminder of your right to be there. Not the development he was hoping for. Add a point for the clerk.

With the subject in tow, proceed to the rack and appear to be looking for the item requested. But rather than examining size labels as he would expect, shamelessly inspect the condition of the security devices instead, even counting the garments aloud. Then respond:

> *"Nope, sorry, no 42s. I don't know what happened to it, but at least these are all tagged. If you want to give me your name and phone number I will order one for you."*

The smirk may reappear as the shoplifter adds a point for the clerk. This is adding up to be a worthwhile adversary. Should you discover any tampering with security devices, or product devoid of tags, or empty hangers, comment on these discoveries with wonderment:

> *"What do you know about that? I could have sworn we had control tags on all of these. Good thing I came back here. I'll bet somebody was trying to steal these too. I think I'll go adjust the camera. If you need me, I'll be right over there."*

A professional shoplifter, bold and determined, but not anxious to be caught, will receive the subliminal message loud and clear. You have met the issue of shoplifting head-on, intimated that resources (whether owned or not) for detecting theft are deployed, and established your turf for a continued presence. That this shoplifter would remain and steal following an encounter along these lines is highly unlikely. He may not move out right away (after all saving-face is one of the prerequisites of returning again), but aggressive (almost confrontational) customer service, as a vehicle to prevent shoplifting, is more effective against the professional, and enlightening for the staff, than mere passive inquiries offering assistance.

Properly chastened from shoplifting, the professional's last ploy may be to goad you in to an encounter that would level the playing field somewhat in his estimation. He may begin rearranging merchandise, shooting furtive glances in your direction, or engaging in gestures that are designed to have the impression he may still attempt to shoplift. Should you react to these deceptions, you could lose your advantage by inviting a confrontation that enables the shoplifter to accuse you of suspecting him of theft. Do not get cocky when you realize that you are being toyed with; allow him a bit of leeway at your expense. You will still get the last point.

Try to ensure that other staff members get a good look at the subject before he leaves. Realizing your intention in this regard will hasten his exit, an exit which should be punctuated with a patronizing *"thanks for shopping with us"* from as many sales people on hand as possible. Making eye contact and brief conversation with the subject will enhance future recognition of him by your staff in the future.

The after-the-fact encounter is more complex than the prevention-minded approach. This occurs when a shoplifter is engaged in the act of theft, which is detected by the employee. Undeterred, the subject has initiated the theft by defeating a security device, removing product tags, or moving merchandise to a place more conducive to concealing it. The employee's choice is to either continue to observe the transgression until the theft is consummated and effect an apprehension, or to seize the moment, using the malfeasance witnessed to interdict the theft before it is completed. Each requires a level of skill by the store associate that may not come naturally to retail employees. That is why a workable understanding of the apprehension criteria (see Chapter 18) is essential in combating the professional shoplifter.

The key to shoplifting interdiction is not to accuse the subject of attempting to steal your product. Rather, it is his handling of your goods in the improper manner indigenous to shoplifting that permits you to respond forcefully and indignantly. To illustrate, suppose you observe a subject move merchandise from one rack to another, then squat down and yank off your price tickets or an EAS tag. You could presume his next step would be to conceal it, so you back off and hope to get a clear observation of his placing your merchandise on his person (or in his bag), then lie in wait to nab him at the door. This is a good plan, but a lot could go wrong. You may not find a vantage point from which to witness the concealment. Then, your stop at the door would be compromised by your inability to state exactly what merchandise is in what place, or to even be sure he has it. He may move on, leaving the unprotected merchandise exposed to theft by a cohort you are unaware of, as you trail him in the store expecting him to return to the stash. You could see the whole theft and make a confident stop at the door, only to get punched in the eye for your trouble. He may break and flee, causing you to choose between a street chase and losing your merchandise.

Or, you could interdict the theft and have grounds to eject the subject based on your observation of his conduct. Once you witness his removal of an EAS tag, or his secreting product other than where it is intended to be displayed, you can make a forceful approach demanding an explanation for his actions:

EMP: *"What is going on here? Why did you put that sweater in among these jackets? Look at these tickets on the floor! I saw you take them off this sweater!"*

SL: *"I didn't do that; it was like that."*

EMP: *"No it was not. I saw you. Why are you lying? What are you trying to pull here? How am I supposed to sell this now? This is ruined!"*

SL: *"I didn't ruin anything. What are you talking about?"*

EMP: *"Right here. Look at this pull in the sleeve. You can either buy it or get out. I don't want your business here."*

SL: *"I didn't do nothing. You can't kick me out."*

EMP: *"Oh yes I can. I have to send this sweater back to the factory to get fixed and re-ticketed. You better leave."*

The concept to this approach is to stay within the parameters of what you actually observed, and attribute no intent to steal to the subject. Merely convey that his conduct is disruptive enough to your operation that you can rightfully demand he leave. The more incriminating the subject's actions (i.e., cutting a cable, removing an EAS tag), the more strident your objection can be:

"Hey, why have you got all these hangers on the floor, and what are these shirts doing all rolled up?"

"I saw you break that cassette case and take the tape out! That case costs money. Give me that tape and get out!"

"Hey! You just pried open that fixture! We don't allow that; get out!"

"I saw you taking these inventory tags off those pants. You're not allowed to do that. Somebody could steal them. Get out!"

"You broke open this set and took two out! You can't do that. Don't come back here again."

The central theme of interdiction involves employee intervention once preliminary elements of the theft occur. Your observation of conduct that damages, defaces, or renders an item less presentable for sale entitles you to confront the subject and his actions for explanation. Your righteous indignation at such conduct, coupled with a subjective assessment of the damage to your operation, leads to the eventuality that the subject's business is no longer welcome, and a rightful exclusion from the premises may follow. At no time is the attempted theft, which is only presumed to be the end result, discussed, as this would afford the subject the moral high ground to dispute your contention. It is the mischief-making that is seized upon to warrant the confrontation. The inappropriate behavior permits the approach, accusation (within the scope of observed misconduct) and lawful removal from the premises (see Chapter 20, Criminal Trespass) as the merchant sees fit. Amid the protestations of your unreasonable response to his benign acts, you conclude the issue matter-of-factly:

EMP: *"Then are you going to buy it? No? Fine. Then leave now or I'll call the cops."*

SL: *"Go ahead and call the cops, I didn't do nothing."*

EMP: *"Fine. We'll do it your way."*

Gather up the evidence of the transgression and walk away, calling to the employee at the front counter: *Joe. Call mall security (or police, etc.).* Your authoritative conclusion to the encounter will result in the subject's reluctant departure, perhaps amid shouted obscenities, but departure nonetheless. As he leaves you may add at your discretion: *"and don't come back here again either, or I'll call the cops."* This effectively serves as a lawful exclusion from your store, a revocation of his right and privilege to enter and remain on your premises in the future. It is strongly recommended that such an event be documented on an incident report should reference to this occurrence be needed in any future dealings with this individual. The outcome of such an interdiction, providing the matter was handled correctly and professionally, is rather favorable to the retailer: the merchandise was protected, the shoplifter was ejected and formally excluded, and employees were not placed at risk by virtue of an apprehension or detention.

Active training of employees for the purposes of boosting their confidence to act in these situations (see Chapter 6, *Employee Awareness*) is essential to preventing shoplifting in stores. Providing parameters of when and how to act — practical applications employees can relate to when they know they are being tested by shoplifters — is the surest way you can keep your employees motivated and your inventory safe. In most cases, employees resent the shoplifting they know goes on but feel powerless to prevent it. They do not like being played for a fool and having to be "nice" to people they know want to steal. They'd like to win a round once in a while, but are inhibited by not knowing how far they can go or where to draw the line. They are uncertain whether management will back them up if they are aggressive. A shoplifter who was successfully deterred by employee vigilance could write a letter to higher-ups complaining of rude treatment, and the worker may be sanctioned.

These are the issues management needs to deal with in order to maximize their most precious resource in preventing shoplifting. You would not fail to train your associates on how to provide service, ring sales on a register, and process delivered merchandise. Do not skimp on active, well-publicized training in loss prevention techniques either.

Employee Dishonesty 9

One of the more intriguing aspects of employee theft in a retail environment has been the coming-of-age of the employer's awareness and recognition of employee dishonesty. It was not so long ago that businesses operated under the premise that "employees would not steal from this company." A "that cannot happen here" attitude prevailed, and workers were trusted. It was a by-product of more genteel times, and instances of employee theft were scandal.

Later, as lessons were learned and sophisticated embezzlement operations were uncovered, employers consoled themselves that such incidents were an aberration, but reluctantly initiated some rudimentary safeguards to prevent such opportunists in the future. At the time, it was the moral fiber of the employee that was defective, and certainly not a deficiency in the way the Company went about protecting its assets.

Yet, as the dollars and cents of losses grew, recognition of employee theft became more prominent. Although the culprits were more or less restricted in thought and mind to the hourly-waged, transient employees "down on the dock," or the ever-available morning porter from "that thieving cleaning service," retailers employed guards, detectives, and investigators to comfortably declare the situation resolved, or at least manageable. The platitude of "employees would not steal from this company" now contained the caveat "and get away with it."

As security departments rolled-up the body counts, retailing progressed into the electronic age: the dawn of merchandise information systems, computerized receiving and distribution operations, and sophisticated point-of-sale networks that managed the Company's burgeoning inventory control apparatus. And during this remarkable period of growth and technical advance, the security department remained in the basement office. Surveillance was conduced by security guards hiding in the rafters, waiting for the stockroom clerk to put a shirt down his pants.

Clearly, opportunities to exploit the new sophistication in retail operations for personal gain were evident, and the security programs to deter such thoughts were obsolete and believed unnecessary. That losses attributed to shortage continued to mount during this time was inevitable given the retailer's tendency to underestimate the industry of an employee predisposed to theft, coupled with the failure to consider the exposure to loss inherent in sweeping procedural change.

Gradually, loss prevention sciences replaced security operations, and progressive retailers began to balance their resources to protect their businesses from the depleting effects of internal losses. Deterring employee theft became a proactive program of education, early detection, and swift intervention.

Modern retail companies now invest heavily in their loss prevention efforts to reduce employee theft, and they do it across departmental lines, illustrating that shortage control is a universal responsibility for all managers. Many of the resources a retail company can employ to manage its exposure to employee theft are simple, effective, and inexpensive. It involves incorporating a standard of integrity into the business environment that is tangible, uncompromising, and simple for employees to relate to.

The indoctrination of employees into this culture of integrity must be clearly evident in all aspects of employee orientation, training, development, and advancement. Key for employee recognition of this corporate mindset is that success is reciprocal. Certainty of sharing in a company's success is a known motivator for productivity and dedication. It must also be conveyed that loyalty is an attribute the Company seeks and rewards.

Loyalty to an employer may be dismissed by some as a casualty of the modern business era, but the company that still has it is a step ahead of its competitor who does not have it when factors that contribute to employee theft are evaluated. Establishing an environment that builds loyalty requires an atmosphere of trust that may seem incongruous with the close scrutiny of employee activity essential to curtailing dishonesty. But the two elements can co-exist as the employee is educated that management is fulfilling its obligation to its customers, shareholders, and its workers by ensuring the integrity of its business practices. Knowing the employer is diligent in this regard becomes a statement of fact, a matter of routine, and is less likely to be interpreted as an intrusive affront to an employee's character.

The first principle for success against internal theft is inclusion of a standard of integrity in company dogma, or The Mission Statement. All companies have them in some shape or form, but too few publicize their commitment to employee honesty in them. Zero tolerance of employee behavior that does not meet the highest ethical standard (so stated) provides the employer with the moral high ground when confronting suspect situations.

It gives the employer latitude to respond quickly and challenge behavior inconsistent with the Mission Statement, and precludes the employer from having to "build a case" before an employee can be called to task for conduct or activity that is perceived as detrimental to the best interests of the Company. It provides a global perspective for interpreting gray areas.

To sustain this policy, certain actions must accompany the words. Indoctrinating an employee begins with the earliest contact that person has with your organization. Ideally, reference to honesty and integrity should appear in the classified ad, but for practicality, we will begin with the application process. It is essential the employment department, or the hiring authority, begin to influence the applicant's first impressions accordingly. Therefore, great care should be taken to impress upon the applicant the value of past employer references in order to enhance the potential for hire. Specific individuals to contact and the position they held in supervising the applicant on previous jobs must be furnished. The onus for satisfying a rigorous background check should fall to the applicant. The interviewer should solicit information by asking the applicant to predict how the reference may answer questions about the applicant's trustworthiness, reliability, loyalty, reason for leaving, and suitability for rehire.

The applicant's point of view on these issues may be insightful, since the reference may be unable to specify these answers due to restrictions imposed at the reference's company. Still, the prospect that you may ask about these concerns may elicit some qualifiers from the applicant that can be useful in judging what may otherwise be tepid endorsements from previous employers. Note separately for future reference any instances of an applicant indicating he was referred to the job by friends or relatives working for the company.

The application process should also include releases for the employer to perform background checks that include any number of database indices of adverse information. Releases to search credit reports, both pre-employment and periodic throughout the duration of employment, should be sought. Whether you actually proceed with this step is a matter of company policy, and a resource whose merits will have to be evaluated with your business needs. But ask for and receive the releases nonetheless. Allowing the applicant to think you are this diligent, even if you are not, is okay.

The same applies for releases to perform checks on criminal background, motor vehicle records, academic achievement, and military history. There is even an adverse information database exclusive to member retailers that disseminates past records of shoplifting, retail fraud, and termination of employment for dishonesty (records that a criminal background check will not uncover since many retailers seldom prosecute). Whether you subscribe to any or all of these database services is academic; the value is in the applicant's perception that you do.

Be certain to discuss point-blank with prospective employees recent periods of unemployment, especially with those applying for management positions that afford unimpeded access to company facilities and cash. It is not uncommon in today's job market for executive personnel to be out of work for three, or up to six, months. The associated financial crunch of this income displacement warrants an inquiry on how the applicant has managed to support himself in that time. Aside from the productivity complications involved when a person is warding off the bill collectors, the urgency for a quick fix to a pressing financial dilemma has frequently resulted in an otherwise intelligent, honest person making irrational, damaging choices.

Other resources available to the employer for an integrity "once over" include on-line paper-and-pencil testing. This industry has improved both the content and application of its tests, as well as the speed and efficiency with which results are reported. Survey tests that gauge an applicant's response to control questions in the areas of honesty, substance abuse, customer service, and employee relations can provide qualified insight into behavioral tendencies that can be an asset or detriment to your organization. This resource is less labor intensive and disruptive to the interview environment than it once was, while coming more in line with the acceptable cost parameters of the employment process.

Another area of consideration at the pre-employment stage is drug testing. Again, this is a matter of company policy, and the merits and cost of such a program need to be weighed against the potential gains of screening out undesirables from the work force. In deciding company policy concerning drug testing, there exists a presumption that employees who use drugs would be more likely to steal from the company to support even casual drug use, and therefore are high-risk. If a correlation can be drawn at all between drugs in the workplace and employee theft, the best is that both activities are illegal, and aggressively pursuing policies that reinforce the notion of zero tolerance for criminal activity in the workplace is the consistent message to be sent.

Having proven their mettle through the application process, the applicant has now become an employee, a trainee to be exact. Establishing an interim status as a trainee is useful to the employer as it suggests to the new employee a probationary period of intense scrutiny. The trainee will usually respond to this attention by exhibiting exemplary conduct to impress his superiors. In fact, the new employee has tacitly accepted a higher standard of conduct, which can then serve as a benchmark for future behavior and performance. Instead of being able to relax his standards following the period of probation, the new employee will come to realize that improvement is expected with tenure.

These concepts lend themselves to the second principle of success against internal theft: accountability. Accountability, or rather management's insistence upon accountability, is the foundation for early detection and swift remedy in cases of suspected employee theft. The seeds of accountability are planted in the orientation process of new employees. Upon accepting the company's employee handbook standards, the new employee agrees to conform to the standard of conduct prescribed by the employer. Detailed training of this material should be conducted in such a way that the trainee acknowledges this understanding, and a representative of management is afforded the opportunity to review the import of this subject matter with the new employee. Direct references to company standards on integrity, and intolerance of unethical behavior, should be stressed.

Retailers need to be especially diligent in this area, as the content of the employee handbook, specifically the rules and regulations section, locks-in the employee's accountability through mandated duties and responsibilities. Failure to specify expectations, standards, and consequences dilutes the effectiveness with which management can respond to the early warning signals of employee malfeasance. Further, the employee is given notice that questionable activity will be challenged, and is therefore less inclined to take exception when asked to cooperate in some future loss prevention inquiry.

As you can see, the initial concepts involve the acceptance of the employer's expectation and the employee's accountability. Essentially, the up-front policy statements, coupled with the employee's acquiescence on compliance, builds a box around the employee, giving management the upper hand to control events. The next phase involves supervisory techniques that provide positive reinforcement of these principles.

A classic rule of thumb retailers have ascribed to when considering the issue of employee dishonesty goes like this: 10% of your employees will steal from you no matter what you do; 10% will not steal ever, regardless of the need and opportunity; and the remaining 80% may steal if you let them. It has long been the goal of loss prevention programs to keep the 80% that are on the fence honest, with strategies that suggest that employee theft does not pay.

Need and opportunity are the factors that ultimately decide whether or not the 80% eventually succumbs to this ill-advised remedy to financial difficulty. Employers cannot fully monitor and respond to those circumstances of need that arise in the course of an employee's tenure with a company. But periodic evaluation of the employee's lifestyle is a constructive step toward building a profile of employee need.

The astute employer should be cognizant of events which effect the employee off the job, and establish a mechanism to alert the appropriate supervisory personnel of circumstances brought to the employer's attention through normal channels. Indicators that an employee may be having difficulty managing personal finances can be as overt as a court-ordered garnishment, or as subtle as an income verification request on a mortgage application.

The benefits department, as sordid as this may appear at first glance, can be a virtual data bank of an employee's capabilities in personal financial management. Establishing a process whereby an appropriate and confidential inquiry, conducted by a tactful human resources executive or qualified supervisor, can assist management in evaluating whether an employee is over-reaching his resources. This is not a green light to place the individual on loss prevention's "Most Wanted" list, but a service to the employee in the long run.

First of all, it reminds the employee that management is concerned about the employee off the job. Second, it alerts the employee that, in this case, the left hand does indeed know what the right hand is doing, which is an example management too infrequently demonstrates to the staff. Third, it plants the seed that his off-the-job activity is not anonymous, and that management is aware of his special circumstances. And last, in a subtle and informal manner, it notifies the employee that his personal affairs have come to your attention, and reinforcing that notion may preclude that employee from making a regrettable blunder.

If this sounds too abstract in determining whether an employee's financial situation makes him a candidate for illicit profit sharing, consider the motives that are expressed by apprehended dishonest employees when reading their confessions: personal problems, mounting debt, medical expenses, eviction, divorce, etc. All of which are changes in lifestyle whose symptoms are discernible with a trained eye in the benefits department.

Since this is an example of harnessing in-house resources for purposes other than its primary function, the following examples are offered for guidance in implementing such a process:

ACTION: The company receives an income verification request for your employee who is attempting to finance an auto loan. The employee has signed a waiver for the employer to release this information.

REACTION: Privately, inform the employee that the paperwork has been received and processed in a timely fashion. Prompt the employee in a conversational manner to provide details about the financing by inquiring about the interest rate he got, is he happy with the deal he got from the dealership, will his insurance go up a lot, is he trying to sell his old car, etc. Always conduct these sessions constructively, with a subtext of: good luck and let us know if we can help. Meanwhile, calculate in your own mind what impact this purchase will have on the employee's cash flow.

ACTION: The employee requests his spouse be covered under your company medical plan, citing her recent termination at her place of employment.

REACTION: Begin by asking details about the spouse's occupation, offering networking contacts you can supply. Be generous: offer to look over the spouse's resumé, allow the employee to make copies of it at work and to even have access to your fax machine for urgent leads. This largesse sets the tone for you to probe the most pressing issue: *"Are you guys going to be okay?"* Reassure the employee these things happen and you will keep his situation in mind when overtime opportunities come up, or when per diem jobs become available that the spouse may be suited for. *"Let us know if we can help."*

ACTION: Employee requests to access his 401K or retirement account citing financial hardship.

REACTION: Certainly by company policy, and in some cases by law, the onus is on the employee to present evidence that the financial hardship meets the criteria set forth in the plan for early withdrawal. Acting on behalf of the employee, referencing the interest and tax penalties for this option, learn why the employee cannot utilize traditional alternatives: *"What about savings? Can you get a loan? Borrow from relatives?"* If the answers to these constructive suggestions are negative, you have a clearer picture of this employee's resources to successfully overcome the stated hardship.

ACTION: Employee requests to change medical plan from family to single coverage, citing divorce action.

REACTION: Ask with empathy how the employee is handling all this. Does he need time off? Would he care to take advantage of the company's professional counseling plan and coverage? Will the added stress affect his work in a way you need to know about? These disarming, but appropriate, overtures may yield an opportunity to discover what you really want to know: *"Are you broke, homeless, angry, and desperate?"*

ACTION: Employee returns from an extended medical leave after recuperating from surgery.

REACTION: You already know the employee's income has been reduced to the two-thirds disability pay the past six months. You already know he's on the hook for the 20% co-pay of major medical (plus deductibles). The out-of-pocket expense coupled with the income reduction has been a financial reversal for this employee. Amid the good cheer and welcome-backs, it is appropriate to inquire if there are any financial concerns the employee wishes to share with you. If this setback has wiped the guy out, let him know the company will reassure creditors on his behalf, and support any debt consolidation plan he has agreed to, or perhaps restructure commission/bonus schedules to ease the burden. *"Let us know if we can help."*

As distasteful as some of these tactics may seem on the surface, it is nonetheless advantageous to get this close to an employee's private life. It bears repeating: these are the reasons a majority of dishonest employees point to in explaining why they stole from their employer. Few have stated *"I took it because I'm greedy."* It is more often than not an overwhelming need that clouds judgment and provokes poor decisions.

Another way to approach this issue is to consider that your employee population is divided into two groups: dishonest employees and latent dishonest employees.

This is an aggressive posture, but one that ultimately strengthens procedural controls. This approach enhances any audit program you wish to implement, since audit programs by definition assume some degree of noncompliance. Any pattern of nonconformity to published policy compromises standards, weakens resolve, and creates a climate of opportunity for someone predisposed to theft.

Worse, operations that play fast and loose with the rules stimulate nefarious thoughts in the minds of employees whose dishonesty is dormant, as they are being indirectly coaxed to test the waters. Bringing that 80% off the fence, or activating the latency of employees who would steal if they could get away with it, will soon overrun your resources and you will hemorrhage red ink.

Once an individual becomes predisposed to theft, one of two general rationalizations has taken place: *"They won't know if it is gone,"* or *"They don't care that it is gone."* In the first case, management practices have demonstrated that inventory control is suspect. Usually, a shipment or delivery has gone awry, and management learns of the incident only upon the chance discovery of the misdirected product. Events of this nature illustrate to the employee that controls do break down, and when it happens, the mechanism to respond to those situations is imperfect. An industrious employee may then test the veracity of these controls and response mechanisms to isolate the prevailing conditions for systemic failure.

The worker may intentionally conceal or misdirect a shipment in order to observe management's capacity to learn of the event and implement retrieval efforts. Swift detection and a rapidly initiated investigation may deter the employee from considering this activity in the future. But failure to respond will embolden the employee to one day take ownership of a desirable shipment. The difference between the two outcomes rests with management's ability to enforce compliance to its own safeguards.

The dishonest employee will attempt to discern what safeguard was ignored, and will evaluate to what degree that omission, that failure to comply, can be anticipated. For instance, in the example of the lost shipment, management may require stores to check in deliveries against a manifest and report discrepancies to a central location.

Suppose Store #5 and Store #15 were each scheduled to receive 30 boxes. Store #5 checked in 30 boxes received, but later in the day learned from the central discrepancy location that Store #15 reported receiving 31 boxes against its manifest listing delivery for 30 boxes. Store #5 is informed that the odd box at Store #15 bore a destination sticker for Store #5.

Further investigation reveals that the third assistant at Store #5 did not, for reasons he must be compelled to account for, count in each box of the shipment. From rote, indifference, malice, or indolence, he placed check marks down the left hand column of the manifest, put the boxes in the stockroom, filed the manifest, and went off to further contribute to the company's success.

In dealing with the aftermath of this situation, management should do all it can to repudiate the rationalizations discussed earlier: *"they don't know it is gone; they don't care that it is gone."* Failure to exploit this incident is an opportunity lost. Instead, management should proceed under the following assumptions:

1. Johnny, the third assistant at Store #5 has never properly checked in a shipment, and the employees at that store know it. There are probably countless other check and balance functions not practiced in Store #5, and the employees there know that, too. Johnny is either (1) negligent, (2) dishonest, or (3) both.
2. The store manager, first and second assistants, are most likely derelict in their duty, either in training Johnny or in their supervisory responsibility of Johnny.
3. The 30th box labeled for Store #5, was intentionally misshipped to Store #15 from the distribution center. In fact, Store #5 is short-shipped by design because it is known that Johnny does not check in the boxes. This was learned from a previous inadvertent shipping shortage which was not detected.
4. That Store #15 was selected to receive the extra box is because the shipper has a cohort at that location who was supposed to abscond with the over-shipment, but due more to good luck than good management, a responsible employee discovered the discrepancy and reported it.
5. This is a division-wide conspiracy, and overreact accordingly.

In all likelihood, these dire conclusions will be proved unfounded. But the impetus of a loss prevention program is to proceed against any notion that management is complacent when procedures are compromised. Where resources permit, an effective response to this incident would be the following:

1. A comprehensive on-site review of Store #5 to determine the depth and breadth of procedural compliance. This audit should be conducted with the store manager and reviewed in the presence of his

immediate supervisor. A report summarizing findings and corrective action to be implemented should be forwarded to the director of stores, with target dates for completion.

2. After determining the degree of culpability regarding Johnny, disciplinary action should be taken in conjunction with a representative from human resources.

3. A shipment movement log should be implemented at the distribution center to identify the packer and loader responsible for ensuring deliveries are shipped to the proper locations. This will permit accountability when "discrepancy central" is advised of future misdirected shipments.

4. A congratulatory note should be sent to the employee at Store #15 who reported the over-shipment, and copied to that employee's supervisor. It should be explained that shipping the extra box is part of a division-wide program that tests the integrity of manifest checking procedures, and that her diligence proves that the company's faith in its employees to safeguard its assets is deserved.

5. Implement a program that seeds shipments to be over and short, and have "discrepancy control" publish store rankings by detection rate.

These steps illustrate a management response that belies the last of the great rationalizations: the low perception of risk. Before an employee crosses the line and engages in theft, the element of risk is weighed. Companies that fail to publicize known losses as an event miss the opportunity to compound a wavering employee's assessment of risk. Further, companies that implement safeguards, purchase new security equipment, identify trends in shrink that result in the enactment of new procedures, and then "keep it a secret" do little to deter a perception of low risk.

To elevate the element of risk, supervisors should aggressively challenge employee's whereabouts (because an employee is often absent from his workplace when staging, transporting, secreting, and removing merchandise), discourage personal phone calls and friends visiting (because communication is essential in collusive rings and often involve outside accomplices), and insist on accountability for unusual transactions (because circumvention of normal sales procedures is indigenous to fraudulent activity at the register).

For example, many retailers require an authorizer's signature for refund transactions. This is the safeguard management has built into the system. The exposure is an employee ringing in a refund transaction for a customer who is not there, and pockets the money. The register will balance because the refund document will offset the cash taken. The safeguard is to have a manager authorize the return, requiring the manager to examine the product returned and speak with the customer. This will prevent fraudulent returns unless the employee is willing to assume greater risk (i.e., selecting merchandise and involving an outside accomplice).

When a manager is derelict in this duty, authorizing the return without seeing the customer and the merchandise, the manager has implied to the clerk the following:

1. Not all rules have to be followed.
2. I trust you.
3. I am above policy.
4. Short cuts are okay.
5. I am not as diligent as I appear.
6. Management safeguards are not a priority.
7. I am unaware of the exposure to loss I have created.
8. I am unconcerned about the exposure to loss I have created.

A manager who sets this tone, even by a single omission of responsibility, has become an accessory before the fact. Supervisors who fail in this regard do a tremendous disservice to their staff. They minimize the risk the employee will assess prior to engaging in theft. Eventually, irresponsibility of this nature will manifest itself enough in other aspects of the manager's performance that the manager will be replaced, most likely by someone more diligent. The employee, however, has become emboldened by success to get over on the system, and dependent on the easy money he has realized from his ingenuity, underestimating the escalated risk posed by the new manager...and they will get caught and pay the price. A manager that fails to sustain a high probability of detection, due to proactive supervisory skills and the ability to ask the hard questions, is remiss in his duty to the company and the employee.

The last opportunity management has to feed the element of risk is to insure employees realize the consequences of employee theft. The blanket statement "all employees will be prosecuted" is an inadequate message. First, all employees will not be prosecuted because, inevitably, cases that are too shaky to pursue in court will arise. Second, employees do not know the consequences of prosecution well enough to make a value judgment — you have to spell it out. They have a perception that the criminal justice system goes lightly on first offenders, especially if all you did was take something from a big corporation. What they do not perceive is that even light treatment from the criminal justice system is traumatic for a first offender.

Some employees may have been through the turnstile before, and they are not intimidated by being put into the system. But the vast majority only know about being arrested from watching COPS on TV. Using case histories is most effective. Employees are anxious to know *"what happened to Johnny?"*

after witnessing his summons from the selling floor and eventual arrest. Exploit the scuttlebutt with a "Life After Theft" meeting that affords management a chance to reinforce consequences and escalate risk:

> *"I know you are all wondering what went on here a couple of three weeks ago when the cops came and took Johnny away. He made some dumb mistakes he did not think we'd catch. But the suits back at Corporate were on him fast enough, and it was not pretty to see.*
>
> *After we interviewed Johnny and he admitted that he stole from us we had to contact the police. Johnny cried when we told him we could not just let him pay back the money and be fired, we told him that would not be consistent with the message we need to send.*
>
> *So the cops came and they handcuffed him (they have to do that) and led him out to the patrol car. He asked if they would take him out the back door, but they said they parked out front. They took him to the station and booked him for grand larceny, fraud, embezzlement, and falsifying company documents. They did his fingerprints and all, then had to put him in a cell because of the multiple felony charges, he'd have to have a bail hearing.*
>
> *The D.A. said he might drop the other charges and just prosecute the grand larceny if Johnny made good on his promise of restitution; but until then, he was still charged with the multiple felonies and he had to stay in county jail the weekend until he was arraigned and posted a $2500 bond Monday. His wife put up the deed to their house.*
>
> *They had a hearing after that and Johnny pled guilty to one count of larceny, reduced to an A misdemeanor. He was fined $350 and sentenced to one year probation and 60 hours of community service.*
>
> *He had to pay his lawyer $600 to represent him, but at least he's out.*
>
> *He has no job anymore, no benefits, a criminal record now, and he still has to pay back $150 a month to the company over the next ten months or they will revoke his probation.*
>
> *Next time you see Johnny down at the car wash, ask him if he thinks it was worth it."*

You may not want to be so folksy about it, and your company may not wish to divulge such information in an open forum, but illustrating the consequences in a tangible way is a service to employees.

In conclusion, preventing dishonest employee activity is first a matter of setting standards of integrity, followed by awareness of the profile for escalated employee need, with a proactive accountability to control opportunity, and finally a policy of response that dismantles the tenets of rationalization and escalates the perception of risk. Practicing these guidelines will significantly reduce your need for Chapter 12.

Sales Audit

10

Sales audit is the business of control. It is the control of your cash, control of your revenues, and control of your margins. It tells you the best sellers from the flops, the rainmakers from the dead wood, and the good from the bad and the ugly. The demands of the retail business to know how fast hot product is moving, or whether a catchy promotion has made an impression on customers, or who the top performers are among a sales force, all contributed to the evolution of sales audit from the tallying of daily totals to the report card of key business decisions. To meet this need, the cash register was replaced with a point of sale (POS) system: a computerized database of consumer transactions which communicated what customers liked and how many times they liked it.

Management information systems (MIS) tailors the tracking of business trends for the consumption of specific disciplines within an organization. The buying line learns what's selling fast, and in what color, size, and style. Inventory control manages the flow of replenishment product from the distribution center to the stores. Advertising is able to identify promotions that customers respond to. Operations can track productivity through transaction analysis, adjusting payroll hours accordingly. The Controller can effect cash control, monitoring deposits, disbursements, and credits.

Customizing MIS programs to deliver information that meets the needs of the business, then shaping a sales audit operation that collects, processes, and disseminates that information, often separates the winners from the also-rans in today's retailing environment.

The collection source for this information is the POS station. A routine sales transaction can be broken down into as many elements as desired for study: date, time, place, item, color, style, size, salesperson, and cost. Was it cash, check, or charge; Mastercard®, Visa®, or American Express®? Did they use a coupon; did they spend a gift certificate; did they get a discount; are they owed a rebate? The detail is limited only by the POS software application the retailer has invested in for this purpose. If the company skimps, the information is slow, manually sorted, and subject to "net down" revisions. If the company splurges, the information is state-of-the-art (and occasionally overwhelming).

The middle of the road, with the flexibility to easily download enhancements and be readily adapted to new generations of the existing software, provides a strong foundation for managing the business. Normal transaction patterns were established as a company matured and a history was accumulated which served to forecast future trends. Norms fluctuated from unforeseen events, but the early-warning system enabled retailers to respond accordingly, and performance could be seen to even out over the course of a season.

Transactions which did not fit the pattern, or impacted the norm in an adverse fashion, were able to be culled out as exceptions. They resulted from voids, refunds, incorrect pricing, no sales, etc. — transactions indigenous to a retail operation. As software applications became more audit-driven, i.e., designed for the edification of specific end-users, certain commonalties became apparent that would benefit multiple users. For instance, the buying line may wish to track a certain sale item which had been discounted for a sale event, in order to better budget mark-down dollars and to evaluate margins. The same information was useful to advertising, as the promotion planners assessed which media formats performed best in select markets.

Eventually, these two factors came together as progressive loss prevention professionals modified their operation to become one of the multiple end-users. They were not a user in the standard sense the program writers had envisioned; LP was not a traditional consumer of the report's face value. Instead, LP coveted the by-product of those reports: the exceptions. Analysis of exception reports gave LP investigators an insight into sales anomalies at a store. When the buyer reviews the exception report and sees a $125 dress that was not on sale, but was sold for $79.99, she is concerned that her markdown dollars are being misallocated, and that her margin has eroded. The LP investigator looks at the same transaction and becomes concerned about a deliberate underring; that a clerk may have undersold an item to a friend. That same exception report will tell the LP investigator whether that dress was later returned for a refund: a $125 refund for a net take of $45.

As the LP organizational structures evolved from a payroll-based culture to a more streamlined operation consistent with its departmental counterparts, MIS programmers were sought out to offset manpower reductions with technological support. Just as closed circuit television surveillance could compensate for fewer "floorwalkers," automated exception reports could reproduce the fruits of plodding, paper-trail investigations. There was the requisite wailing and gnashing of teeth in the process, and management did not initially make LP initiatives a lofty priority for its MIS brain trust, but gradually talented people collaborated to customize exception reporting to furnish investigative leads and produce evidence of defalcation.

There are several aberrations in transaction patterns that are evident when an employee engages in the systematic circumvention of procedure to effect a theft at the register. Cash and merchandise flow through the POS station, and therefore becomes the focal point where the dishonest employee's intentions are manifested. The following pages detail transaction irregularities that should be collected, formatted, and stored for LP review.

LP Exception Reports

Voided Transactions

Implications

An initiated sale was aborted, but the circumstances of the event are represented to the company only at face value, offering the dishonest employee a vehicle to duplicate a legitimate process to steal cash or merchandise.

Reporting Parameters

Voided transactions occur for many legitimate reasons: clerk error, finical customers, decline of check or credit, system default. The challenge for LP is to separate the valid from the nefarious in order to verify the appropriateness of the transaction. This is best accomplished by measuring the frequency of voided sales by clerk. Employees with a propensity for voided transactions are indicating several tendencies to management: their training is suspect, their ability to "close a sale" may need to be refined, or they are systematically deleting sales for personal gain. As with all reports that measure activity, context is essential for interpreting the data. To properly evaluate a clerk's frequency of voided sales in context, the report must measure the clerk's activity against established norms. In this case, the report should rank the clerk against other employees at that location. That location should be ranked against other stores in the district. That district should be ranked against other districts in the region; and the region be ranked against other regions in relation to the company norm.

The end result may show the following anomaly, worthy of management inquiry:

The company norm for voided sales levels out at 5% of total transactions. Region 4 is highest at 8.5%; region 2 is the lowest at 3.8%. In region 4, district 3 performs at 13%, clearly the market that accounts for the disparity to norm for region 4. Within district 3, stores 308 and 309 account for 30% of voided transactions, nearly double the average of other locations in the district. At store 309, it is determined that user 007 accounts for a dispro-portionate number of voided transactions.

Management can take one of two courses at this juncture. User 007 can be interviewed by his manager to elicit his explanation of the unusual fre-quency with which he voids sales. A satisfactory response could put the issue to rest, and the subject would be made aware the company has resources to monitor activity from afar, a positive reinforcement to walk the straight line. Or, the user could be "run" against other exception reports that measure different factors (price changes, refunds, register imbalance, etc.) to deter-mine if his user ID "pops up" as contributing to other exception irregularities; especially if it is learned that user 007 recently transferred in to Store 309 from Store 308, and has apparently brought his POS techniques with him.

But before we hang user 007 out to dry, let's revisit the context issue. Mere frequency is not necessarily indicative of negligent performance. User 007 should be further ranked against his total transactions. To illustrate, if user 007 voids 50 sales per week, but records 1,000 weekly sales transactions, his activity is 5% of total, matching favorably to the company norm. Compare that to the part-time weekend clerk who may only void 5 sales a week, but initiates only 50 sales transactions on her shift; she performs at twice the company exception norm.

Enhancements

As with all exception reports, they should be designed to foster accountability for transactions at the register. Most POS procedures call for the user to complete some sort of document that accounts for exception activity. In the case of a void transaction, the clerk may have to fill out an exception slip, which lists the transaction number voided, the new transaction rung (where applicable), the reason for the void, and perhaps obtain a manager's signature authorizing the void. The exception slip is then included with the daily sales media and filed at the store or forwarded to a central location. In order for this information to be challenged, it must first be retrieved, manually sorted, and logged to determine such factors as user reasons and common authorizer.

POS software that enables the user to bring up on the screen an auto-mated exception slip would facilitate the audit process immeasurably. The user would complete the information by cursor-prompt, using reason codes, and the authorizer could enter their approval by passcode. The information could be electronically stored and accessible for sales audit and LP review.

Refund Transactions

Implications

Merchandise is returned for store credit or cash, and a disbursement of funds to a third party is initiated. A dishonest employee could recreate the circumstances of a legitimate return in order to pocket cash from the drawer without creating a cash imbalance. Also, in concert with a cohort, the clerk could reconstruct the elements of a merchandise exchange, to move product out of the store without ever receiving returned merchandise in the transaction.

Report Parameters

As with void transactions, frequency of this exception can be plotted against company norms, and aberrations can be "kicked out" on an exception report. The context can be measured in clerk productivity reports which can assign the percent of return transactions recorded against total transactions, as well as percentage of dollars refunded against recorded sales. An arbitrary number of plus/minus 20% vs. the company norm can be the breakpoint for management review and investigative follow-up.

Unlike the void summary report, the refund activity report can also track customer refund activity by name, address, or other identification provided in the return process. The program can cross-reference activity between locations, identifying customers with significant refund histories. Instances where an original sales receipt is presented can be isolated to determine if a specific clerk is ringing a disproportionate amount of the original purchases which ultimately result in a cash refund (this could indicate a dishonest employee withholds valid cash receipts from unsuspecting customers, later allowing an accomplice to present identical merchandise for return with a legitimate receipt). This could also prove beneficial in identifying potential shoplifters who have eluded detection in the stores. Taking action against customers who simply return a lot of what they buy is not advised; identifying them, however, could be useful in future encounters from a service standpoint. Frequent return activity unsupported by the original sales receipt is noteworthy as well. Being able to cross reference names with multiple addresses could show a customer is deceptive when providing identification, and common addresses to which mail refunds are being sent for multiple customer names could red-flag a potential mail drop for an organized shoplifting ring at work in your stores.

Enhancements

The automated exception slip would again prove useful in collecting data on return activity electronically. This would give MIS programmers the needed latitude to format and save refund transaction history to simplify retrieval for future audit and investigation.

Discount Activity

Implications

Probably the most prevalent exception captured in the sales audit process is discount activity. High volume transactions involving pricing exceptions make sifting through price change activity for employee malfeasance a daunting task. The reason is that the prolific number of legitimate price changes provide "cover" in the report for unauthorized discounting.

Report Parameters

Most inventory control systems involve electronically scanning an item at the register. This generates the sale information for item tracking as well as the current retail. Price changes for promotional or clearance merchandise is usually downloaded to the stores from the home office. But in practice, many occasions arise when the information is not processed in time to correspond to the sale event. This results in "price overrides" being recorded at the register, as is the case when the customer presents an item from a display clearly marked 20% off, but the monitor displays full retail when the item is scanned. A management level employee usually will enter an authorization code to override the scan price and permit the discount price to be entered. This event results in an exception being reflected on the exception report. Voluminous events render the report unwieldy and difficult to analyze. Other discounts appear as exceptions as well, with coupons, two-for-one promotions, and employee discounts being among the most frequent.

Exception reports designed to track "off-price" events by clerk need to break out by reason code employee discounts from coupon redemption from known sales promotion. Employee activity can then be evaluated in more narrow contexts of company norms. This is best managed by assigning different function keys to each discount event:

F7 Enter → Discount Event

Alt 1 Enter → Employee Discount

The automated exception slip appears and the information on the purchaser and authorizer is entered. This screen can lock in a single discount percent (e.g., 20% off) established by the employee discount policy to prevent excessive discounts from being allowed on employee purchases.

F7 Enter → Discount Event

Alt 2 Enter → Coupon Redemption

The automated exception slip appears and the information to identify the specific coupon event being redeemed by bar code is entered. This too can be promotion-specific, permitting only the face amount of the identified coupon to be discounted.

F7 Enter → Discount Event

Alt 3 Enter → Sale Price

The automated exception slip appears and the price change authorization code corresponding to the scanned item is entered effecting the authorized price change.

From here, the standard comparison reports by discount type can be run, which are especially helpful in identifying potential for employee discount and coupon redemption abuse.

Enhancements

A "second generation" discount exception report is run that details transactions where the established discount price was overridden for the purposes of entering a new price. This effectively culls legitimate exceptions from the "off price" report forwarded to LP for review, yet retains discount information on employee sales and coupon redemption on the primary report for separate investigations related to those events. If "override lockouts" are employed on the pre-established discount functions, i.e., only 20% on employee discount, only markdown authorization percents permitted for sales event discounts, etc., another function key can be allocated for the infrequent events that fall outside of the prescribed discounts:

F7 Enter → Discount Event

Alt 4 Enter → Discretionary Price Change

The automated exception slip appears and a manager can authorize an open price change per reason code, e.g., 50% damage, $9.99 blowout sale, customer accommodation, zero sale (100% off) for products taken from stock and used in store display, or awarded to employee contest winner, etc.

No Sales

Implications

For integrated cash drawer and POS operations where transactions must be entered to access the cash drawer, the no sale function is employed. Dishonest employees can access the cash drawer with an apparently legitimate purpose, but in fact use it to prepare or effect a cash theft. The no sale receipt can also be substituted for a valid cash sale receipt and passed off to an inattentive customer, with the dishonest employee retaining the original receipt for later use in voids and refund fraud.

Report Parameters

Legitimate reasons, e.g., cash counts, interim drops, and change requests, are documented on the no sale ejection receipt, perhaps authorized, and filed with the daily sales media. The manual retrieval, sorting, and compilation process this entails inhibits diligent monitoring. The automated exception slip should be designed to lock-in accountability by reason code. For example, if the reason code for the no sale indicates "interim deposit," then an automated tally of cash sales could lockout this reason if the amount taken in is less than a predetermined figure. The lockout would appear on the exception report for management to question why the clerk attempted an interim deposit with minimal cash on hand.

The cash count reason could be set up to only engage with a manager's code, since the automated tally function can provide the information without opening the drawer, and the physical counting of cash in the drawer would only be necessitated by a cash audit, which is a manager function. Beyond the "request for change" reason, clerks would have few legitimate causes to transact no sales. Standard frequency comparisons by clerk of no sales recorded will highlight persons engaged in excessive no sale activity.

Enhancements

An exception report that cross referenced no sale transactions that were preceded by a voided transaction would red flag situations where the opportunity to remove cash tendered in a legitimate transaction was created following the intentional voiding of that transaction to cover the theft:

Exception Sequence: cash sale → void → no sale

The money went in; the sale was voided; the money came out.

Price Look-Ups (PLU's)

Implications

Oftentimes, a clerk is requested to scan an item for a customer unsure of its price. The sale information appears on the screen, and the "print screen" function may allow this information to print out and be substituted by a dishonest employee for the legitimate receipt not produced when the eventual sale is not recorded.

Enhancements

Lockout the print screen function from all transactions where this function is unnecessary.

The Underground Currency

Implications

Retailers produce legal tender for merchandise purchase and product discount that a dishonest employee can substitute for the cash he steals and still balance his cash drawer. This currency comes in many forms: gift certificates, manufacturer's coupons, gift-with-purchase coupons, ("get a free roll of film when you buy a camera"), frequent shopper coupons ("punch cards worth $10.00 when you buy x amount of items"), and the dollars-off coupons that accompany many promotional mailers. When a closed-end loop to "frank" or cancel this currency is not in place, the dishonest employee can recycle this tender over and over, removing its equivalent value in real cash or merchandise each time.

Report Parameters

Sales audit reports are designed to primarily identify redemption activity associated with specific promotions, providing ROI information to advertising and sales promotion. This is done either by specific bar codes or generic event codes that identify a particular promotion.

Exception reporting of these events should concentrate on the end-of-day reports designed to separate cash from gift certificates or from coupons in calculating daily cash sales. Reconciliations where the cash is twenty dollars short; but the gift certificate/coupon count is twenty dollars over, are too often dismissed as a clerical error. In fact, it is more indicative that store currency was substituted for hard cash.

Redemption activity needs to be carefully monitored in store to store comparisons to identify locations which report excessive redemptions. These locations should be targeted for control audits in the field to determine that proper safeguards of gift certificate and coupon stocks are in place, and that the process for removing redeemed certificates and coupons from circulation is followed. Locations with high redemption rates coupled with poor performance in cash over and short activity, should be prioritized for field audit. Redemption frequency by clerk, in the context of the clerk's transaction rate and the store redemption rate, should be tracked.

Enhancements

Gift certificates sold should be plotted against gift certificates redeemed to identify locations that take in more gift certificates than they issue. Although this can be accounted for in companies that have multiple store outlets in a common market, excessive discrepancies should be challenged to ensure the market has not been flooded with stolen/counterfeit store currency. Serial numbers or item-specific bar codes should be used on gift certificates to readily identify lot numbers of stolen or compromised paper, and to enable a cross reference to provide the sales transaction that ensures a redeemed certificate was indeed sold.

Similarly, store coupons that are earned by customers in frequent shopper programs need to be controlled. To continue operating programs where the customer presents a filled-in punch card or stamp book and receives a store coupon worth cash or product from a spindle at the register offers the dishonest employee too much opportunity for obtaining those coupons fraudulently. Frequent shopper bonuses can be tracked electronically on customer account histories, and the POS can issue the coupon to the account when the criteria has been satisfied.

Accommodations for electronically franking tendered certificates and coupons make for less reliance on manually canceling these documents with magic marker X-outs and "redeemed" stamps. Oversights in this process, either unintentional or by design, lead inevitably to recirculation. Centralized redemption centers offer little comfort to national retailers, where clerical employees tasked with reconciling redeemed certificates have been known to abscond with unfranked paper themselves for use in their home market, or recycle them back out to cohorts in the field.

Petty Cash and Paid-Outs

Implications
Disbursements from the cash drawer are netted down from cash sales and represented to the company at face value. Dishonest employees can misrepresent these disbursements with manufactured supporting documentation (bogus service bills, receipts off the floor at the supply store, postal receipts from personal transactions passed of as company expense, etc.) and pocket the cash.

Report Parameters
The automated exception slip can format generic paid-outs for travel, postage, supplies, etc., by reason code, and can be readily accessible for sales audit review. Expense categories can be budgeted against expense forecasts by location, and exceptions reported when the expense exceeds the monthly allotment. Documentation from these disbursements must still be retained at the store level or forwarded to the home office, but electronic auditing will assist the company in allocating its field audit resources.

Summary Reports

Summary reports offer a profile of store-specific or employee-specific exception activity. Enhancements to POS software that permit cross referencing of multiple exception factors identify trends which may not be evident in individual exception reports that are item-specific. For instance, for stores that experience unacceptable shrink results and perform in the top percentile of a cross section of exception activity, a program designed to reduce exception activity through scrutiny of, and accountability for, key exception events can be an important element of recovering the shortage performance within a single inventory period. Further, employee-specific cross referencing may bring to light areas of opportunity for an investigator to approach a subject who is under suspicion for theft, but whose method of operation has been elusive. It would also lend itself to moving against the subject on procedural issues unconnected with the suspected theft activity, but useful nonetheless in placing him on notice that his performance has come to management's attention.

It is essential for companies designing their POS software applications that the loss prevention benefits of detailed exception reporting be considered. Rigid software packages offering little flexibility to customize reporting formats are ultimately restrictive to the company's ability to control and manage events at the POS station, and the price for bargain-basement software will be exacted in inventory losses.

Retailers anticipating sustained periods of growth face hard choices in buying for the future or settling for a system that adequately meets the needs of today. The far-reaching costs of a POS conversion program down the road should be factored in to the decision, as well as the rewards of a strengthened base from which to expand.

Section III

The Finer Points

Overview

As suggested by the title, Section III contains elements of loss prevention practices that are best designed, implemented, and managed by loss prevention professionals. However, not all retailers have the luxury of in-house LP expertise, yet they require the same benefits from these programs as companies that do.

Many members of the senior management team have LP proficiency in certain areas. Assigning program development of the finer points to a committee of human resources, legal counsel, finance officer, operations executive, construction manager, and an agent of the company insurance carrier can be a starting point for policy review.

Another resource for guidance in the areas presented in Section III would be retaining the services of a loss prevention professional to consult with your executive committee. A schedule of quarterly vulnerability reviews in conjunction with management training seminars is an inexpensive and worthwhile investment for bringing your shortage program to the next level, and insulating your corporation from liability.

Exposure to liability is a by-product of LP functions, specifically in the areas of investigation, apprehension, and prosecution. Retailers have become more disciplined in operational standards that curtail incidents of general liability and workers compensation by promoting safety in the workplace. So, too, must retailers bring the same diligence to the arena of false arrest, tortious conduct, product liability, and negligent hiring.

In reviewing the procedural recommendations proffered in Section III, the retailer needs to recognize that good faith and best intentions alone will not deter civil action. A proactive and verifiable training program in the field, borne of clear policy and sound judgment, is the determining factor for avoiding ruinous litigation.

Investigation and Interview

11

In most retail settings, investigations come about when unexplained losses or activities indicate that possible employee malfeasance has placed assets at risk. There are ample opportunities to initiate investigations where external forces are at work defrauding the company: bad check passers, refund operators, credit card fraud, organized shoplifting rings, burglary, etc., but those investigations are more often coordinated between store operations and law enforcement agencies once the deed has been discovered and a formal complaint has been filed.

For a company to begin an internal investigation, it is usually predicated upon reports, observations, or audits that suggests a pattern of activity likely to be associated with employee theft. There may be apparent losses to support this conclusion, or simply the activity itself may be suspect. As with all expenditures of company resources, investigations need to have a goal. The primary goal of investigations is to stem the losses. This is usually accomplished through the detection and apprehension of the culprit(s) responsible, although it is not unheard of that the investigation process itself results in the abrupt cessation of criminal conduct without ever discerning for certain the identity of the participants.

The secondary goal of investigations is to expel persons engaged in theft permanently from the workplace. For this goal to be realized, a case for termination needs to be presented to Human Resources in a such a way that no recourse for reinstatement is available. Misdeeds or procedural transgressions must be so apparent as to prove gross negligence, dereliction of duty, or willful violation of policy that results, or could have resulted, in a sustained loss.

Ancillary to these goals may be the objective of criminal prosecution to illustrate the company's intolerance of employee dishonesty. For this objective to be achieved, the investigation must conform to the protocols of evidence which sustain the burden of proof in a criminal proceeding. Trained investigators are capable of building a case for prosecution through proven surveillance techniques, interview skills, and the presentation of evidence in such a way that indictment and conviction will follow.

The recovery of assets, either through the voluntary return of stolen property, restitution, or civil recovery, remains an objective of investigative work in the private sector. This objective is attained through negotiation in the interview process, or in some cases, as a result of a court order in the course of case disposition.

For most retailers, investigations are conducted by LP personnel operating in the capacity of field investigator, or by a qualified operations executive capable of achieving the primary and secondary goals described above. The resources a company allocates for investigations, both in the means to conduct them and the quality of its investigators, determine to a large extent the likelihood of success the retailer can expect in stemming the losses, removing the culprits, concluding a successful prosecution, and recovering its assets.

The investigation is more often than not initiated by a lead, which emanates from statistical review, incident reporting, or defalcation unearthed through sales and operational audits. For both the professional and amateur investigator, recognizing and developing leads is essential to the investigative process. Sometimes, the most provocative lead is generated by a location's annual or semi-annual inventory shrink performance. When the disparity between the accrued shortage forecast and the actual shrink results is significant, factors may be at work suggestive of collusive employee theft. However, other avenues to which shrink aberrations can be attributed, i.e., the inventory taking procedure, receipt verification, shipping discrepancies, inter-store transfer activity, price changes, etc., should be explored in the inventory reconciliation process before committing investigative resources.

Should the results of the inventory reconciliation process be inconclusive, then an investigation into the possibility of employee theft accounting for the swing in shrink performance may be indicated. There are preliminary steps an investigator can take prior to pursuing an active investigation of surveillance and interview.

A review of store incident reports within the context of the known shortage results is helpful in determining such factors as employee awareness, shoplifting patterns, external fraud activity, known thefts, and the degree to which store personnel practice loss prevention. An above average frequency of loss prevention-related incidents is indicative of staff training and response to shortage-causing elements, as well as theft activity in excess of initial assessments.

The level of compliance at which the store operates with respect to procedural standards and company policy is evident in audit scores and operational reviews, and the history of audit performance should be taken into account when determining a course of action. Consistently high audit reviews belie the atmosphere conducive to employee theft; repeated deficiencies and dwindling scores are indicative of "slippage" that promotes opportunities for employees to circumvent procedures and controls, which offer the ideal environment for undetected employee theft.

Employee personnel files warrant scrutiny by the investigator in the initial stages of an investigation. Match the employee population against the target profile for dishonest employees established for the company: short service, short hour, below-average performance appraisals, absenteeism, etc. Follow the review guidelines for need and opportunity presented in Chapter 9.

Further, examine the sales audit exception reports and plot the location's exception rates for select transactions against the company norm, as presented in Chapter 10. Low exception activity for voids, refunds, cash over and short, coupon redemption, and discount pricing is inconsistent with circumvention of POS procedures; high activity is a red flag. Should an automated inventory replenishing system be in use, then a correlation between sales and reorders should be evident. Requests for stock reorders that are not generated by sales activity, transfers, or recalls, and are not substantially accounted for on known theft reports, is indicative of missing product being known to the store, but not reported through normal channels.

An examination of alarm history reports during the inventory period is advisable as well. Note after-hour activity that points to unauthorized entry, early opening/late closing patterns, or "cause not found" events resulting in response back to the building after closing. Enhanced monitoring reports as detailed in Chapter 2 are invaluable in determining building usage for nefarious purposes.

These research topics all provide the basis to form fair questions, the fodder for investigations where no primary suspect is indicated through lead information. Armed with fair questions and a noble cause (shrink reduction) the investigator can then proceed with an on-site investigation with an expectation of cooperation from store management.

An LP audit, along the lines described in Chapter 7, would follow in sequence as the "ice-breaker" upon arrival at the store. This event may be precipitated by a pre-opening or closing surveillance by the investigator in order to get acquainted with the store routine and evaluate procedural compliance first-hand. But it is the audit function which serves to open dialog and provide a training forum for shortage awareness.

In the course of the audit, information and policy compliance issues will come to light which can narrow the scope of means and opportunity. Audit findings, specifically chronic deficiencies, offer the investigator benign, informal interview opportunities from which he can gauge employee response in a non-threatening atmosphere. Later, in an issue-specific encounter, changes in an employee's demeanor will be more evident. With background research and on-hand findings, the investigator can evaluate the likelihood of the shortage performance being the result of employee negligence or employee theft. Employee negligence will be the result of substandard training or employee indifference, brought about by poor supervision and morale and the absence of a management response to prevailing violations and conditions that compromise accountability. Employee theft will be manifested by way of unresolved discrepancies and the absence of a management response to challenge, investigate, and report incidents of sustained loss attributable to employee deviation from procedure.

Either way, the investigator's conclusion is clear: the problem is the people, so the course of action is to stem the losses and terminate those culpable. One strategy the investigator may employ would be to muster resources for a prolonged investigation:

- Install covert cameras
- Authorize surveillance
- Use mystery shoppers
- Introduce an undercover operative into the employee population

These tactics enable the investigator to build a case of fact, one that would have a high probability of detecting criminal wrongdoing in a reasonable amount of time, and lead more readily to the bonus package of prosecution and recovery of losses. The subsequent interview process of the employee caught red-handed would shed considerable light on the depth and breadth of employee dishonesty at this location, as well as identify the procedural weaknesses which facilitated the theft. Some of the more comprehensive policy revisions that improve controls have come about as the result of a thorough investigation and substantive interview. Or, the investigator may instead decide that cold interviews based on the circumstantial findings of preliminary research, coupled with the serious policy infractions uncovered on site, is sufficient to effect the separation of the more blameworthy employees, as well as afford the opportunity to probe for admissions of theft in the interview process.

Setting the environment for an interview encounter is a fundamental part of the preparation process, but one that should not be overplayed. If you have a strong case, you can conduct a successful interview on a park bench. If you have a weak case, the trappings of a Russian gulag will not help your cause. The essential factors are control and privacy: the interviewer should be in a position to control the environment (i.e., access/egress, temperature, communications, refreshment), and the element of privacy consistent with confiding information should be present. The subtext of the setting should reinforce the interviewer's expertise and authority over the matter at hand, while diminishing the subject's resolve to evade and deny. An orderly array of labeled files, computer print-outs, sales media, and reports suggests to the subject that the interviewer is prepared, deflating his hopes for a fast exit. Do not overdo it with the props, however. The success of the interview hinges on the merits of the case.

Arrange for no unplanned interruptions. Forward calls to another extension, and see to it that no one enters uninvited. A decanter of water and clean glasses should be available. A pack of gum is nice, but discourage smoking. Tissues do come in handy. The desk, with the interviewer seated behind it, and the guest chair positioned in such a way as to facilitate eye contact, all tend to meet the subject's expectations of a formal setting.

The reputation of the interviewer can establish expertise and authority in the mind of the subject, but where the quantities are unknown, the subject will assess the interviewer by job title and demeanor. A business-like, matter-of-fact approach that conveys a dispassionate, professional attitude affords little comfort to the subject who is gathering himself for battle. Although this initial distance the interviewer has placed between himself and the subject will have to be overcome later as the interviewer seeks to establish a rapport, it is effective in setting the proper tone, reveals nothing the subject may perceive as a weakness to exploit, and facilitates the interviewer's presentation of a credible investigation for discussion.

The dynamic of the interview process is a fascinating study of human behavior. The interviewer must present himself as knowledgeable of facts he may not have, and certain of events he did not witness. The interviewer must appear to the subject to be competent, trustworthy, and empathetic in order to foster the right atmosphere for an admission of wrongdoing. These attributes must be conveyed to a nervous, wary, and dishonest subject, conflicted by trepidation and remorse, with a steeled resolve not to confess.

Yet, once the admission is obtained, the interviewer must present the consequences of the admission in such a way that does not connote betrayal of a trust or underhanded tactics, but is nonetheless mindful of the naked manipulation he has engaged in to reach the admission stage. The subject, now rightly accused, feels compelled to show remorse he may not feel, and attempts to restore his personal honor and dignity that was forfeited by the admission he probably regrets making.

This dance of wills is played out in the back offices of retail stores every day. The interviewer presents the circumstances of a loss in such a way that warrants their discussion. The subject acknowledges the predicament, but can offer very little by way of explanation. The interviewer presses lightly, showing means and opportunity. The subject agrees but will not implicate.

The interviewer suggests motive; the subject downplays it. The interviewer offers proof; the subject alibis. The interviewer dismantles the alibi, suggesting deception; the subject denies, admitting error. The interviewer introduces multiple occasions, citing a pattern; the subject denies, claiming he never knew better. The interviewer produces documentation he did know better; the subject is at a loss to explain it.

Before the cycle can repeat itself, the interviewer offers a resolution in the form of a "soft accusation." The soft accusation is effective because it addresses one of the subject's needs by referencing conclusion: *"Look, this can all be over with if you will tell me the truth here. I know you're involved. It's no accident this investigation lead me to you."*

The burning desire of the subject in this "voluntary" interview is to be done with it. Since few initiate the conclusion on their own (i.e., *"I'm sorry I can't help you. I'd like to go now"*), the soft accusation enables them their first glimpse of light at the end of the tunnel. Relief from the interview is the first tangible benefit they can attain by cooperating with the interviewer, and they weigh it against the envisioned consequences of an admission. Oftentimes the benefits are seen to pale against the consequences, so an admission will not be forthcoming at this stage. The skilled interviewer, however, begins to build the benefits by presenting the balance of the interview as an opportunity for the subject to lessen the consequences.

They move to round two, where the misdeeds are more specific and the denials less emphatic. Evidence of wrong-doing mounts to the point where both can agree that the employee engaged in systematic procedural violation. The interviewer will allude that the violations are serious enough to bring dismissal; the subject will acknowledge he will probably be fired. The loss of employment was one of the consequences the subject feared might result from his admission of guilt. This consequence has been effectively overcome, and another barrier that feeds the denial cycle is broken down. In round three, the interviewer will move toward eliciting an admission of theft in an isolated transaction. Without trivializing the incident, the interviewer will allow the subject to get a sense that his transgression, in the big picture of big business, is not such a big deal, that maybe the subject has overestimated the consequences, and that by cooperating now, the most feared sanction (prosecution) may not be exacted. The subject can discern this in a softening of the approach by the interviewer, perhaps by buying in to some of the rationalizations the interviewer offers for the theft, all designed to diminish the consequences.

The interviewer will allow the subject to wrestle with these demons while he positions himself to make the direct accusation. The interviewer will reestablish the credibility of the investigation in the subject's eyes. He may cease downplaying the scope of the subject's involvement, changing course to suggest magnifying it. The subject will seek to bring the interviewer back around to a position more sympathetic to the subject (like before when the consequences seemed lessened) and be ready to offer a qualified admission to a direct accusation.

The interviewer will return to the procedural violations, saying he is certain they were deliberate and made for personal financial gain; the subject will counter it was not intentional and that it was for somebody else. The interviewer will concede that the subject's role may be minimal; the subject will insist his take was small. The interviewer will stipulate any take is wrong; the subject will admit it is, and apologize for letting people down.

The interviewer needs to accomplish two things at this point: reinforce the notion the subject has made a good decision and is on his way to making amends; while nailing down the specifics of the admitted, single incident of theft. Reassure the employee that the worst is behind him, that he and the company have reached the only truthful conclusion to their mutual problem, and prepare the subject to furnish a written statement.

The written admission fulfills the interviewer's secondary goal: it will effectively support the termination of the subject for theft. The primary goal, that of stemming the losses, can only be reconciled once the interviewer is satisfied that the persons responsible have been identified and eliminated, and the procedural controls to prevent future losses are reinstated. The written statement, once executed, gives the interviewer leverage in extracting additional admissions more representative of the subject's true degree of involvement in the store's shortage picture, and coaxing the names and activities of other employees suspected of theft.

Knowing that the interviewer possesses a signed confession is debilitating to the subject who wishes to deny more involvement or protect co-workers from discovery. The interviewer can press more and the subject deny less. There is a dependence now implicit in their relationship: the subject strives to satisfy the interviewer, lest the interviewer withdraw his support for the subject in the disposition process. To touch on the disposition process for a moment, realize that the uncertainty of their fate is burdensome for the subjects. The consequences they so dreaded have not as yet been spelled out, but they sense their continued cooperation is in their best interest in this regard. They are permitted to conclude that the interviewer, by no means the sole arbiter of their destiny, can tip the scales in their favor by putting in a good word at the right time, and to frustrate the interviewer by holding back on matters the interviewer is intent on finding out is unwise. Interviewers who purport themselves to be the lone decision maker of whether or not an employee is prosecuted do themselves a disservice, even when they in fact have the final word. It is much more advantageous to tell a subject that they must present the matter to a higher authority for disposition. The subject may then view the interviewer, his former adversary, as his advocate to upper management, and will be more attentive to the needs of the interviewer who is still trying to assess the impact of this employee's actions on the overall shortage performance of this location.

The interviewer can explain to the subject that upper management will want to know if the interviewer believes the subject has provided all the information he has pertinent to the investigation: *"How can I tell them you told me everything when I know you're holding out about Joey?"* And, *"I can't tell them the two of you just cooked up this scheme last Friday night, when I've got documentation that this has been going on .for five months ! There is a $15,000 problem in this store!"*

Once the investigator is satisfied the subject has been truthful about the theft activity he and others have engaged in, he should then prepare a supplemental statement to the first admission detailing these events as well. In written statements, the investigator should have a pretty good idea of where the case disposition is heading, because that will determine whether or not the statement itself is likely to be introduced as evidence in a criminal proceeding.

There are three types of written statements investigators need to be familiar with in an interview setting:

1. The **evidentiary statement** documents a criminal act and is intended to be entered into evidence against the subject in a criminal proceeding, or offered as proof of employee malfeasance in a labor relations hearing.
2. The **statement of procedural** violation, documents the willful disregard of company policy resulting in a loss, or potential of loss, sustained by the company, and intended to support formal disciplinary action against the employee.
3. The **informational statement** documents a witness account of unusual incident, or is collected as supporting information relevant to an investigation, and is intended for inclusion in the case file.

The evidentiary statement is one of the more misunderstood documents among loss prevention practitioners. For many years LP professionals went to great lengths to format the quintessential employee statement. First, the interviewer could write it and present it to the subject for signature. Then, the subject had to write it, because it was more convincing as a "free and voluntary" confession if written in the employee's own hand. But the employee failed to capture the essence of the case in his hand-written statement on many occasions, and the interviewer wound up directing several rewrites until he was satisfied that this free and voluntary statement given by the employee met the criteria required of the investigator by the company. This often resulted in a case being more compromised by the length of time the subject was detained to write the statement than by any questions that could be raised over the appropriateness of the interviewer writing the statement for the subject. Next it was determining the wording for the statement's concluding paragraph. Specific language spelling out criminal acts had to be incontrovertibly present. The employee wished to write, *"I admit I took the coat."* The investigator was required to present a statement which concluded: *"On the above date and time I did take, for my own possession and use, certain articles belonging to the ABC store for which I made no payment, nor did I intend to make payment, and I admit that I intended to steal, and in fact did steal, one leather coat size 42 valued at $199.99."*

Then came the meticulous documentation of evidence, initialing cross-souts on the statement, initialing tops and bottoms of each page, initialing sales checks and receipts used in the investigation, recording of serial numbers of currency and initialing each bill, and the ceremonial signatures of persons witnessing the statement — all this while still representing to the employee no decision has been made about whether or not they will be released or prosecuted. The problem with all this protocol is that it places far too much emphasis on the statement, and not enough on the merits of the case. It is the observation of theft, the possession of stolen property, and the document trail that is offered as evidence in testimony that wins cases in court. A written statement that may, or may not, be considered free and voluntary should never be the case in chief for a prosecuted case of employee dishonesty. The private sector had assumed incorrectly that they would be held to the same standard as police agencies in the collection of written statements to be entered in evidence as confessions. The preambles of statements were written to include Miranda Warnings at one point, and the employment history was detailed ad nauseam throughout the biography. Step-by-step events leading up to the theft event were re-enacted on paper, culminating in a conclusion of qualified admissions so convoluted with intentions and actions, past and present, that only Oliver Stone could appreciate!

Gradually, with the less structured LP departments of specialty stores leading the way, a streamlined format became more acceptable. Realizing that the effect of the written statement served more to blunt a prosecuted employee's willingness to reject a plea bargain and go to trial than it would turn the tide of a verdict solely on the way it was structured, the written statement assumed its rightful place in the case file: a story about an employee who thought he could steal and get away with it, and how he got caught (in his own words).

In practice, having the interviewer prepare the statement then present it for signature presents no greater risks for the test of evidence than the employee writing it himself. The advantage is that a skilled investigator can include the pertinent elements of the case, while excluding extraneous information such as excuses and apologies that often punctuate statements written by the subject. The investigator's familiarity with the vocabulary of the retail industry, together with an intimate understanding of the investigation which lead to the interview, lends itself to a concise presentation of fact and evidence a prosecutor can follow easily in the pursuit of a criminal conviction.

In constructing an evidentiary statement, think of the format having four parts:

1. The Preamble: an introduction of the subject and the content
2. The Biography: the relationship of the subject to the company
3. The Body: the statement of facts
4. The Conclusion: an admission of criminal acts

A sample evidentiary statement follows:

Preamble:

"I, John Doe, residing at 100 Main Street, Anytown, U.S.A. wish to make the following free and voluntary statement concerning my theft of money/merchandise from the ABC store on April 1, 1995."

This preamble cuts right to the chase and is not laden with Miranda Warning inferences such as *"knowing I need make no statement,* and *that any statement I do make can be used against me in a court of law"* and, *"I have been advised of my right to have a lawyer present."* This is very intimidating language and chances of getting the employee to read beyond it without his being suspicious of the interviewer's agenda is remote.

Biography:

"I was first employed by ABC Company on December 1, 1994, as a sales person at the Highway 123 store for the Christmas season. Upon my employment I received orientation and training about the company and about my duties. I learned to operate the cash register, record transactions, receive merchandise from the warehouse, and service customers. I received a copy of the company's rules and regulations booklet which I read and understood."

This biography serves as a recitation of the training the employee received, which can effectively refute an attempt to disguise his theft as an innocent mistake brought about by the company's failure to provide adequate training. It further illustrates a knowledge of POS functions and merchandise handling procedures which he may have circumvented to facilitate the theft.

Sample Body 1:

"On April 1, 1995, I reported for work at 12:30 p.m. and went about my usual duties. At 3 p.m., I withheld a customer's credit card from transaction 345 and then used it to purchase $400.00 worth of goods at 5 p.m. on transaction 789. I placed the merchandise in a bag and gave it to my friend, Mary Jones. I didn't have permission or authority to use the credit card of customer Ben Taken. At about 5:10 p.m. I was asked to come to the manager's office where I met the store's loss prevention investigator and was interviewed about the transactions described above, and subsequently, I admitted my role in the fraudulent use of a credit card to steal merchandise."

This is a clear, clean, precise, easy-to-follow sequence of events describing the theft of merchandise. The investigator's report can include all the nitty-gritty details learned in the interview: that the employee called Mary Jones shortly after withholding the card, that they planned the 5 p.m. rendezvous. If necessary, the investigator's testimony of these verbal admissions is just as admissible and credible as a written admission. The copy of the sales check with the itemized purchases need not be entered line-by-line on the employee's statement. The investigator's report file can include that information, along with the customer's statement, and that of the co-conspirator, Mary Jones.

Sample Body 2:

"On April 1, 1995, I reported for work at 12:30 p.m. and went about my usual duties. At about 3 p.m., I was summoned to the back office to check in today's shipment from the warehouse. While checking off the cartons against the manifest, I noticed three boxes of watches had been shipped, but only two were listed on the manifest. I decided I would hide the third box in the corner of the stockroom to see if anybody would notice it was missing. After the day manager left and the night manager didn't seem to know a box was missing, I moved the box from the stockroom to the employee lounge, and placed it into my knapsack with my books. I then went back to the selling floor and completed my shift without incident. When the time came to lock up the store at about 10:30 p.m., we were approached outside by the day manager and a corporate executive I now know to be the loss prevention manager. They checked everybody's bag who was leaving, and the watches were discovered in my knapsack. I was asked to come back into the store and explain about the watches to the day manager and the loss prevention manager. At first I told them I got them from somebody at school and was trying to sell them to people at work to raise money. But they did not believe that and after a while I told them the truth: that I had stolen the box of watches valued at $1500 from today's shipment. I was informed several shipments to this store were unaccounted for, and I realized they also knew about the box of earrings I stole last week and the carton of expensive wallets I took last month. I further admit to having taken the shipment of toiletry kits that were supposed to be given to customers purchasing cosmetics sets around Christmas that everybody was looking for. I would place the retail value of my combined thefts at $6000."

The times, dates, manifest numbers, and itemized inventory of stolen product can be accommodated in the investigator's report, where the essence of the investigation from the Distribution Center to the parking lot can all be detailed. This statement of fact would hold up in any criminal court and be welcomed by the prosecutor for its matter-of-fact simplicity. But the conviction would be attained by virtue of the investigator's testimony recounting the investigation, the appropriateness of the stop in the parking lot, and the physical discovery of the stolen product in the subject's possession.

Sample Body 3:

"On April 1, 1995, I reported for work at 12:30 p.m. and went about my usual duties. At about 3 p.m., a customer approached to purchase a pair of ladies gloves at $25. The total with tax was $26.50, which the customer gave me in exact change. She told me not to bother bagging them as she would wear them out. I asked her if she wanted a receipt, but she said she did not need it and left. I placed the $26.50 in the drawer without recording the sale. Later, about 4:30 p.m., I took two $50 bills from the register and placed them into the change bag to bring to the back and get ten $10 bills. I also placed the $26.50 into the bag. When I got to the back, I made the change for the $50 bills out of the safe, and placed the $26.50 into my pocket. When I got back to the register, the store manager and district manager were waiting for me. They asked me to balance the register. I did and it came up even. They asked me to show them the sale transaction for the gloves. I told them I did not have a chance to ring it up yet. They asked where the cash was. I told them in the drawer. They told me the cash count should be $26.50 over if the cash was in the drawer. I told them I may have put the cash into the safe by accident. They told me I put the cash into my right pants pocket. I said they were wrong. They then asked me to go with them to the back office. I did and when we got there they showed me a camera which was hidden in the air vent over the safe. They asked if I needed to see the tape. I told them I did not and produced the $26.50 from my right pants pocket and returned it to them. They then showed me a series of register graphs that showed shortages of cash over the past 60 days totaling $770 on the days I worked. I admitted taking about $400 in cash during that time."

The Investigator's Report can detail the register plotting investigation, which lead to the camera installation and the use of a mystery shopper in this case. The subject's statement sufficiently details the crime, but the videotape and testimony of his returning the money from his pocket to the two executives is the incontrovertible evidence the prosecutor will look for.

Conclusion(s):

Sample One:

"I admit that I used the credit card of customer Ben Taken unlawfully to record the purchases of $400.00 worth of merchandise. I have instructed Mary Jones

to return the stolen property to the store in order to credit the customer's account. In the subject's own hand: *I have read the above statement and it is true and correct to the best of my knowledge."* (Signed/Witnessed)

Sample Two:

"I admit by my above stated actions that I have stolen shipments amounting to $6000.00 from the ABC store since my employment began in December, 1994. I shall return to the store representatives all of the merchandise still in my possession. (In the subject's own hand) *I have read the above statement consisting of pages one and two, and it is true and correct to the best of my knowledge. No threats or promises have been made to me with respect to returning the stolen property I still possess."* (Signed/Witness)

Sample Three:

"I admit by my above stated actions that I have stolen approximately $400 in cash from my register over the past 60 days. If permitted, I would like to pay back the money I stole. (In the subject's own hand) *I have read the above statement and it is true and correct to the best of my knowledge. No threats or promises have been made to me with respect to paying back the money I took."* (Signed/Witness)

A separate statement (an addendum) can be taken detailing the terms of restitution and/or return of product. Subjects wishing to reimburse the store for product taken that cannot be returned by way of some type of payment plan can be effected through a standard form promissory note.

Restitution is tricky business. The store cannot be perceived as waiving prosecution on the condition of cash payment. Such an arrangement would be entered into under extreme duress by the subject, and his payment in exchange for freedom may be deemed extortionary. If the company does plan to prosecute, this should be told to the employee, even though it diminishes his incentive to pay up. The store officials can tell the subject that they will inform the prosecutor when restitution is made, and that perhaps the prosecutor will place that into consideration when determining how to proceed.

If the company does not plan to prosecute, the subject can be told that proceeding with a prosecution is not contemplated at this time, but the company does have up to 30 days to file a complaint if it so chooses. No linkage between payment of restitution and letting the matter drop can be inferred.

A sample procedural violation statement follows:

Preamble:

"I, John Doe, sales associate at the ABC store on Highway 123, wish to make the following free and voluntary statement concerning my violation of company policy on April 1, 1995."

Biography:

"I was first employed by the ABC store on December 1, 1994, as a sales person at the Highway 123 store. Upon my employment, I received orientation and training about the company and about my duties. I learned to operate the cash register, record transactions, and receive merchandise from the warehouse service customers. I received a copy of the company's rules and regulations booklet which I read and understood. Around February of 1995, I became the full time shipping clerk at the store, responsible for checking in shipments, processing returns, and maintaining the receiving logs. I received training in these duties from my manager, and read and understood the sections of the Operations Manual relating to these duties, including sections 2-1 and 2-8."

The embellished biography in the procedural violation statement is essential to demonstrating to human resources that the employee was sufficiently trained in his job responsibilities, and was aware the actions to be chronicled in The Sample Body constitute a willful disregard for company policy that lead to a sustained loss, or would have, had the actions not been detected by management.

Sample Body:

"On April 1, 1995, I reported for work at 12:30 p.m. and went about my usual duties. At about 3 p.m. I was asked to go to the receiving dock and handle the warehouse shipment which had arrived. In the course of checking in the boxes, I noted three boxes of watches were shipped, but only two were listed on the manifest. Procedure 2-1 states that I am required to notify the distribution center discrepancy control desk of any misshipments. I had intended to do this when I finished off-loading the truck, but by the time I was done, the control desk was closed. I further understand that shipments from department 007 are supposed to be secured in the security cage, as stated in procedure 2-8, but I neglected to put it there, leaving it in the stockroom unattended. At about 5:30, the store manager called me in to the stockroom and pointed out the carton of watches he discovered behind the cleaning supplies on the corner shelf. He asked how the carton got there and I told him I didn't know. He was upset with me for not calling the discrepancy into the warehouse as I was supposed to, and could not understand how I failed to place the carton into the cage, either. He pointed out that only him, Joey, and me were working between 3 p.m. and 5:30 p.m., and that they had been together on the selling floor the whole time, and that neither one of them could have placed the carton on the shelf behind the cleaning supplies. He said I must have done it, but I told him again I left the box on the counter. He asked if I properly secured the back door after the truck left and I told him I did. He asked if I properly secured the stockroom door when I was done and I told him I did."

In this case, the manager found the employee's stash and confronted him. The employee lied, but the manager was smart enough to realize the employee violated important security procedures in attempting the theft (as must happen), and is prepared to move against the employee, not for theft, but for procedural violation. It is important to note, however, that even though the employee's alibis and excuses are absurd, the manager had no qualms about allowing the employee to lie in his statement, as they serve to illustrate a wanton disregard for company assets. Having "no explanation" does not amount to an explanation. The employee remains accountable.

Conclusion:

"I admit by my above stated actions that I have violated company policy in that I failed to notify the distribution center of a shipment discrepancy as required in Procedure 2-1. Additionally, I admit that I violated Procedure 2-8 by failing to properly secure the shipment in the security cage as required, thereby exposing it to loss. I realize this incident constitutes an act of gross negligence and dereliction of duty. I further realize that my inability to explain how the shipment became concealed behind the cleaning supplies in the stock-room, when the box was in my sole custody and I acknowledge no one else had access to it, casts doubt upon my ability to perform my prescribed duties and safeguard the assets of the company, as required in the company rules and regulations manual."

(In the employee's own hand) *"I have read the above statement and it is true and correct to the best of knowledge."* (Signed/Witnessed)

A more self-serving conclusion would be hard to find, but illustrates why the interviewer should write the statement and submit it to the employee for signature. By holding the employee's lies up to ridicule in the written statement, the manager is able to compound the infractions to demonstrate the employee's failure to perform. Human resources and the district manager should easily determine the employee is at least untruthful, if not dishonest, and have little concern in terminating the subject for admitted gross negligence and dereliction of duty (key phrases human resources looks for in imposing the ultimate sanction).

Sample Body 2:

"On April 1, 1995, I reported for work at 12:30 p.m. and went about my usual duties. At about 3 p.m., a customer approached to purchase a pair of ladies gloves at $25. The total with tax was $26.50, which the customer gave me in exact change. She told me not to bother bagging them as she would wear them out. I asked her if she wanted a receipt, and she said she did not need one and left. I placed the $26.50 into the cash drawer without recording the sale. At

about 4:30 p.m., I took two $50 bills out of the register and placed them into the change bag to bring to the back and get ten $10 bills. I also put the $26.50 into the change bag. When I got to the back I was approached by the store manager who asked what I was doing. I told him I needed to get change for the two fifties, and he watched me take the ten tens from the safe. He then asked what the other cash in the bag was, and I told him it was from a sale I was going to ring up when I got back. The manager asked why I had waited to ring it up, and I told him the customer just wanted to leave. He asked why I did not ring it up right away, and I told him I wanted to check the price again. He asked how I could let the customer leave without knowing for sure what the price was, and I told him I was pretty sure it was $25.00 plus tax. He asked me how long ago the sale had taken place, and I told him about 20 minutes ago. He then corrected me that it was about an hour and one half ago. I then told him I thought I should put the cash in the safe since it was not rung up, and that I was going to put in a note explaining why the safe fund was over $26.50. I felt that it was better than having my drawer out of balance at the end of my shift. The manager disagreed with this tactic, stating that excess funds in the safe that are not accounted for would be exposed to loss. He further pointed out that I had closed and locked the safe after making change for the fifties without placing the $26.50 inside. I told him I thought it would be best to make separate safe transactions so the two would not be confused. The manager told me he believed my thought process in this incident was seriously flawed, and that POS Procedure 4-2 and 4-3 clearly state all sales must be recorded and all cash tendered for sales must be placed into the cash drawer and nowhere else"

Simply knowing the employee was going to take the money, and proving this was his intent are two separate issues. The manager, however, knew he could rely on procedural violation to hold the employee accountable for the infractions he committed (as must happen) in attempting to steal the cash. Linking two procedural violations with the exposure to loss inherent in the infractions, plus including the employee's irrational alibis which the manager dismantled with little effort, allows the manager to present a case for termination.

Conclusion:

"I admit by my above stated action that I have violated company policy governing cash handling procedures in that I failed to record a sale as required in Section 4-2 of the procedure manual. In addition, I failed to properly safeguard that cash by removing it from the cash drawer in violation of Procedure 4-3. I further wish to state that I initiated an unauthorized safe transaction, when I intended to deposit the proceeds from a sale I failed to record into the safe, creating an imbalance in the change fund. I realize that these events constitute an act of gross misconduct on my part, and that such acts are listed

in the employee handbook as serious violations leading to disciplinary action up to and including termination."

(In the employee's own hand)*"The above statement is true and correct to the best of my knowledge."* (Signed/Witness)

An aggressive human resources would see the manager's intervention for what it was: the interruption of an employee theft, and would approve a separation. However, HR must be mindful of issues such as length of service, precedent, etc., and must carefully consider the employee's performance record with the company as well as the documentation that training was inclusive of procedures 4-2 and 4-3, and feel certain all bases were covered before determining violations of this nature warrant discharge. At a minimum, however, the sanction will be severe enough to ensure any future irregularity involving this clerk and his cash drawer would meet with immediate termination, and the diligent manager will have a reformed employee no longer stealing cash, or an open job to fill, in very short order.

A sample informational statement follows:

"I, Ben Taken, residing at 500 Main Street, Anytown, U.S.A., telephone number 555-9999, wish to make the following statement concerning an incident which occurred at the ABC store on Highway 123 on April 1, 1995. At about 3 p.m. I purchased a watch for $125 on my credit card #0123 456 789. A young man with the name tag "John" waited on me. He rung up my purchase and I left. At about 5:30 p.m., I received a call from the store manager inquiring if I had left my credit card behind at the store. I checked and found I did not have it, and the manager stated he had it at the store. I was later informed that the clerk "John" had used my card without my permission to charge $400 worth of merchandise to my account. The store will credit my account the $400 and take appropriate action against John. I do not wish to press criminal charges at this time." (Signed/Witness)

This statement is short, sweet, and to the point. The chances of the customer ever having to testify in a criminal case the store brings against John is remote. But the customer should be offered the opportunity to pursue criminal action if he so chooses.

Sample Two:

"I, Joey Newguy, employed at the ABC store on Highway 123, wish to make the following statement concerning an incident which occurred at the store on April 1, 1995. I have been employed by the store for two weeks, and am still in my training period. On today's date I was learning register systems with my manager when I remember the manager sending John to the back to handle the truck. I don't know how long he was back there, but neither my manager

nor myself left the selling floor during the time John was back there. It was a little after 5 p.m. when John came out to relieve us at the register. The manager and I went to the back, me to clock out for dinner, and him to prepare a supplies requisition, when the manager showed me a carton that looked like a new shipment on the shelf with the supplies. I do not know where it came from or how it got there. The manager then told me to hold off going to dinner until he was finished talking to John, and I went back to the register to get him.

(In the employee's own hand) *"I have read the above statement and it is true and correct."* (Signed/Witness)

Not that John had much of a leg to stand on anyway, but this informational statement does verify that no one went in to the stockroom while John was receiving the shipment, and serves to ensure the manager could not be accused of moving the box to the supply shelf.

The use of handwritten statements serves to illustrate that employees suspected of theft need not be caught red-handed for the astute manager to effect their removal from the workplace permanently, and stem the losses incurred from their dishonest activity. Recognizing procedures are compromised when employees attempt to steal permits management to seize the moment, and turn the symptoms of employee theft into the instrument of the dishonest employee's undoing. But it is incumbent upon companies to provide stores with explicit procedural guidelines in order for store managers to have maximum flexibility in resolving the theft issues they encounter.

Employers who direct internal investigations should be cognizant of the Employee Polygraph Protection Act of 1988. This act restricts the use of polygraph examination (lie-detector tests) in the private sector except in very narrowly defined circumstances.

Limited use of polygraph tests are permitted in three situations:

1. As part of on-going investigations of economic loss (theft, embezzlement, industrial espionage/sabotage) in the pre-employment stage of the hiring process for certain security positions,
2. By drug manufacturers or distributors in connection with hirings,
3. Criminal investigations involving controlled substances,

However, these limited exemptions come replete with strict administrative procedures regarding the use and disclosure of test results, which must be followed in order for the exemptions to apply. Specifically, an employee may not be terminated, disciplined, or otherwise penalized due to the outcome of a polygraph test or the employee's refusal to take the test.

Only in circumstances where additional supporting evidence provided by other elements of the investigation independent of the polygraph results can an employee be disciplined. For example, suppose one employee is accused by another of stealing, with the accuser having observed the act of theft. Motive means and opportunity support the allegation and the witness testimony is credible.

A known loss can be established without any doubt when a skilled interviewer has documented inconsistencies in the subject's story and concludes the subject is being untruthful. Yet, the employee will not admit to theft and maintains his innocence.

Although, by strict interpretation of the guidelines the company can, in this case, make a proffer to the employee of submitting to a polygraph, restraint should be exercised nonetheless. Should the employee decline, no inference of guilt can be derived from the employee's refusal to take the polygraph exam, and the company is compelled to resolve the matter as it would have if no offer for polygraph was made.

Should the employee fail the polygraph exam, i.e., show deception, disciplinary action cannot be forthcoming based solely on the test results. The test results may be considered in toto with the fruits of the investigation, but other supporting evidence should be shown as sufficient to warrant the disciplinary action on its own merit. Indications that the company considered the test results as conclusive proof should not be apparent. Should the employee pass the polygraph exam, then those results should be considered sufficiently exculpatory to warrant further investigation.

Under these guidelines, the routine use of polygraph in investigations of loss in a retail setting should be discouraged. Should an invitation to take a polygraph be raised with the employee, the employer's latitude in moving ahead with disciplinary action could be compromised by the employee's refusal to take the test. The employer could be later accused of disciplining the employee because he would not submit to a polygraph, which is a clear violation of the act. Of course, the employee would have to prove this contention, but the door to litigious action has been opened.

Similarly, the employee who agrees to be tested and fails, can attribute his dismissal solely to the results of the test, and the supporting evidence would have to be considerable to demonstrate the employer merely considered the test results and did not act unilaterally based on the outcome of the polygraph. In cases of major theft and significant loss, where a polygraph may be deemed worthwhile, the company should seek to have the investigating law enforcement agency broach the subject and sponsor the test to better insulate themselves from culpability under the act (the company need never be formally notified of the employees who refused or of the results). But police departments are hesitant to serve as the agent of a polygraph exam as well, preferring instead that the complainant handle this request with its employees, especially in matters where they believe the corporation has sufficient investigatory resources to arrange for and conduct the test itself.

Lastly, an employer should not be maneuvered into providing a polygraph for an employee who formally requests to take one. If polygraph examinations were not considered a viable strategy by the investigator to begin with, this unexpected development should not change that assessment. You cannot prohibit an employee from arranging for and taking a test on his own; but you have no obligation to review or consider the test results as part of your investigation.

Civil Liability

12

Retailers' exposure to civil liability has exploded with the onset of our litigious society, and the business community is in the cross-hairs of the "lotto-mentality" that permeates jury awards.

Loss prevention weighs into this arena bearing a two-edged sword: on the one-hand, LP is the company's primary inspection and investigation resource; on the other, LP practices, especially in the areas of apprehension and prosecution, are the fattest targets to exploit.

On the plus side, in its capacity as auditor for compliance and standard-bearer of employee awareness, LP can supplement the ongoing efforts of store operations to identify hazards in the field that lead to charges of unsafe conditions, negligence, and unfair labor practices.

Persons assigned loss prevention responsibilities should broaden their areas of expertise to include aspects of the company's safety program. Although responsibility for safety inspection should fall within the purview of store operations, LP should be mindful of safety standards when visiting stores. And in the event a situation involving employee or customer injury occurs, and where the exposure to the company is significant, LP personnel should be called upon to coordinate the accident investigation. Interviewing witnesses, taking statements, collecting evidence, and providing testimony are all specialized talents of a trained investigator.

Further, these same skills can and should be utilized in the context of human resources investigations. EEOC violations, charges of sexual harassment, and concerns with respect to violence in the workplace often come to the attention of the personnel department before proceeding to court. Tapping the in-house resource of a skilled investigator can at least minimize, if not prevent, costly litigation and damages.

On the downside, LP practices are often the most prolific source of charges a company may be subject to. Every confrontational encounter between LP representatives and customers or employees is a potential lawsuit.

Unilaterally dispensing with confrontations of an LP nature is not practical, so there is an element of risk that must be recognized.

There are fundamental steps a company can take to reduce the incidents that lead to litigation, and lessen the exposure to costly settlements when they do occur. The first line of defense is having sound, practiced procedures disseminated to the field — procedures on worker safety that prescribe safe work habits to reduce worker compensation claims, procedures on customer safety that prescribe safe practices for housekeeping and merchandise display to reduce injury claims, procedures for employees to follow in the event of an accident (who to call, what to do, the notifications to be made, and what forms are to be filled out), and strict, unambiguous guidelines for detaining shoplifters and interviewing employees suspected of theft.

The retailer can begin insulating himself from liability by taking the modicum of protection offered by procedural enhancement. First, the subject matter has to be deemed correct and complete. Then the trainer must be proven qualified to disseminate the information. And, without fail, a reliable program to document the training of the employees has to be established.

These steps go to the element of duty, the first of four prerequisites a plaintiff must prove in order to make a case for negligence. Merely acknowledging your duty, as is done through a combination of procedural enhancement and training, does not relieve the retailer of his obligation to fulfill that duty, but is effective in demonstrating that you do not operate with wanton disregard for public safety.

In establishing operating procedures, take care to ensure they reflect reasonable standards. This is essential since the second prerequisite for an action of negligence is unreasonable conduct on behalf of the defendant.

For instance, you do not prescribe for floor waxing to commence 30 minutes before opening. But on a rainy afternoon, a person is just as likely to slip on your wet tile floor, and your failure to maintain a safe environment, given your duty to do so, is deemed unreasonable conduct. But waxing your floor 30 minutes before opening, that is not only unreasonable, it is reckless.

The third prerequisite for negligence is forseeability. In order to be proven negligent, the unreasonable conduct you had a duty to prevent must be interpreted as very likely to cause injury. It is considered common knowledge that a waxed floor is slippery. It is therefore a foregone conclusion that walking on a waxed surface exposes an unsuspecting person to peril. Since potential for injury is forseeable, and the operator has failed in his duty to provide a safe environment by permitting unreasonable conduct, the operator is three fourths of the way to an indefensible action for negligence.

Forseeability used to be a difficult element for plaintiffs to prove when bringing negligence action against a retailer in cases where customers sustained injury or loss as a result of being the victim of a crime occurring on the retailer's premises. For instance, when a customer's handbag was stolen while she was trying on shoes, the customer would seek redress for the retailer's negligence for inadequate security. That the retailer has a duty to provide adequate security is a given, and to do less is unreasonable. But the proprietor could counter that this act was not forseeable, and could petition for dismissal since the plaintiff could not demonstrate this element of the four prerequisites. Similarly, mall management would defend a negligence charge in the same vein when a customer's car was stolen.

However, criminal activity in malls and shopping centers is so well documented today that these events are now, in fact, forseeable, and proving this element for the plaintiff takes little more than a statistical summary of 911 calls and complaint reports handled by the local police department servicing the mall. Retailers, too, keep statistical information on the number of arrests they have initiated and losses they have sustained, and corporate data of those records can be subject to subpoena. These recent developments have limited the retailer's ability to deny property crime on their premises was forseeable.

This leaves the last safe haven for defending negligence — the requirement that the plaintiff prove the defendant's actions were the proximate cause of the injury. If a retailer's employee creates an unsafe condition that the retailer has a duty to prevent, and the actions of that employee are deemed unreasonable, since it is forseeable they will cause injury, then the employer's agent becomes the proximate cause for the injury.

If a customer slips on your wet tile floor that was mopped by your employee, then you are negligent, especially if you failed to abide by one of your own procedures, i.e., mopped areas must be cordoned off and signed. If that same customer, however, slips on an ice cream cone spilled by another customer, it may be determined that you are not the proximate cause of the injury; another party owns that element. You may have contributory negligence culpability in this matter since you failed to maintain a safe environment, especially if you erred in following one of your own procedures, i.e., posted signs *No Food or Drink Allowed.* But your actions are at least defensible as not being the proximate cause of the injury, and your exposure to damages is significantly reduced.

As the reliance on the forseeability element has become more tenuous, so too is the proximate cause issue becoming more and more open to interpretation in the courts. Recent rulings have begun to explore the notion that retailers and mall operators have a higher duty to ensure public safety based on the premise that customers have an expectation of safety. Failure to perform this higher duty tends to offset the argument of proximate cause in some cases.

The hotel industry was the first to be cited in negligence rulings as having a higher duty based on strict interpretation of what had been outmoded mandates governing innkeepers in common law. When the victim of a crime sued a hostelry citing negligent security, the hotel offered that the perpetrator, not the hotel, was the proximate cause of the injury and that the plaintiff failed to meet the prerequisites for proving negligence. The court instead held that the operator failed to meet a higher standard of duty as prescribed by law, and that that failure was the proximate cause of the injury. Degrees of duty were now an area of contention.

So far, precedent decisions assigning a higher duty to retailers and shopping center operators have not been cited in negligence litigation involving store owners. But the day may come that the car thief may not be held as the proximate cause of the stolen car at the mall. Therefore, when considering procedural guidelines for company operations, it would be beneficial to design them to serve more than simply a general duty to provide a safe environment; strive for them to meet the standard of a higher duty as well.

The issue of negligence liability, as essential as it is to a profitable operation, is the most benign of the litigation pitfalls a retailer must contend with when assessing the potential exposure inherent in its loss prevention operation. As costly as a finding for the plaintiff can be in a negligence case, it pales in comparison to an unfavorable ruling in a matter involving the intentional torts.

Torts are wrongful acts for which a civil action can be brought. Negligence is an unintentional tort, and as such redress is sought by way of compensatory damages that compensate the plaintiff for financial losses, pain and suffering, and any adverse effects that the defendant's negligence has caused. When a plaintiff's negligence is also found to be done with malice, an intentional tort is committed. In addition to compensatory damages, the court may also award punitive damages to the plaintiff. The difference is significant: although your liability insurance carrier generally pays out compensatory damages in the settlement process, the defendant company, not the insurance carrier, is culpable for punitive damages.

Exposure to charges from the list of intentional torts rests prominently with a retailer's security operation. The actions of the retailer's agents, employees, or contracted third parties in the course of conducting their assigned duties could include the following:

False arrest (i.e., false imprisonment, false detention): limiting a person's freedom to go by words or acts with no legal right

Assault: unconsented or unprivileged physical contact, or privileged physical contact that is excessive or punitive

Malicious prosecution: prosecuting with malice

Defamation (libel and/or slander): a statement that injures one's reputation or character that is false and that is published to a third party

Tortious interference with employment: maliciously interfering with the employment of another person

Invasion of privacy: infringing upon someone's reasonable expectation of privacy

Tortious infliction of emotional distress: intentionally or maliciously inflicting emotional distress on another person

These intentional torts were designed to protect people from abuses of what we call the powers of citizens arrest. Protection from abuses in the course of arrest by law enforcement officers is granted in the Bill of Rights and early amendments to the Constitution. These constitutional guarantees prevent unlawful and malicious conduct by government agents, i.e., police officers. But persons making a citizen's arrest are not subject to the same criteria; they are instead accountable to the Law of Torts, and the imposition of considerable financial damages for unreasonable conduct.

In order to be insulated from the punitive damages of intentional tort litigation, the retailer must ensure that sound, practical policies for the detention of shoplifters and the interview of employees suspected of theft are practiced. That means they must be written, disseminated, trained, and documented in such a way that the company can distance itself from the reckless conduct of a company agent acting with wanton disregard of company policy. This will not prevent a civil action, but it may lessen the company's culpability in the award or settlement.

Specific individuals, i.e., loss prevention professionals, store management, and corporate executives, should be designated as having the authority to initiate the detention of a person suspected of committing a criminal act on your premises. Such individuals must be capable of initiating this action within the guidelines of the company's apprehension criteria, policies that are driven by the protections afforded retailers in the General Business Law.

Most states have language written into the General Business Law that afford a merchant certain latitude in effecting citizen arrests. This protection, sometimes referred to as The Merchant Statute does not permit retailers any special privileges in citizen arrest, but merely provides an affirmative defense to charges of tortious conduct. An affirmative defense is effective in defusing the contention of malice, which can be the difference between the intentional and unintentional tort, hence the difference between compensatory and punitive damages.

The affirmative defense holds that retailers may detain a person for a reasonable amount of time, and in a reasonable manner, in order to ascertain the ownership of property. The statute will not define what is considered a reasonable time, nor will it state what constitutes a reasonable manner. The standard of reasonableness rests with the court's assessment of how a situation was resolved within the parameters of common sense, good faith, and best intentions.

To put the merchant's statute in context, a retailer could defend an action that involved stopping a customer whom the retailer believed had placed unpaid for merchandise into a briefcase for the purposes of inquiring of the customer if this indeed happened. If the customer agreed to open the brief-case to show the retailer no such action took place, the customer would be less able to subsequently sue the retailer successfully for false detention/false arrest. If, on the other hand, the customer refused to cooperate with the retailer, and the store owner ripped the briefcase from the customer and spilled the contents onto the floor, the court may rule the merchant's statute does not apply, since the detention was not conducted in a reasonable manner. Similarly, if a retailer and a customer come to an impasse over opening the briefcase, it may be considered reasonable that a police officer be summoned to resolve the issue. But if it took 3 hours for the police to respond to the scene, the court may agree that the detention was made in a reasonable manner, but the detention exceeded the boundaries of a reasonable time, and the merchant would be unable to invoke the affirmative defense.

Many factors come into play that extend from the lawful detention. Two that the retailer has to be particularly attentive to are the use of force and search and seizure of property. The law does not distinguish powers between a citizen's arrest and a police arrest in this regard. Once a lawful arrest has been initiated, that is, the rights of an individual to go have been impeded by word or deed, based on the first-hand knowledge a crime has been committed, then the citizen making the arrest may use necessary force to restrain and detain the person arrested. Too, a person making a citizen's arrest may search a detainee and his belongings for weapons to ensure a safe detention environment. Knowing where to draw the line in an apprehension environment is what separates a trained loss prevention professional from a well-intentioned, but amateur, store manager.

As always in matters of this nature, the standard of reasonableness must be observed. Necessary force cannot deteriorate into excessive or punitive force. A person who cooperates in the arrest and poses no threat to flee need not be handcuffed or locked in a closet. Nor would the court look kindly on strip-searching a teenage girl under the auspices of establishing a safe detention environment. Although these extremes may be policy in the arrest procedure for some police departments, they have no place in the private sector.

In cases where a theft has taken place, i.e., the store owner has witnessed a customer conceal merchandise and exit the store without payment, care in the approach, accusation, and custody of the shoplifter must be taken. Merely winning a conviction in criminal court for larceny will not preclude responsibility for the manner in which that arrest and detention was conducted when scrutinized in a civil court. It cuts both ways: the shoplifter is liable for his conduct in criminal court, and the retailer is liable for his conduct in civil court.

Incident reports, containing detailed documentation, are essential for retailers to defend their actions. Written statements by witnesses, coupled with a summary report of the matter by management, are indispensable when facing a hostile deposition two years after the fact. Company procedure should mandate incident reporting by defining the contents of a file that accompanies all situations where a customer has been stopped, accused, detained, or prosecuted by a store representative. In addition to witness statements and summary reports, copies of police reports, court dates and disposition, and verifiable chain-of-custody information regarding evidence (recovered cash, merchandise, credit cards, sales receipts, etc.) should be included in the case file.

In applying the standards of reasonable conduct vital to limiting exposure to civil liability, employers must recognize that employees are afforded the same considerations as customers. A common misperception is that the rights of employees are somehow subjugated by virtue of the employer-employee relationship. The line between persuasion and coercion is often blurred in the conduct of employee investigations, especially when those investigations are handled by persons other than loss prevention professionals.

Employers often seek cooperation from employees when conducting internal investigations. However, implicit in the employer-employee relationship is an element of intimidation and control that is susceptible to abuse. Marathon interrogations and back room confessions, although still practiced and for the most part not illegal, certainly are suspect in the purview of reasonable conduct.

It is no longer a prudent idea, although at one time this would have been considered routine, for a manager to tell a 17-year-old salesperson, whose register came up $20 short at closing, that "*we are going to stay here until we get to the bottom of this!*" Regardless of any criminal wrongdoing uncovered in your after-hour investigation, imagine trying to defend the reasonableness of keeping a minor in your store, late at night, interrogating her without the benefit of parental notification, and turning her out to a deserted parking lot at 1:00 a.m., alone and distraught.

There is a tendency for amateur investigators, in these instances, to overstep the boundaries of fair play, and remain blinded to the consequences of their well-intentioned actions. Often, nonexistent evidence is alluded to, in an effort to get the employee to confess. Threats and promises are made that seriously undermine the legal merit of any admission gained. Evidence is gathered through tainted means, and as such would be inadmissible in court. For instance, a search is made of a suspected dishonest employee's handbag. Stolen property is found, and confronted, the employee confesses and is prosecuted for theft.

As defined later legal searches are permitted by warrant, by consent, and as incidental to a lawful arrest. In this example of a warrantless search, the stolen property is not found incidental to a lawful arrest because the search preceded, rather than followed the arrest. It was the discovery of the stolen property which prompted the arrest, so the fruits of this search could be challenged for admissibility. The employer could maintain that the employee consented to the search, and the fruits of that search should be admissible. The employee could counter that although consent was given, it was not a free and voluntary consent; rather, consent was given because the employee feared the consequences of refusing her employer. The employer would then point to the employee handbook which states as a matter of policy that employee handbags are subject to inspection by management, claiming the employee gave consent in the employment contract. The employee would rebut that argument by claiming she would have withdrawn that consent had she not feared retribution from the company in the form of disciplinary action.

In either case, the consent could be proven tainted, and absent a warrant and a lawful arrest from which the search could be incidental, an evidentiary hearing could suppress the stolen property and any subsequent statement of admission made by the employee in the course of the interrogation, on the grounds they were obtained by coercion.

Without the property evidence or statement of admission to present at a criminal trial, it is doubtful a conviction could be gained. The employer could then have to answer charges of false arrest, malicious prosecution, invasion of privacy, and wrongful termination in a civil suit.

Now the legal maneuverings described above are extremely rare. It is more likely that both the property evidence and the subsequent confession would be admitted in a criminal proceeding because the courts hold private persons making a citizen's arrest to a lesser standard concerning matters of search and seizure than they do a law enforcement officer.

The point to be made is that an employer must be cognizant of the intricacies involved when initiating investigations and interviews with respect to employees. No lesser consideration of an employee's rights to due process should be practiced due to a misguided notion that workers are somehow compelled to accede to the demands of management. Company policies may never supersede constitutional protections, and juries will award harsh reminders to overzealous corporations.

This venue of reasonableness carries over into two more areas of concern for those conducting loss prevention investigations: surveillance and entrapment. Covert surveillance of activity in the workplace, once considered a matter of management prerogative, is now facing government regulation. Businesses may soon have to define the scope and intent of electronic surveillance, notifying employees of the type, duration, and purpose of surveillance equipment deployed on the job. Electronic surveillance is defined as cameras, recorders, and equipment that monitors employee activity, and could well be inclusive of MIS software that monitors transaction information and employee productivity, as well as devices that prevent unauthorized employee use of company telephones, copiers, and fax machines.

This development is in no small part attributable to abuses and excesses of surveillance privileges. Ill-conceived security programs, involving hidden cameras and unauthorized wire taps in the name of asset protection, have been subverted to satisfy a prurient interest in locker rooms and office romances. As a result, the company is exposed to major liability for invasion of privacy, and a valuable resource for legitimate loss prevention inquiry is jeopardized.

So, too, have the investigative benefits of undercover operatives been compromised. Infiltration of the employee population by agents of management, usually contracted from security agencies, has uncovered many of the most damaging, collusive, dishonest employee rings. Yet, poor technique in the follow-up investigations, coupled with the unilateral termination of implicated employees, has focused scrupulous attention on the agencies that provide operatives, the companies who use them, and the capricious action taken against employees based solely on the investigative reports by what amount to paid informants.

Not surprisingly, management gets in over its head: the agency wants to deliver in order to justify its weekly billing; the company executive that contracted the agency wants the operation to culminate in "the big bust" in order to display his investment prowess; and the company itself is anxious for a forum in order to demonstrate to the employees-at-large that crime does not pay. But see who has the deep-pockets in a lawsuit for defamation and wrongful termination when the tactics used by the security agency are deemed akin to entrapment by the court.

This chapter, by no means, is designed to make the retailer hesitant in his pursuit of a crime-free workplace. On the contrary, providing the fundamentals for avoiding civil liability should serve to strengthen a retailer's resolve, making for more aggressive management of loss prevention resources, and stimulate improvements to procedures that protect the company from frivolous litigation.

Robbery Prevention

13

This chapter affords us a good opportunity to evaluate loss control measures in relation to company policy, field operations, and training effectiveness. Company policy will dictate the cash handling procedures that safeguard the company's greatest assets: its people and profit. Field operations, with respect to its capacity to comply with corporate policy, will be tested by practical, but tedious, procedural mandates. And the four key ingredients for evaluating the effectiveness of a company's training function come together around this issue.

First, the subject matter is interesting; you will have the attention of the participants. Second, there are divergent points of view concerning which policies work best in an effort to deter, and in some cases survive, an armed robbery attempt. Third, the subject matter is important; after all, retail employees do face a life or death situation in some cases. And last, the information presented in this chapter is in demand by the employees involved in the training.

As represented by the four sections of this book, let's first examine the physical security measures companies should consider when designing a retail location with an eye for preventing robberies. Store layout is an important factor in determining susceptibility to a robbery attempt. Point of sale (POS) stations should be located in the front of the store, so as to be visible to pedestrian and parking lot traffic. A person is less likely to attempt a hold-up if there exists a strong possibility that this activity can be witnessed by a passerby. This will not preclude a robbery attempt (none of the measures we discuss will), but if a choice exists between a secluded POS area and an open area that presents an unobstructed view, the secluded station is more likely to be targeted. To this end, when locating a register at the front of the store, be certain that promotional window displays and advertising posters do not defeat your purpose. The POS station should be secured with a self-locking gate, or Dutch-door, that prevents unauthorized entry when the station is unattended. Cash drawers on registers should be key-locked or accessed only by employee code so that an unattended, unlocked cash drawer does not tempt the opportunist to make a move.

Many times a simple cash larceny, the theft of money from an unattended register, escalates into a robbery situation when a till-tapper, a scam artist who is attempting only to access a register cash drawer, is detected and confronted by an alert employee. Many flee, but some, panicked at being caught, stand their ground threatening the employee with harm, or in some cases producing a weapon, and then taking the cash by force. In this case, a register station that could have been protected by a barrier (the lockable gate), and a cash drawer that should have been secured in a fashion that would deter the till-tapper, was instead deemed vulnerable and targeted for a hit. The intrusion of the vigilant employee was the catalyst that turned a larceny into a robbery, and management must now cope with the aftermath: lost profits and a traumatic experience for the employee, with all the associated labor relations fallout. The lesson learned here is that the physical security of the POS station in some cases can at least prevent robberies that were intended by the perpetrator to be something less spectacular.

Another example of physical security devices available for robbery prevention is closed circuit television (CCTV). As discussed in Chapter 4, the benefits of such an investment in security hardware go beyond its usefulness in deterring shoplifting and detecting employee theft. Visible cameras have proven to be a significant deterrent to armed robbery attempts, but selecting the best application for this resource is the subject of on going debate in the loss prevention community.

First, camera benefits include: a live camera, positioned to capture the image of a person committing a robbery, is something some robbers would take notice of during a walk-through, or "casing," of a target. This feature alone has been cited as reason enough to move on to a more attractive location. In the event a robber is not disposed to casing an establishment, but instead targets your location solely on the basis of his perception that the risk is acceptable, then the deterrent value of your camera is lost, but the detection value remains. If the monitor that displays the video from the POS station is positioned in a back office location, then perhaps a manager or other employee would observe the robbery remotely and be able to alert the authorities.

In addition, a CCTV system that records activity at the POS station on a VCR would also be invaluable for police investigators in their efforts to apprehend the perpetrator. Many retail robberies are "serial robberies," a spree that only ends with the arrest of the robber. In an after-the-fact kind of way, the ability of retailers to assist the police is a form of robbery prevention in its own right.

So far, CCTV surveillance has acquitted itself well as a device which can deter, detect, and in some cases help apprehend persons committing robbery. It would seem a prudent tool for robbery prevention, and as such, universal application should be strongly recommended. Is there a downside to this prevention approach? Certainly there is, and not because of anything inherently wrong with the logic of CCTV application. The downside involves the unpredictable nature of persons engaging in armed robbery, and the risk to employees and customers that flows from unforeseen responses.

For instance, a potential problem with the scenario described above could arise when the manager, viewing the robbery on the monitor in the back office, becomes involved. The manager may have a visual understanding of what is happening, but he may not know the audio portion. He may not know the robber has just asked the employee "is anybody in the back?" and the employee responded that no one was there. Then, in the course of the robbery, the robber observes the red light next to Line 2 activate on the telephone when the manager attempts to call the police, and shoots the clerk. Was this outcome predictable? Certainly not. Was this tragedy preventable? Possibly.

It was possibly preventable because a basic tenet of surviving a robbery was not followed. We are all taught when confronted in a robbery situation to cooperate with the robber. The credo "the money can be replaced, the employee can not" has been recited for decades. When the manager, operating with best intentions, attempted to do more, to take an extraordinary step in a perilous situation, he unknowingly put the employee at greater risk than the employee may have been in otherwise, had the manager allowed the employee to hand over the cash. The robber may have fled. The robber may have shot the clerk anyway. We do not know. We do know that summoning the police did not save the clerk, and by virtue of that fact, was a needless risk, not because it backfired, but because it did not allow the robbery to unfold naturally. The natural progression of a robbery is that the person with the upper hand controls the situation, and the person at a disadvantage acquiesces. Once satisfied, the percentage of robbers who flee is higher than the percentage of robbers who remain and do violence. It is not an absolute, but the percentages are significant enough to encourage the victim to cooperate in order to satisfy.

Earlier, we had discussed the merits of a CCTV system that recorded the POS activity on a VCR and suggested this feature would assist in the subsequent police investigation. Is there a downside here as well? There is when we consider the unforeseen and the unpredictable.

There are documented cases where the robber, having observed the camera at the POS station during a robbery, got his cash, then insisted the employee hand over the videocassette from the VCR. It is not a widespread phenomena, but experienced professionals who identify the camera surveillance as the only deterrent to a particular target have been known to plan this step as the means to overcome the deterrent.

In the perpetrator's mind, if the camera removes the target, then removing the camera (in this case the videotape) restores the target. A prolific method of operation? No. But the risk potential has to be weighed when considering CCTV application. The risk here is that a robbery with no camera may be concluded at the register when the cash is handed over. When the presence of the camera (and perceived videotape) is factored in, the robber may now want the videotape. Instead of being out the door making a getaway, the robber is now marching the employee to the back room to get the tape.

The back room is last place the employee needs to be with an armed robber. No longer exposed to incidental observation by a passerby, the robber's incentive to flee is diminished. The impulse of greed replaces the impulse to run, and the robber may become emboldened to now demand the contents of the safe, now visible to the perpetrator. Or worse, the potential to assault the employee escalates because the robber's leverage in the situation has increased. Sexual assaults of female employees in robbery situations occur far more frequently in the secluded back office than on the exposed selling floor.

In addition, the employee senses the level of peril has increased and may now lose control; fighting back, attempting to flee, or becoming hysterical. Each of these responses is incompatible with the robber's usual intentions, and as the level of cooperation wanes, the potential for violence surges.

To presume we are in this position due solely to the benign presence of a CCTV system, installed primarily as a deterrent, is a stretch. It is, however, demonstrative of the unpredictable outcomes that occasionally occur in the course of a robbery. Failure to anticipate even the potential downside of otherwise prudent measures to prevent robberies can and does result in unforeseen tragedy, the repercussions of which linger a very long time.

Chapter 2 touched on another physical security system applicable to robbery prevention measures, the burglar alarm system. Primarily employed to detect unauthorized after-hour entry, most systems feature silent, or passive, alarms that signal the alarm company of an emergency situation.

Commonly referred to as a "hold-up button," this device is placed covertly at the POS station as a means for an employee to surreptitiously summon aid in extreme conditions. For years, retailers deployed these devices to enhance an employee's comfort zone in the event a robbery takes place. The device reminds the employee that they are not alone, and that help is only minutes away. Initially, these devices were successful in facilitating a rapid response by police units that resulted in many robbers being caught in the act. No doubt influenced by television crime shows that depicted sly bank tellers tripping the silent alarm using the hidden floor button, clerks at retail locations would mimic this action with predictable outcomes: many were shot.

Robbers soon began to admonish clerks "don't try anything funny" and retailer's policies followed suit by instructing employees to use the device after the robber fled, still counting on that rapid response to the scene. With the onset of the 911 emergency systems nationwide, the function of the hold-up button has changed. Alarm companies receiving a hold-up alarm used to call the precinct house and report a robbery-in-progress at your location, hence the rapid response. Today, hold-up alarms at most national alarm monitoring stations are received centrally, and the alarm company dispatcher uses the 911 network to report receiving a hold-up alarm at your location. That call is handled and dispatched by the 911 operator in the standard fashion that prioritizes emergencies. Your urgent call for rapid response via the hold-up alarm is in competition with the cardiac arrest, back-alley shooting, house on fire, and jumper off the bridge emergencies that permeate the airwaves. Since we no longer use the hold-up alarm as a means to a swift and dramatic arrest of the robber as he flees the store, one must consider the downside of this application carefully. The very nature of the device is contradictory to the best advice available: cooperate and hope he leaves.

Only in the event that the situation deteriorates is further action required. But by definition, the hold-up alarm involves the employee in an attempt to facilitate the capture of the robber: a function the employee is not trained to do, not encouraged to do, and in all likelihood, will not accomplish.

Just suppose, instead of notifying the police, that the alarm company dispatcher calls the store to report an alarm was received. This is the standard alarm company response to many alarms received during business hours, alarms that monitor fire exits, receiving docks, smoke detectors. It is not the standard response to hold-up alarms, but just suppose the alarm company misreads the zone received as something other than a hold-up and telephones the store instead of the police. Or worse, suppose this is your company's procedure: that due to the propensity of false alarms (and the ensuing fines) you have instructed the alarm company to check with the store first before dispatching the police on all alarms, and maybe you have worked out some kind of code-word to convey an emergency situation. Why don't you just shoot the clerk yourself! Since this is the likely outcome of such a policy!

The two lessons we have learned in evaluating physical security measures for robbery prevention are (1) these situations are unpredictable; and (2) do nothing that conveys anything less than full cooperation. Owning, deploying, and using hold-up alarms is a catalyst to unpredictability and conveys only resistance.

Is that to say hold-up alarms have no merit in robbery prevention? As a deterrent, no. After all, you never see signs posted that say *"Warning: Hold-up button available under counter."* But in the aftermath of a robbery, the hold-up button remains an alternative means of communication to an outside agency in the event the telephone is disabled. There are cases where robbers have unplugged the desktop telephone unit and taken it with them in order to impede notification. Also, employees may feel management has abandoned them to their fate without the emotional security a hold-up alarm system provides. Is there a low-risk application for hold-up alarms? Yes.

Consider the situation where the robber is dissatisfied with the "take" at the register and orders the clerk/manager to the back office to empty the safe. This situation has clearly deteriorated because the primary objective of facilitating the perpetrator at the register in order to hasten his exit has failed, and the staff person has become further imperiled with the prospect of being isolated in the back office with the robber. Indeed, in some cases the level of cooperation encountered at the register can be over-accommodating, encouraging the robber to up the stakes.

In this case, a hold-up alarm located in the back office area may be an asset to the properly trained employee. Attempting to distract or trick the perpetrator in order to send the alarm is inadvisable. Only in cases where imminent, serious injury is about to occur, should an employee attempt to thwart the robbery. But in the event an employee is injured or incapacitated in the aftermath of an office robbery, an accessible hold-up button may be the only means available to summon aid.

Since being herded into the back room in a robbery seriously escalates the potential for harm, it is worthwhile to consider a tactic which can possibly preempt this development. Install a small "drop safe" (key-locked, not combination lock) at the POS station and seed it with two or three sealed deposit envelopes containing about $200 each in marked $20, $10 and $1 bills. If and when the robber states he wants the employee to go to the back and open the safe, the employee can respond that the stores' "change fund" is kept at the counter and offer to open the drop safe. Handing over this unanticipated windfall may satisfy the robber and he will leave, without making the trip to the back office. A truly innovative application of the hold-up alarm system would be to have a pair of recessed contacts installed on this drop safe that sends the hold-up signal to the alarm company anytime that safe is opened. This drop safe, of course, would serve no other function in the store operation except to send an alarm in the event an unwanted trip with a robber to the back office is unavoidable.

However, this application is not without risk. The employee has crossed the line from cooperation to (passive) resistance, and this strategy is only acceptable if the employee feels an encounter alone in the office will go badly.

This is a lot to ask of an employee under these circumstances, but company policy should afford the employee-victim some control and latitude of the situation by providing the resources and training for the employee to exercise prudent options.

For instance, an assistant manager is alone in the store at opening. A man walks in, produces a handgun and orders the manager to empty the register. Dissatisfied with the opening change fund, he then tells her to come in the back and open the safe. Literally shaking with fear, she gets to the office door only to find she does not have the key; she left the key ring at the register. The robber tells her to go get them, and she hurries to the register counter. Then suddenly, without really thinking about it, she bolts right out the front door, and keeps running to the restaurant across the street. In this scenario, instinct took over. Whether cognizant of it or not, this employee determined she was better off risking a bullet in the back than the potential consequences of "cooperating" alone in the back office. Because she comes away unscathed, she is lauded by her superiors for courage and quick-thinking. But this does not mean corporate should issue new policies that state employees should run for their lives at the first opportunity in a robbery. Employees should be taught to do what they think is in their best interest. And because initial cooperation and a willingness to comply is generally in the employee's best interest, that is what they should be taught first. Only in the most precarious situations are finesse tactics, such as the one described with the drop safe, justified.

To conclude our discussion on hold-up alarm usage, the best application to maximize their effectiveness with minimal risk is to establish an alarm-triggering mechanism that is consistent with carrying out the robber's instruction. Retailers may want to look into an ambush code for combination locks on safes that activates the alarm while still permitting the safe to be opened per the robber's orders.

Similarly, a device can be installed on the safe room door that will send a hold-up alarm anytime that room is entered. Only by "shunting" the alarm with an external switch prior to entry will the alarm mechanism be deactivated. Therefore, in complying with the robber's instruction to open the door, the employee has, in effect, triggered the alarm. These passive applications are useful for retailers that are prone to robberies perpetrated by individuals intent on getting into the safe, such as jewelry stores, supermarkets, and convenience stores doing a brisk lottery business. In such cases, the robbers can be well-armed and are prepared to be brutally intolerant of a flinching, hesitant employee.

But as with all security protocols, they can be undermined by the unscrupulous "inside man," a present or former employee peddling inside information. Instructing a manager to use the ambush code when opening the safe during a robbery, without knowing the robber has been fully briefed on this tactic by an ex-manager fired six months ago for stealing, should make any retailer rethink how creative one needs to be. Remember always in planning physical security measures that deter, detect, and impede armed robberies that responses are not always predictable and are fraught with unforeseen consequences.

That is why the strongest preventive measures come not from hardware, but from LP programs and procedures that minimize exposure and emphasize training and discipline in the store operation. Establishing cash handling guidelines is the first step in securing your assets and protecting your employees. Make sure cash on hand is discreetly managed. Never flaunt a full cash drawer or make references in front of customers about cash drops or deposits. A manager passing the POS station with a bag under his arm should not stop and inform the clerk *"I'm going to the bank now."* I've heard this while in line at a store more than once, and I'm sure we have all witnessed incidents of indiscretion concerning retail employees' handling and transport of cash. *"Can you ring this customer up?" "Sure, as soon as I finish this drop."*

Sound familiar? It is the result of employees becoming complacent over what they consider mundane tasks: counting down the drawers, recording interim deposits (or cash pulls), and closing out a register at shift change. These are necessary, prudent measures in managing cash, but the message has been lost at some establishments. The employees feel that these procedures are designed to protect the cash. It must be emphasized that these policies are followed to protect the employee.

When training an associate on cash handling procedures, management should make clear that maintaining minimum cash on-hand at the register prevents repeat-robbery situations. To illustrate:

> Suppose a store that averages $1500 daily in cash sales is robbed one hour before closing, and the perpetrator gets away with $1200 from the register. This is a nice haul for the type of robber specializing in quick-hit, at-the-counter, in-and-out commercial robbery. As stated earlier, many retail robberies are serial crimes, a lone or small band of criminals targeting a specific strip mall or commercially zoned section of highway. The success of the caper in this example is likely to keep this retail location on the target list — it was fast, easy, and profitable — worth the risk in the criminal mind.

Now take the same situation where company policy dictates cash drops be made from the register to the drop safe every 4 hours, or any time the cash count exceeds $300. The robbery now yields less than $300 instead of $1200, and the likelihood of this location being identified as a prime target for a repeat performance is reduced.

Procedures that lessen the prospects for armed robbery confrontations are more likely to be followed by employees when explained to them in this light, instead of being presented as another task to be performed because policy says so. POS software is available to retailers that prompts the clerk when an interim cash drop is required. By tracking the cash tendered to a predetermined amount, the register will alert employees a cash drop is overdue. For companies that wish to ensure this procedure is not compromised by an inattentive clerk, the program can be modified to lock out future cash sales until the drop is done. Only a manager's override code will permit the register to function in lieu of an interim deposit.

Discreetly managing cash in the store can be accomplished with training and understanding. But retailers who require their management personnel to make bank deposits of the daily receipts need to elevate the awareness level among their management staffs in order to minimize the exposure to the employee.

In keeping with the thoughts previously presented, daily bank deposits are essential to keeping a store off the prime target list. In the event a robbery is perpetrated by a thief who goes for the safe as well as the register, a haul that nets two or three days' worth of deposits (in our example this would approximate $3500), would of course be considered in the criminal mind a worthwhile take down. Netting $1500 instead because previous days' receipts were deposited each day would be more of a mediocre reward for such a risk, and not necessarily doom the location to a place on the list for a return engagement. Remember, serial robbers successful once are emboldened to return since they now know more about the store layout and the willingness of employees to offer no resistance. It is essential that the profitability, or lack of it, of hitting your store offsets these factors.

Consider the potential outcome if a robber hits your safe on Monday for $3500 because weekend bank deposits were not made. Then he returns on Friday, expecting $3500 again, but getting only $1500. Would he think the store manager was holding out on him? Would he sense the willingness to cooperate has waned because he did not hurt anybody last time? Would he pistol-whip or shoot the manager because he feels cheated? Examples like this are helpful in motivating store management personnel to follow daily bank deposit policies more closely.

Let's assess the risks involved in the bank deposit process. First, the selection of a bank location should take into account the logistics of making the deposit. How far away is it? Is there customer traffic at the bank during the times you anticipate making deposits? Does it facilitate after-hour drops? If so, is it well-lighted? Indoors or outdoors? Will your employee have to leave his car? If so, is the route from the parking area in open view? Of course, retailers in malls should most certainly avail themselves of any banking resource sharing space in the mall.

Don't hesitate to ask bank officials or the local police if there is a history of people being accosted at this location prior to establishing your account there. Ask the bank if it is their policy is to inform commercial depositors of an incident that may occur in the future. All too often victims learn after the fact that depositors were robbed on previous occasions, but the bank failed to alert regular customers to these events, and an opportunity to modify your schedule of deposits was lost.

Payroll grids and staffing levels will dictate whether deposits are made prior to opening or midday when staffing overlaps or after closing. But retailers should strive for optimum deposit conditions in planning store coverage. First, only a person from the management team can be assigned this function. For reasons of accountability, trust, and practical business sense, staff people should be excluded from the process wherever possible. Next, no member of management should ever be requested to make the deposit unescorted, even if this necessitates involving an hourly employee as an escort. Be certain to include this function in the job description, especially for cases that do require staff participation in the process. The prospect of informing a grieving parent that their son or daughter was injured taking your money to the bank when the parent believed their child's role in your business was to wait on customers or stack shelves is disconcerting.

Also, review with your corporate legal and insurance people the liability issues involving an employee using their own vehicle for company business. In many cases, young managers at the assistant level have spotty transportation resources to get to and from work. Will using their parents' or boyfriend's car for your company business pose a liability problem for your carrier? Find out.

There are upsides and downsides to each deposit scenario: morning, afternoon, and night. The pre-opening deposit poses a scheduling dilemma: is it feasible to assign two management-level employees to the opening shift, the traditional prep-time and slow period of a retailer's business day? It usually is not, and for this reason, staff-level employees are often involved in the pre-opening deposit process. Another downside is that your cash receipts have been left overnight in the store safe, susceptible to loss from after-hour burglary.

An industrial safe and functional alarm system should be adequate to frustrate all but the more professional burglars, and assigning a trusted employee to escort the manager (preferably in the manager's vehicle) is a calculated risk. But the upside is attractive. It is daylight out. Rush hour traffic has passed. Providing that the deposit is completely prepared and ready to go by the night manager, the opening manager and employee would be absent from the store for a minimal period. The bank itself may be open for business, and the manager can enter the bank proper rather than be exposed to the risks associated with after-hour deposit drops. Also, the manager can obtain the deposit receipt in the transaction, reducing the chances of discrepancy later with the bank, as sometimes happens when deposits are made without the benefit of a teller's participation.

With the pre-opening deposit, the window for greatest risk exists with the manager's initial entry into the store, and his exit a short time later. Having arrived to the store, the manager should remain is his car while awaiting the arrival of the second employee. He should use this time to scan the parking lot, making note of vehicles and persons observed. When the second employee arrives, the manager should exit his vehicle and enter the store under the watchful eye of the second employee; once inside, the manager can then admit the second employee. This dual-entry tactic should discourage a criminal lurking for the purpose of forcing his way into the store with the opening employees to commit a robbery.

Similarly, the exit to leave for the bank should be in two stages. One employee exits and enters the vehicle. He then signals the other employee an all-clear to exit with the deposit. (This staggered exit policy should also be the rule when the closing shift leaves at night). Once at the bank, a careful survey of the route inside is still advisable. Only the manager needs to enter the bank; the other employee should remain in the vehicle out of harm's way. These are merely common sense, personal safety techniques that people should practice on and off the job for their own good. People are often victims of crime because they are less diligent than they should be with respect to their surroundings, become distracted or preoccupied, and fail to heed the subtleties of a dangerous condition.

Likewise, morning deposits can become a routine for management, another chore to be done on an endless list of tasks. The sense of urgency dissipates, one's guard is lowered, the complacent become careless, the lazy become stupid, and the criminal takes advantage. The tendency for ill-advised short-cuts is more prevalent with the pre-opening deposit because over the course of 365 days, one or both employees will arrive late. In the ensuing rush to get back and forth from the bank, safety will be compromised. In the event an orderly pre-opening deposit cannot be made due to unforeseen circumstances, the manager should be able to use his discretion to put off the deposit to a more opportune time. This decision should not be made unilaterally by the manager, but in conjunction with his regional manager to whom he should communicate this breach of policy. If your immediate supervisor must be notified each time you fail to comply with procedure, how often will failure to comply be an issue?

The midday deposit has similar scheduling downsides to the pre-opening deposit. Even if two managers are present for the midday shift, both cannot leave to make the midday deposit because one has to remain and manage the store. Again, the eventuality is that a staff person will be assigned escort duty. Also, the store is at risk to the type of robber we call the "bell-ringer." His method of operation is to enter the store just after opening, when customer traffic is marginal and staffing low. Had the deposit been made prior to opening, then the deposit would be safely in your account and the robber's take would be only the opening change fund instead of the entire previous days' receipts. The point here is not how much money is lost, but on how attractive the endeavor was for the robber, and how the outcome effects his determination whether or not to return another time. The upside of the midday deposit is considerable. Pedestrian traffic and parking lot activity is brisk; it is still daylight; and it is harder for a criminal casing your patterns to determine exactly when you are going to leave the store with the deposit. In the pre-opening deposit, a person observing your actions for a couple of days can easily determine you will come out between 9:05 and 9:15. That is because the criminal planner will know how far away the bank is, how long it takes to make the deposit, and that you have to be back by 9:45 to open at 10:00. You always are.

With the midday deposit, the manager has more latitude in selecting the time of the deposit, say anywhere from 11:30 a.m. to 1:30 p.m. This window takes into account the arrival time of the second manager, as well as the cut-off time at the bank for same-day credit on deposits. The midday deposit affords the manager the most opportunity to vary both his time and route to the bank; an edge that may offset the inherent vulnerability to the bell-ringer.

The last option involves the closing deposit. Seen mostly with mall retailers utilizing bank drops within the mall, night deposits under these conditions are not as precarious as they may seem. There is usually pedestrian traffic along mall corridors up to 30 minutes after the mall is closed. Mall security officers are usually visible during these times, making their rounds and ushering people out. Robbers may be reluctant to attempt a grab-and-run of the deposit in a mall after hours because they are uncertain of the best escape routes and doors being manned and/or locked by mall security as customer traffic dictates.

Also, the likelihood of two management persons being available for the deposit on the closing shift is higher, reducing the need for involvement in the process by a staff person. And a considerable advantage to mall tenants is not having to keep the deposit overnight in the store, where neither the safe nor the alarm system is up to the specs of those traditionally found in free-standing stores.

For non-mall locations, the night deposit brings few, if any, benefits that offset the substantial downside: criminals like to work under the cover of darkness. Thirty minutes after a strip center closes, parking lots are desolate, highway traffic is moving too quickly to notice trouble, and the employees are isolated when they leave. A robber who knows the employees are leaving with the deposit is in his element to accost the closing manager under the cover of darkness and pull off what is to him, a low-risk crime.

Assuming the closing manager makes it out of the parking lot safely, the ride through the after-hour bank drop is a lonely one. Robberies of bank customers at ATMs and after-hour depositories happen overwhelmingly at night. Unless your policy is for the manager to take the deposit home with him at night and stop by the bank on the way in the next morning, (I did not think so), night deposits from free-standing locations is imprudent at best and needlessly endangers employees at worst.

The other aspect of the cash management program is the check and balance of field compliance. This is best facilitated through the home office, developing a method that alerts management to instances of stores failing to make a bank deposit. Companies traditionally used the monthly bank reconciliation reports to compare cash sales reported against cash deposits made at the bank. This summary report confirms the monthly totals of deposit activity, and discrepancies are handled through field operations channels for resolution. Even when totals match, companies are unable to determine from this report that deposits were made daily without exception. Most POS software in use today transmits daily deposit information to the home office, i.e., the amounts scheduled for deposit. This does not necessarily mean that the deposit was actually made; only the daily examination of the franked deposit slip receipt would confirm that the deposit was indeed received at the bank. Since it is unrealistic for multi-store chains to audit this type of daily operations function, another method should be considered.

Some companies have arranged with their banks to do daily sweeps of all remote accounts, transferring the funds to a central account. The amount of the daily sweep, or location withdrawal, is determined by the amount reported to sales audit via POS transmission of the scheduled deposit. In the event the deposit has not been made, the wire will "bounce" and the home office will know within 24 hours which stores failed to make the daily deposits. An exception report identifying stores which failed to comply can then be generated for immediate follow-up action with the field. There are some cost implications to this program. Banks often charge service fees per transaction, and will levy penalties for bounced wires much as they do for personal checks. For chains with hundreds of locations, the cost may be significant, but the benefits are substantial: the field becomes cognizant of an electronic supervisor monitoring their performance.

An interim solution may be to initiate this program for three or six months until deposit accountability becomes ingrained with the field. Then to minimize the cost of this approach, the home office can discreetly reduce to weekly sweeps. The supervisory effect on the field may endure even though the program has been diminished. The finer points of robbery prevention involve the training support management can provide to store personnel. Policy-in-a-vacuum, the company-wide circulation of Do's and Don'ts, will not replace on-site meetings that allow for dialog with employees. This approach affords management a rare opportunity to address employee concerns in a way that demonstrates the company's commitment to worker safety and training.

Employees are accustomed to attending training sessions designed to sell more, do more, and use less. For the company to send a corporate representative to regional operations meetings to address an issue of genuine employee concern, allows management ennobles in the estimation of its workers. As discussed, successful LP programs depend on the employees' caring about the company's success and contributing to it. Here is an occasion for management to illustrate its caring for employee well-being, and publicize measures the company has taken to enhance their safety.

For instance, if you sense employees are resentful that cameras have been installed to monitor them, point out that the cameras serve as a deterrent to armed robbery as well. If managers are resentful of having their schedules altered to accommodate morning or midday deposits, explain the benefits to them in terms of risk reduction. If the staff complains that mandatory interim drops are a nuisance and inconvenience customers, assure them these procedural steps are designed to protect them, not your money.

Never allude to the equipment or resources you have employed to prevent robbery as a program that will preclude robbery. Explain instead that these measures are recommended by informed individuals and police agencies as methods that reduce the potential for robbery. Point out that strategies change, that what was once thought prudent (under-the-counter hold-up buttons for example) is now considered risky. Tell them you may very well be back in six months with more program modifications, because the company will continue to explore new options and seek advice from experts.

Be prepared to listen and negotiate. A store that has been victimized by robbery may insist upon armed guard coverage around the clock. If the store expense structure cannot support this demand, do not dismiss the request out-of-hand, even if you believe this to be a dubious investment. Challenge the store manager or regional manager to come up with a cost saving proposal from other areas, i.e., payroll, supply, outside services, etc., that would sustain periodic guard coverage at times store personnel feel would be most beneficial. Further, it is not uncommon to see an increase in sales during night hours that guard presence is scheduled. Customers have been known to comment that they feel safer coming to the store knowing a guard is there evenings, and the hike in revenue alone may support the coverage.

If a store wants a camera on the back door so they can determine whether the person knocking is the delivery man or an armed robber, but you feel LP equipment can be better allocated and this suggested application would not be cost effective, compromise on installing a peephole. Keep it constructive, be diplomatic, and promise nothing you cannot deliver.

Where applicable, instruct a management executive (especially your senior manager of real estate/construction) to contact mall management to discuss their security arrangements for tenants with respect to escorts and response to calls about suspicious persons. Above all, teach them to follow their own instincts. Identify suspicious activity for them, and encourage them when and how to call the police before the fact. This is a crucial point, because some store managers are hesitant to "cry wolf," fearing the repercussions of sounding the alarm prematurely, and mistakenly ignore the hair rising on the back of their neck.

Give examples store personnel can relate to: It is 9:50 p.m. and the store closes at 10:00. Two guys have been in and out twice in the last hour, each time browsing, then leaving. They have moved their car up in the parking lot, and now one has returned and is looking at you and his watch. Clearly, their presence and purpose has unnerved you and your assistant. The last customer is about to leave. The store manager should pick up the phone at the POS station and call the local police station, not 911, but the local department. Use the register telephone instead of the back office phone for two reasons: going to the back room may encourage the inside bandit to follow you into the room; and seeing you on the phone at the counter may delay any move to the register he is contemplating.

MGR: "Hello. This is the manager at ABC store at the XYZ shopping center on Highway 123. This may be nothing, but there are two guys here that have been in and out all night. We're getting ready to close, and I think they might try something."

PD: "What do you mean?"

MGR: "You know, I'm getting the feeling they might try and rob us or something."

PD: "Have they done anything or said anything to threaten you?"

MGR: "No, not yet. But I'm afraid they're going to. I'd like it if you would send a car over here to make sure they leave."

PD: *"We can't do that unless they actually do something. Why don't you tell them you are closing, and call us back if they give you any trouble."*

MGR: "Because I'm afraid they'll stick a gun in my face if I do, and I don't think they'll let me call you back. Why don't you *hold on* while I tell them we're closing, and I'll let you know he says."

(*Pause*)

MGR: "He said 'okay,' but he doesn't seem to be moving along."

PD: "Well, I'm sorry, but we really can't dispatch a unit just because you feel uneasy about someone. We're very busy here."

MGR: "Look, officer…what's your name? I'm a woman alone here and I'm telling you I want a car sent over now! There's been seven robberies along this highway this year and I don't want to be number eight! Some police officer spoke at our tenants' meeting at Christmas and said we should call anytime we feel we need help. Well, I'm calling!"

Note: None of these details, i.e., being a woman alone, citing robbery activity, attending a mall meeting, etc., need to be true. But it is persuasive and indicative that you're not going to be easily blown off by the dispatcher. (*Citizens are permitted the luxury of panic and exaggeration!*)

MGR: "Oh shit, (the expletive is necessary to communicate your heightened anxiety) the other one just came in. Are you gonna send a car or not?"

PD: "I'm sorry, we really can't. But I will see if there's a unit nearby I can have come by, but I can't say when they will be there. We're very busy."

MGR: "Fine. You do that. I'll just pull the fire alarm here because at least the fire department comes without any bullshit!" (Again, the expletive is necessary to communicate your anger and frustration).

PD: "I wouldn't do that. Sending in a false fire alarm is against the law."

MGR: "Okay. I'll drop a match in the wastepaper basket first."

PD: "Arson is against the law too."

MGR: "Fine. Then send an ambulance over because I'm gonna have a heart attack any minute!"

PD: "Okay lady, you have made your point. I'll send over a unit. You stay on the line with me until they get there. But we can't be doing this every time you get spooked."

MGR: "I know. I've never done this before. It's just that I'd rather be safe than sorry."

It is important for your staff people to know they must be aggressive with police agencies in order to receive attention (see Chapter 16). In the past, store personnel could pull their hold-up button and summon the police without lengthy negotiation. But that practice has been discouraged by some police agencies, and businesses with lengthy false alarm histories have been heavily fined, and in some cases, have had their alarm permit suspended or pulled.

Your employees should know that the company will stand behind them in these situations, and any reasonable actions they take will not be met with criticism. Some retailers are hesitant to approach this topic in an official manner with store employees. They are concerned about raising fears and inviting costly demands for coverage, equipment, and resources they cannot afford. Perhaps a training video would soft-sell the issue and still communicate the company's care and concern for employee safety.

One approach that has been successful involves "Personal Safety Training." Invite a qualified speaker, or a police community-affairs officer, to speak at the home office about personal safety and videotape it. The subject matter is benign, offering tips on awareness and habits that reduce a person's chances of becoming a crime victim in the home, on the job, in the parking lot, in an elevator, at the ATM, etc. Then plan for the speaker to segue into commercial crime and robbery, establishing how the same awareness tips work on and off the job for retail workers. Use it as a forum to validate your procedures in the minds of employees, and to demonstrate that the policies you have enacted are sanctioned by an expert. Then distribute the video to your stores requesting they contact an appropriate company executive with their thoughts and comments. This approach sends a message that the company is concerned first for the employee and not the cash they take in, and that the organization is prepared to address sensitive matters important to the employee population.

In addition to training and awareness, management has to consider a delicate subject with labor relations implications: selective staffing. If the purpose of this chapter is to provide insight into the realities of armed robbery and strategies to prevent them, it would be remiss not to point out that robbers prefer to hit targets staffed by female employees. There are no studies to be cited that offer conclusive evidence of this assertion, but if the run-of-the-mill street hood, predisposed to robbing a convenience store, was shown three locations: one staffed by two women, one staffed by two men and one staffed with one man and one woman; and this urban predator was asked to rank the locations in order of preference for target susceptibility, the ranking should be clear. The private sector has been able to overcome gender bias in employee performance and opportunity. The criminal element, however, remains more of a throwback to simpler times: survival of the fittest and the strong over the weak. This is an unfortunate predicament for progressive companies proud of their accomplishment in equal opportunity and loathe of discrimination in the workplace. Yet the criminal, by definition, is not fair and does not play by the rules. His assets are intimidation, brutality, and force. In his estimation, these assets are more readily exploited against women than men. This notion is stereotypical, insensitive, and indefensible, but prevalent in his thinking nonetheless. It bears mention only as a finer point in the context of this discussion. A robber will assess a location from the perspective of capacity to resist. His impression of how formidable a store staff appears may be a factor in his choosing to move on to another target. Companies should confer with their human resources executives, field management, and police crime prevention experts regarding this issue, seeking input on the value of physical fitness of its staff personnel as a deterrent.

In the context of security operations, companies may be considering the use of armed car services as an alternative to sending store personnel to the bank with the deposit. The merit to an armored car program is that store employees are not exposed to the hazards of moving cash from one location to another. Your cash, and more important, your employees, never leave the building to effect your bank deposits. Your exposure to armed robbery is reduced significantly, and both your cash and management staff are better protected. Armored car service is also a deterrent to in-store robberies, as many companies provide signage with armored car logos for your entrance which admonishes would-be bandits: *"No cash kept on premises."* Many retailers believe deterrent signage regarding robberies is essential, and indications of this belief are commonplace: *"NOTICE: Manager cannot open safe. Dual key required. Time-lock safe in use. No access possible."*

Time-delay safes and dual-key locks (store personnel have one key, the armored car service the other; therefore neither can access the safe without the other), are effective in deterring the robber predisposed to casing a target before initiating a robbery. The impulsive, reckless perpetrator, high on crack and irrational, may not observe these warning signs, or may disregard them as a bluff. If indeed these techniques are employed, the store manager will be unable to satisfy the robber's demand. This inability may be read by the bandit as an unwillingness to cooperate, and the situation can deteriorate.

Before deciding on any of the security measures described, seek input from local law enforcement agencies on what criteria they would use in establishing robbery prevention measures. If your store is on a retail strip with several chain restaurants and gas stations that all employ time delay safes or armored car service, your establishment may by targeted merely by default if you do not prescribe to the prevailing wind. On the other hand, don't let a fast-talking vendor or eager field executive talk you into posting deterrent signage if you don't have the services to go along with them. This is much different than sticking a sign in your lawn at home saying you have a burglar alarm system when you really don't.

Your employees will be unable to distinguish the man with a gun in front of them as the wanton-disregard type who isn't fooled. Cognizant of the signs posted, a nervous employee may tell the robber he can't open the safe when he really can. The robber will read the hesitation, the flicker of doubt in the employee's eye as he concocts this empty resistance, and the robber will beat the crap out of him. You're not doing service to your employees by permitting them an avenue to be a hero. And don't discount the potential of the "inside man" who alerts the robber that your signage is a bluff, and the manager can open the safe. Any attempt to outwit a criminal who is clearly in control by virtue of his weapon and determination is foolhardy.

In conclusion, a combination of security equipment, sound cash management policies that are consistently applied, skillful training that heightens employee awareness and addresses their concerns, and perhaps the utilization of outside services and devices that restrict safe access, are all elements of robbery prevention.

Whether or not your company is prepared to invest heavily in robbery prevention, the outcome of such an event will always be unpredictable. If a clerk is willing to unlock the door five minutes after closing to admit a person who swears he "needs to pick up one item real fast," even though the employee knows this is against company policy, all bets are off.

Scams, Frauds, and Bouncing Checks

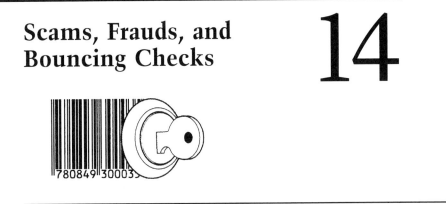

14

Con-men (and con-women), swindlers, and schemers have plied their trade in retail establishments since the beginnings of public commerce. The three essential components to profitable scams are (1) fast-talking, (2) sleight-of-hand, and (3) the substitution of items of less value for items of greater value, the victim taking the loss and the scammer reaping the profit. These characteristics can be successful independent of one another, or coordinated in a unified "attack."

The fast-talking element is designed to first engage the "mark" (the intended victim) in a disarming conversation meant to dispel any suspicion and lower any guard which may be evident by virtue of training or common sense. Once a certain comfort level is attained, the conversation escalates into a series of anecdotes, non sequiturs, and solicitations meant to befuddle the mark and create the opening for the "sting."

A good example of this approach is the "short change artist" who is able to confuse a sales clerk into returning change for a bill of large denomination and the bill itself, along with the merchandise "purchased." As difficult as such a transaction may be to imagine, the scam works like this: After an exchange of pleasantries and inquiring about the price ($3.00) of an accessory item, say a pack of batteries or a magazine at the checkout, the scammer will proffer the exact amount in cash. The clerk will revise the amount to include sales tax ($3.18), and the con artist will place pocket change (never enough) on the counter in an attempt to meet the price with tax. Upon discovering he does not have enough change, he will tender a $50 (or even $100) bill for the purchase, leaving his initial outlay exposed on the counter. When the clerk returns his $46.82 change, he will combine the two pools of money and declare he does indeed have the $3.18 in exact change after all. The puzzled clerk will try to make sense of this inane statement, while the con man pushes

$3.18 toward the clerk requesting she take the exact change and give him back his $50.

As ludicrous as such a scenario seems on the surface, it has in fact been practiced successfully with cashiers that are inattentive and easily distracted, especially those who roboticly comply with customer requests. Naturally, such a scam is easy to detect in its initial stages because it requires the purchase of a nominal item with a bill of large denomination. That in itself is often problematic for retailers, as they reflexively resist depleting their change reserve by asking the customer if they have anything smaller. If clerks learn to associate this type of scam with the natural impulse that surfaces to request a smaller bill, then they can be instinctively alerted to exercise caution in the transaction.

The more prevalent short-change scams involve the "you gave me change for ten and I gave you a twenty" routine. This used to be effective in the days retailers took customers at their word. Now, rather than blindly hand over the $10 in dispute, store management would "balance the register" in the customer's presence, explaining if the customer was correct, the register would be "over" by $10. The short change artist today is prepared for this eventuality, and is ready with a rebuttal. The scammer puts his faith in percentages. Cash drawers, for a variety of reasons, do not always balance to the penny. The till will either be (1) over, (2) short, or (3) even. The short change artist figures he has a two-out-of-three shot for some sort of imbalance which he will hang his hat on to at least plead the clerk has obviously made some mistake should the count not come out even.

A skilled debater, which many of these players are, can fluster a manager with a barrage of arguments to prove his point. If the register is over, he will claim the difference must be his money. If it is short, he will tell the manager the clerk is stealing from both the store and the customers. He will use the imbalance event to demonstrate something is not kosher, and demand that at least he be made whole while the store works out its own problems. If it is even, he may have taken the preemptive step of having a cohort plant a "marked" $20 bill in the register during a previous transaction.

The scammer will then show the manager some distinguishing feature, red dye smudged in his hand for instance, and point out to the manager that one of the $20 bills in the drawer has the same red mark on it which proves it must be his bill. Another ploy to recover a planted bill is to tell the manager he examines serial numbers as a "hobby" for playing "liar's poker" with friends. He will then recite the serial number of a $20 bill in your drawer as proof it is his. A page out of the same book is for the scammer to remember he wrote his Aunt Tilly's phone number on that bill after he called directory assistance. He will then rattle it off, and sure enough, there will be $20 in the drawer with that number scrawled on it, planted earlier by an accomplice.

Managers who are uninitiated into these practices will be caught off-guard by such a convincing argument, and absent proof of a scam, often capitulate and return the disputed amount. These losses rarely impact operating profits with any significance, and therefore generally go unreported to the police and the short change artist moves on to the next shop. The real exposure for small stores is what kind of undetected shoplifting is going on by the scammer's other accomplice in the back of the store while the clerk and manager are engaged in the passion play at the register?

The sleight-of-hand con is probably where the "artist" in con-artist came from, for it is impressive to observe but painfully expensive to experience. Practiced mostly against jewelers, a well-dressed couple will muse with the sales clerk over several items. Equipped with "flash cash" and an aristocratic demeanor, the female will sample a few pieces with the male apparently intent on purchasing her something she likes — a necklace perhaps. The target piece has been identified in previous visits, and a facsimile, worth a tenth of its value, has been secured for the scam (for true professionals, duplicating store tags for the phony is not a problem). The fake necklace has been affixed to the back of her dress collar, hanging down inside the back of the dress. The genuine article is tried on normally, around the front of the neck to be clasped in the back. As the female tries to clasp the real necklace behind her, she will turn from the counter, putting her back to the male and ask his help. The male will slip between the clerk and the female customer, and the female will drop the real necklace forward down the front of her dress, while the deft hands of the male extracts the phony necklace from its perch in the back of the dress, fastening it with a single, practiced move. The female will decide this necklace is not for her, and depending upon the con-team's assessment of the clerk, will hand back the phony and leave with real necklace safely concealed in the bosom of the female. If in the course of the scam the team believes the clerk to be a worthy adversary, they may have a contingency plan to further distract her. Prior to returning the bogus necklace, the female will spy an item she absolutely must have.

This will be far more expensive than the necklace now being shown, and the clerk will change gears and try to sell that one, failing to carefully examine the one given back. In the clerk's haste to match the female's enthusiasm for the expensive piece, the phony necklace is replaced in the showcase, and the expensive one brought out. Now the team decides this is the one for purchase, and the clerk takes that piece and a credit card which will be declined (by design) to the register. Everybody is soon disappointed when the sale does not go through, but the gentleman asks to please put it on hold while he makes a visit to the bank. Then they leave, still with the first necklace safe and sound.

Elaborate team rehearsals are not necessary for the sleight-of-hand exchange to work. A single player can accomplish it easily with a ring or watch, as jewelry for the hands is precariously close to the sleeve, and there is something up their sleeve. Although established jewelers have gemologists on staff skilled in spotting the substitutions of precious stones, department stores and other outlets for medium-priced bracelets, chains, and sport watches often do not.

A variation on this theme is a kind of "poor man's" sleight-of-hand where the substitution of worthless product for live merchandise is made outside of the store, then returned. Practitioners of this scam scour flea markets and yard sales for old "commodity" items: irons, toasters, electric shavers, radios, tools, etc. — name brand products still for sale in stores with little change in design. They then purchase the new item in the store, switch the old item into the new packaging, and return it to the store for exchange, using the receipt from the purchase. They request an "exchange" at the return desk because it is less likely that the returned item will be examined closely when the "customer" claims it is defective and merely wants a new one. The supporting receipt is often enough for the clerk to authorize the customer to go ahead and select a new one. No cash is being paid out, so scrutiny is bypassed in favor of tossing the return into the defective bin at the service desk. The scammer now owns two perfectly new items and one valid sales receipt, which he presents for a cash refund for one of the items on his next trip. At home, he has a brand new toaster he did not pay for, and the retailer has a yard sale model in the stockroom, with bread crumbs in it to boot.

Again, this type of activity does not contribute to significant losses in the big picture; in fact, many retailers will get full credit from the manufacturer even for the crummy toaster, and no loss is sustained; except for the expense of processing, shipping, inventory depletion, and the labor cost of customer service wasted on a scammer.

Bad check passers, on the other hand, do account for losses retailers need to contain. Retailers are most often victimized with two varieties of bad checks: checks stolen from the rightful owner, but not yet reported stolen; and checks deliberately written on accounts with insufficient funds to cover, known generically as "NSF" checks. Since legitimate sales transactions relieve the merchandise "purchased" with bad checks from the store's inventory, the losses are usually captured in a "bad debt" account rather than the shortage number under most accounting systems. Regardless, a comprehensive LP program should address this issue as it would any other factor which contributes to company loss.

Most retailers protect themselves from bad debt incurred from bad checks by implementing procedural guidelines that seek to verify the customer's identification. A person trying to pass stolen checks would have to obtain picture-ID of the person whose checks he is passing in order to use the checks. Unfortunately, this is not a major obstacle for the professional check passer, who obtains impressive photo-IDs with little difficulty. Production of counterfeit driver licenses, social security cards, passports, birth certificates, and other official identification is a thriving underground industry, and securing the necessary identification is considered "overhead" to the passer of stolen checks.

Stolen checks have a short "shelf-life," as they are only negotiable up to the time the owner reports them stolen and the account is closed by the bank. Therefore, the professional will move for big ticket items; electronics, jewelry, designer apparel, and gift certificates are most often cited. Retailers, as anxious as they are for customers on shopping sprees, must discipline themselves to raise an eyebrow when a "customer" makes a substantial purchase with little regard for price.

Sales people should be accustomed to customers looking for value in major purchases; they consider the price carefully, ask for promotional discounts, and want little extras thrown in at no cost. Most legitimate buyers haggle about price, and a sales person must really work to sell top-of-the-line merchandise at the full retail price. The bad check passer has no such concerns about bargain-shopping; the money is not his — he wants the best regardless of price. He does not invest the same time and care in selecting product that legitimate patrons do, and acts almost "hurried" to spend.

A customer exhibiting shopping habits like that in today's economy is an exception, and should be viewed as such by the astute sales person. Too often, hunger for volume and commission overrides prudence, and when the check is proffered for payment, everybody has their fingers crossed. The bogus ID is duly noted on the stolen check, home and work phone numbers (ultimately to be found *not in service at this time, thank you*") are exchanged, the account is entered into the POS terminal for authorization, and the dice are rolled. Heads (approval) he wins; you lose. Tails (declined) he does not win; you lose (a great sale), but wait! He might take a double-or-nothing shot with the same victim's credit card.

NSF checks are more fashionable because they carry less risk. Passing stolen checks is a felony the first time through, plus the user's woes are only beginning if it turns out the checks were stolen from a robbery or homicide victim. But the person who writes checks on his own account, an account that is still open but the balance is drained low, risks running from the bill collectors, not the police, the first few times. Some check operators use phony IDs to open legitimate checking accounts. They seed the account with an opening deposit, withdrawing the money back through ATMs. Shame on banks whose drive for new customers makes them susceptible to passing out pads of blank checks to anybody that would ask, but a few do. Armed with his "own" checks and "valid" ID, the check operator cruises the mall, stopped only by the electronic safeguards progressive retailers have had to install at their own cost to protect their interests. And even those safeguards lie dormant while much damage is conceivably done. In order for a check to be declined through the on-line authorizing services most often employed by retailers, a negative history must be accumulated on the checking account in order to trip the "circuit breakers" that result in the check being declined. For a negative history to be established, specific account characteristics are carefully monitored and updated by the authorizing agency. Prior history of bad checks will stop subsequent checks, protecting the subscribing merchants from further loss until the owner has made good on bad debt and has demonstrated consistent improvement. Then the check-writing privileges are restored until the issuer slips-up again and the account is re-flagged, and the subscribers' protection from future abuse is back in force.

The problem for retailers is the exposure they endure from the time a person starts passing checks until the time sufficient factors become evident to the authorizer to flag the account. That exposure can be mitigated by purchasing "insurance" from the agency which will reimburse retailers for losses incurred from checks authorized by the company. The fees are based on a percent of sale volume generated by all transactions where personal checks have been tendered. The percentage is similar to the arrangement with credit card institutions, and reimbursement follows only when strict identification criteria established by the authorizing agent is followed.

To recap that point, check-clearing services do exist which permit the retailer to access their negative database to determine whether there is a statistical probability the check is no good. A small percentage of the total sale is charged for this service, and the retailer can accept or decline the check at his own risk based on the agency's recommendation. A second tier of protection is also available, one which will reimburse the merchant for checks approved by the agency and yet still bounce (most likely due to insufficient factors or frequency being accumulated which creates the negative history), provided the retailer followed rigid guidelines when the check was accepted.

The cost for this protection is naturally higher than the fee for merely accessing the database and making your own call. Scanning only high-risk checks, i.e., starter checks, out-of-state checks, checks without printed address and phone, etc., will not endear you with the service provider, as they make their money not by covering your mistakes, but by collecting on the voluminous good checks you tender.

A good rule of thumb for retailers considering whether or not the savings of subscribing to such a service warrants the expense incurred from bounced checks is to review your bad debt accounts and calculate the aggregate fees vs. losses. Many retailers have realized that screening checks over a certain dollar value, all checks over $75 for instance, reduces their exposure to major losses, while sustaining their margin on smaller transactions.

Credit cards are not as risky because the authorization obtained on charge purchases suggests the account is valid and the purchase is within the prescribed credit limit. However, financial institutions can be sticklers for detail too when their card holder advises them a purchase was charged fraudulently. Since supporting identification is not required for credit card purchases, the banks want to be certain the card is "swiped" and the clerk has examined the signature carefully. Manual entry of an account number into the register, as opposed to swiping the card through the magnetic reader, gives the authorizing institution pause to consider whether the card is actually present for the signatures to be inspected; and frequent transactions without the magnetic reader results in the credit card company flagging the account.

Retailers feel the squeeze of credit card fraud most often in mail and phone order business. Since neither the customer nor the credit card are present for these transactions, the onus on the bank to honor charges, even when approval codes are obtained, is reduced since the merchant cannot fulfill its obligation to scrutinize signatures. Fraud operators access credit card account numbers from numerous sources, most notably discarded receipts. They then establish a mail drop to receive merchandise shipped from companies after placing fraudulent mail and phone orders charged to the unsuspecting cardholder's account. Postal inspectors have even documented cases where incarcerated prisoners have used pay phones in the prison, and their cell block as a "suite number," to carry on the same mail fraud operations that landed them behind bars.

Retailers understand that a certain amount of loss to fraud is inherent in the aggressive customer service approach they must pursue to sustain ambitious sales forecasts. The loss prevention efforts in this area should be instructive in the telltale signs of fraud and active in identifying organized rings that prey on the retailer's desire to serve. Onerous procedural controls that strangle customer service discretion and inhibit the merchant's ability to exploit a spendthrift customer need not be enacted. Prudent safeguards coupled with awareness training and rigorous collection efforts can reduce exposure and satisfactorily contain the costs.

Civil Recovery and Civil Demand

15

What if there was a way to exact monetary penalties from those who stole merchandise from retailers, not just recovering the value of the goods stolen, but penalties in addition to your losses. Suppose a civil fine could be imposed upon persons who so inconvenienced business people with their antisocial behavior (theft) that they would be required to compensate merchants for the trouble and expense it took to stop them.

In a perfect world, shoplifters should be compelled to pay for the security systems retailers must invest in to stem the losses incurred from shoplifting. Shoplifters having to buy the cameras shopkeepers use to catch them is akin to speeding motorists being compelled to pay for more radar guns. But, much as legislation is on the way to require tobacco companies to pay the medical costs incurred by smokers, retailers can indeed recover damages from the perpetrators of retail crime to help defray the costs of security.

State statutes cover the criminal aspects of theft in their penal codes. The state penal codes define crimes and set forth sentencing guidelines used by criminal courts to punish offenders. Civil redress for the theft of property is also offered by the provisions of civil law, historically known as "conversion" under English common law, which is the basis for much of our legal system. The principle of conversion is once a person has unlawfully taken the property of another and converted it to his own use, the guilty party is liable for the value of that property to the rightful owner.

Retailers have traditionally restricted their pursuit of compensation for losses incurred from theft to the use of restitution agreements. To avail themselves of the remedies accorded by the conversion principle, companies would have to file suit and bring a civil action against a shoplifter/dishonest employee for reparation. Given the sheer volume of theft activity, this was deemed an impractical course of action. Instead, retailers sought the more readily enforceable entitlements of voluntary restitution.

Voluntary restitution, i.e., where the defendant seeks to reimburse the victim for losses, differs in that in lieu of the litigation surrounding conversion, the two parties enter into an agreement and a voluntary assurance of restitution is proffered as settlement. The written contract serves as a promissory note of a debt to be paid, and properly executed, would be a binding agreement enforceable in civil court in the event of default. Therefore, in matters of collection of a debt owed through a restitution agreement, the retailer has a primary recourse for recovery from the conversion principle, and has a secondary course of action for recovery by way of the promissory note. Courts view this instrument as a basic tenet of commerce, and it can be counted on to rule in favor of the holder of the note.

Restitution carried with it some troubling aspects as well. Although pursuing payment was more expeditious with a promissory note (because a debtor-creditor relationship was legally established facilitating salary garnishments, negative credit reporting, etc.), the specter of extortionary conduct was raised. Overzealous agents of the retailer would sometimes compel a subject to enter into a restitution agreement in "exchange" for a promise not to seek criminal prosecution.

It may not have been a stipulated quid-pro-quo, but a general understanding was allowed to creep into the negotiation that restitution was demonstrative of cooperation, and a subject's willingness to cooperate was weighed heavily in determining the company's course of action. It is undeniable that some apprehended dishonest employees (including juveniles), intimidated by the prospect of prosecution and hoping to "catch a break," signed restitution statements at the investigator's urging; agreeing to pay back sums to the company that, if challenged, the company would be hard pressed to prove were ever stolen. Too often the dollar figure was established by investigator supposition, known (and unknown) losses, and an employee admission in what could be deemed a coercive environment.

Some of the restitution arrangements were so unreasonable that the subject naturally defaulted, and when the retailer moved to collect, the "voluntary" aspect of the agreement came into question. On occasion, a subject was able to prove to the court that the agreement was entered into under duress, and the court vacated the contract. Absent a binding agreement, the subject was then free to file against the retailer for damages incurred by virtue of the retailer's "malicious" pursuit of collection, and the intentional infliction of emotional distress.

Clearly, retailers had to regulate the practice of restitution, and over time, the rigorous pursuit of those in default waned. Many companies adopted an informal policy: "if he pays great, if he doesn't, what can you do?" Going to court for remedy under the conversion principle was not cost effective, and exacting sanctions for defaulting on the promissory note was becoming a minefield of its own.

A new approach was needed, and relief slowly emerged from the state legislatures in the early 1980s. Beginning in the state of Oregon, the first of the Civil Recovery Statutes was passed and subsequently affirmed by the state Supreme Court. Other states followed suit, and presently a majority of states have enacted statutes exclusively for the retail community, enabling merchants to recover a penalty over and above the valued amounts of goods stolen. This process, known as civil demand, establishes a schedule of civil "fines" (amounts do vary jurisdiction to jurisdiction) which are imposed by statutory provision.

The reader should be clear of the distinction between civil recovery and civil demand. Civil recovery is an embellishment to the conversion principle and it relates solely to crime against retailers. It permits retailers to recover the value of losses attributed to thefts by an individual and contains the provisions to impose a monetary penalty for the criminal act. This is more than an allowance to merely recover losses, because the civil demand component in effect awards cash damages to the merchant as a compound sanction for the criminal act.

The schedule of damages, or civil penalties, vary from state-to-state, some establishing minimums by the dollar value stolen, some by the frequency of the offenses committed against the retailer, and others a flat rate regardless of circumstances. Some allow discretion by the retailer, establishing a scale of fines that the retailer can petition for in a cause brought against the shoplifter/dishonest employee. In some jurisdictions, juveniles are exempt; in others, the parent or legal guardian is liable. In most, but not all, civil recovery can be pursued absent the criminal prosecution of the subject.

In order to collect civil penalties, the retailer needs to notify the subject of the merchant's intention to seek compensation under the state's civil recovery statutes. A notice is sent to the subject citing the applicable statute, and the amounts sought for both the value of product stolen and the prescribed cash penalty. The subject is advised to submit payment upon receipt of the notice, or contact the retailer to work out a payment schedule. No promissory note or voluntary spirit is needed as payment is required by statutory authority.

Failure to respond generates a second notice, with the admonitions of collection agencies, civil suit, interest, and court costs referenced. Should the subject continue to ignore the correspondence, the retailer may refer the matter for collection or institute a civil case.

As often happens with the onset of statutory regulation, a cottage industry has sprung up to service the retailers in their quest for civil recovery and civil demand. Service companies now provide their retail clients with a civil recovery program, an agreement to act as an agent of the retailer and manage your civil recovery affairs in exchange for a percentage of the amount recovered.

The vendor will write the letters, handle the replies, negotiate the settlements, and file civil suits on your behalf to collect what is due the client. There is no cost to the retailer, as literally all that is required is to forward your criminal cases to the service provider, and then sit back and collect regular checks (less the agency percentage) from those who stole your merchandise. The merchant does not have to appear in court (the agency will), the defendant (not the plaintiff) is responsible for court costs, and the considerations of coercion and duress associated with restitution agreements are no longer a factor.

But, since we all know that there is no free lunch, there are some risks to be mindful of. The retailer must be selective in choosing a vendor representative to act as a lawful agent. Contracting an established company with a reputation for integrity and quality control is essential because you need to make sure the cases you submit are bona fide candidates under the applicable statute. The vendor should supply some in-house expertise, preferably legal counsel on staff, to establish criteria and screen your cases for suitability (i.e., that the subject is an admitted and/or convicted shoplifter or dishonest employee, with the supporting documentation available to prove culpability of a criminal act). A national company with definitive research on multiple jurisdictions and a proven track record for results without client litigation would be the optimum choice.

Some retailers find it administratively feasible to manage their own civil recovery program. Using the resources of corporate counsel, and a combination of clerical support, a couple of law school interns, support from the collection department, and strict procedures governing the preparation of case files obtained from security, they operate an expense center with a tidy profit margin, saving the payout which would be allocated to an agency.

Much of the revenue (after expenses) is reinvested in loss prevention equipment, financing the capital expenditures for closed circuit television, EAS systems, and providing offsets to security payroll. It is a lot like the concept behind the Iran-Contra affair. except it is legal.

Violence in the Workplace

16

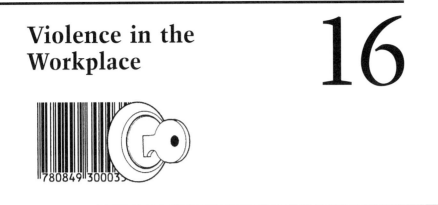

There used to be a time when resolving disputes in the workplace took one of three forms: resignation (putting up with it), negotiation (working it out), or arbitration (third party settlement). In more recent times, there exists a perception that a fourth alternative has made the list: violence. It has become apparent that people are less reluctant to resort to violence as a remedy to a real or perceived wrong than at any time since the frontier justice days of the old west.

Despite government statistics that cite little appreciable change in reported incidents of violence in the workplace, the perception among workers is that violence is on the rise. Companies should develop programs that address this issue not only for the peace of mind of its employees, but for the fact that even a single incident can have a disastrous effect on business as well.

The consequences from a humanitarian point of view are tragic; no employer would downplay its significance. But to further motivate employers to recognize the urgency of this issue, it may be helpful to point out some of the debilitating economic effects. An incident of workplace violence disrupts the status quo and has a negative impact on productivity. It is usually associated with damage to property, leads inevitably to litigation, and effects worker compensation policies. It lowers morale, leads to increased turnover, and can cause lasting damage to the psyche of remaining workers. The associated adverse publicity can cast the company in a poor light, driving customers away for good. Dealing with this issue in a straightforward, decisive manner therefore serves the common good.

A work force is comprised of a cross section of society. Within that society are people who are ever more resorting to violence to solve their interpersonal difficulties. It follows, then, that without a careful screening mechanism, those persons can find their way into your employee population.

The recent phenomenon of victimization, i.e., a perceived entitlement to react as one sees fit in response to a wrong inflicted by another, has desensitized both the aggressor, and to some extent society as a whole, to the recourse of violence as a remedy. This victim-aggressor metamorphosis is a a cultural anomaly, distinct from the criminal-type for whom violence is way of life. A "prompting" takes place that triggers a violent episode, usually the culmination to a slow-burn built up over time. For employers, the realization that the catalyst for such an explosion on the job can often be the work environment itself has been slow in coming.

Job-related stress is a fact of life in the competitive, performance-driven, streamlined business world that is "Corporate America." Many workers have adapted, excelled, and reached new heights in professional achievement. Others have been left behind, burned-out, disgruntled, and coping with failure for the first time. The need to place blame often focuses on the company.

Most people are able to overcome any lingering resentment rationally, and with support of family, friends, even co-workers, recover from setbacks and adjust satisfactorily to changes in the workplace. Others, however, ill-equipped to cope due to a fragile self-image and perhaps dormant personality disorders, harbor deep grudges and deteriorate into a state of clinical depression and paranoia. These individuals often indulge in fantasy, either fanciful delusions of self-importance and success, or malevolent musings of retribution. When a person becomes unable to distinguish reality from fantasy, the potential for antisocial behavior increases, and is often manifested at the work place. The antisocial behavior can be passive, discernible by the deliberate drop-off in productivity, absenteeism, tardiness, and rumor-mongering. It can be more active, with the employee feigning an injury to collect benefits, engaging in sabotage of company equipment or systems, or allowing the employee to rationalize theft from the employer. In extreme cases, the behavior can turn violent.

Retailers have a double-dose exposure to violence in the workplace to contend with. The primary exposures to criminal violence are indigenous to the business: interaction with the public creates an open-door policy where anybody is entitled to enter the workplace. Employees work in small numbers, sometimes alone, in high crime areas, often at night. They exchange money with the public in a visible way, and are perceived by the criminal element in the role of safeguarding desirable products. That retail employees stand between hardened criminals and the valuables they covet escalates the incidents of violence in the retail workplace.

Remember, violent incidents do not necessarily have to take the form of machine-gunned tellers so often dramatized in the media. The slaps, punches, kicks, pushing, shoving, cursing, spittle, threats, intimidation, and general battery endured everyday by retail employees preventing crimes in stores are all assaults upon their persons and psyches. Tumultuous encounters with customers make their heart race, their muscles tense, the corotid artery pulsate, and their body shake. It is hardly as traumatic as the workplace shoot-outs that make the news, but it has a cumulative effect on how they perceive their safety on the job.

Couple this primary exposure with the secondary one of violence at the hands of co-workers, and it is understandable why the retail industry ranks right up there with cab drivers and cops for job related homicides and assaults. Since other sections of this book discuss retail crime and preventive measures retailers should implement to protect both employees and merchandise from external factors, this chapter will focus on the trends and programs that address the concerns of violence emanating internally, from within the employee population.

Insufficient data (thankfully due to the scarcity of incidents) exists to provide a concrete formula for predicting a violent episode or designating a surefire profile of persons most likely to engage in violence on the job. There has been, however, enough experience garnered to discuss tendencies to which antisocial behavior, including violence, can be attributed. By studying the common denominators of workplace violence, it is possible to identify and predict the abnormal behavior patterns that are often characterized in the reported incidents. People who derive an unhealthy amount of self-identity from their jobs are apt to feel most threatened by any change to the status quo in the workplace. Those whose measurement of self-worth is inextricably tied to their occupation tend to view modifications to the corporate structure with skepticism, even alarm, and find re-organizations especially unsettling. Apprehension that the routine will be disrupted, anxiety over the ability to perform or measure up, and edginess over the uncertainty of the future sets in. Realize that we are not talking about a particularly well-balanced individual to begin with. But the familiarity, comfort, and stability of a job with moderate demands provided refuge, often masking the underlying inadequacies and inability to cope that characterize a defective personality.

The job is the saving grace for many of these individuals that allows them to lead a normal existence. Once that safe haven is threatened, by mergers, downsizing, or layoffs, trepidation sets in, and the fragile control mechanisms that were only functionally effective in the best of times, are now over-matched. Consider for a moment the typical plant closing scenario which accompanies many acquisitions, and imagine the impact this has on a psychologically-troubled warehouse worker who is soon to get the news his job will be eliminated. To help illustrate the characteristics of what can at best be described as an emerging profile, we will embrace every stereotype in order to touch upon the known tendencies contributing to violence in the workplace.

Our employee is male, in his late 30s, a classic underachiever who came to work ten years ago as a merchandise handler in the warehouse. He got a high school GED while in the Navy for two years. He comes to work, does his job, and goes home. He lives alone; his frugal lifestyle enables him to support himself with some discretionary income, and he lives what would best be described as a mundane existence. He is not married, but may have been once. He seldom dates, and has hobbies or interests that do not require the participation of others. He gets along at work, but rarely takes part in company-sponsored events, nor does he socialize regularly with other employees off the job. The guy could be a regular Joe, or a time bomb. Up until now, there has been no way to tell and no cause for concern. But a significant change that will forever alter his status quo is about to take place.

On Monday, the corporate "suits" arrived at the warehouse and announced that ABC Company has been acquired by the XYZ Corporation. This event is hailed as a glorious day for ABC, as together with XYZ, their combined market share will dominate the industry. No one need be concerned about their job; there is plenty of work for everybody, and all ABC workers will get to share in the wonderful benefits program of the XYZ Corporation. The meeting concludes with the assurances from the suits that better days are ahead, and everybody should go about their duties with business as usual.

Within three months, several members of ABC's senior management group have resigned to seek other opportunities. Young bucks from the XYZ Corporation have assumed their positions and introduced many changes in the medical, dental, retirement, and profit-sharing plans, which are all better than ABC offered, but intangible to the ABC folks until they meet their enrollment eligibility requirements. Accrued vacation has been converted to a new formula, and job reviews with their accompanying merit raises have been pushed back to conform with the XYZ performance appraisal cycle.

Corporate culture has begun to encroach upon the old ways, with dress codes, productivity schedules, shift work, and the incessant training in new procedures and new systems that has been burdensome and confusing. In a heated discussion behind closed doors with the new VP of Operations, the distribution director walked out; rumored to have been fired, but later acknowledged to have resigned. The new director has held so many meetings with the management staff in the office that workers have slacked off noticeably, and complaints from stores for replenishment product has created only crises and foul-ups.

In true trickle-down fashion, "Regular Joe" has not been spared in these developments. His immediate supervisor is under the gun, and the pressure to meet production schedules is intense. It did not seem bad when Joe got a "promotion" to work leader, but it was on the midnight shift and he has never quite adjusted to the new routine. He would have gone to the doctor for the colitis that flared up from poor diet and jittery nerves, but his $10 co-pay has been replaced by a $250 deductible, and he did not bother.

He has tried to fit in and to go with the flow. He has made suggestions that were ignored, and has gotten yelled at for things that were not his fault. He has not made any waves, and he even canceled the annual hunting trip he has gone on faithfully with a buddy because he could not get the time off; but it would have been hard to go anyway with the freeze on overtime. As if his problems were not bad enough, the rumors started. It seems the XYZ Corporation operates another warehouse in another state. There's talk they might close the ABC facility and merge the two distribution operations out there. If that were to happen, everybody would get laid off. The big boss dismisses such talk, saying only that if people work hard and do their jobs, management would have no reason to close the warehouse. But things are not going well. People who leave are not being replaced, broken conveyors and heavy equipment need servicing, and the stores are still complaining. The rumors continue with talk of people "being screwed." Supervisors he trusted are leaving, replaced by "company men" who do not seem to care about the workers. Upper management continues to deny a closing, but "word on the street" is that everybody should start looking. The entire staff is scheduled to attend big personnel meetings next week. There is a rumor that they are going to announce severance packages for everybody who stays till the end of the year.

As melodramatic as this presentation is, it does allow us to put into context many of the characteristics which lead to the antisocial behavior that is ultimately manifested in violence in the workplace. Keep in mind that the overwhelming number of "Joes" who encounter this bump along the road of life move on to another job in another place with little disruption to their lives. It is the exception that cannot cope, the individual with personality deficiencies and a lifetime of accumulated abuse, rejection, and failure that snaps. They blend in, perhaps, in the good times but surface with adversity.

The first operative that works on an employee predisposed to violence is the despair brought about by the futility of their position. They feel powerless to control the events that are shaping their lives, and channel that resentment toward those whom they perceive to have power over them.

The next stage is criticism — the need to commiserate and complain about the changes taking place in the workplace; changes in the routine, the new procedures, the training, the benefit plans, the new bosses. Being natural loners who internalize much of the conflict in their lives, withdrawing into a sullen, brooding demeanor is preferable to vocal objection as a means to express their dissatisfaction.

Another trait that eventually sets in, paranoia, results from the isolation brought about by their incommunicative behavior, and the conjured perception that they are being cheated out of their birthright: the status quo. The paranoid delusions are fed by misinterpretations of events on the job as being directed squarely at the employee, that management has conspired to make his life miserable. Modifications to benefits, vacation, compensation, and job description that may arise from the assimilation of one corporate culture into another, are construed to be part of management's diabolical plot to get him. In short, he takes it personal(ly). When promises and commitments made by management fall short of his inflated expectations, the paranoia operates to make him distrustful, regarding management (authority) with suspicion and disdain.

The last ingredient to the formula for violence is the seething hostility that goes unchecked as company officials, oftentimes caught up in their own troubles, become desensitized to the problem cases in their quest to "treat everyone fairly" in a downsizing operation. Caught in the predicament of (1) saving their own jobs, and (2) trying to salvage positions for favored employees, and (3) trying to do both while appearing to do neither, supervisors can become oblivious to telltale signs of stress in others that precipitates a violent event. The duplicity sometimes practiced to get the job done while placating estranged workers is perceived as deception, further distancing the disgruntled employee from participating in any of the outplacement and counseling services which may be offered.

Layoffs and plant closings represent the more obvious circumstances that can prompt a violent event. Oddly enough, the behavior does not manifest itself immediately. More often than not, persons return to the workplace in the agitated state to commit violence after a period of displacement from the work force. In the months following separation, the full impact of the disassociation with the company is realized, along with the deeper isolation, financial reverses, and feelings of desertion and bitterness that accompany job loss. It is while influenced by these factors that the subject is overwhelmed, and a rampage ensues.

Employers must also contend with random outbreaks of violence that occur where no disruption in the work environment is underway or even contemplated. These result from grudges between employees caused by obvious factors such as spurned love interest, uncollected debt, or racial intolerance;

or as the culmination of more subtle, but persistently offensive behavior, such as teasing, pranks, and ridicule perpetrated by one employee on another. Unstable people, ill-equipped to neutralize harassment on the job through conventional means, can lash out violently as a last resort.

Another invitation to workplace violence occurs when the domestic problems in an employee's life spill over into the job, unbeknownst to the employer. Out of nowhere, the psychopathic husband of Sally Nobody in the typing pool marches into the office with an AK-47 convinced she is sleeping with the boss and kills them both. It is a stunning incident which ripples through the whole organization. It was not expected, and unless strict access control to the workplace is in effect, it is virtually unpreventable unless there was a way for Sally to communicate her domestic trouble to responsible executives with whom she could share her concerns. At home, this event may have been predictable, with her husband making threats that revealed his paranoid delusions concerning her relationship with the her boss.

Employees who are in abusive relationships, or have experienced some of the elements involved with stalking, must have a means to confide their fears in trained company representatives who can take steps to reduce the exposure to external retribution. Extreme as these examples are, the company must conform their security policies and hiring practices to plan for all contingencies. Employers are restricted in many ways from conducting the kind of thorough preemployment screening that may identify applicants as high risk. Medical histories, disability claims, and workers compensation records are not readily available for review. Therefore, it is inevitable that some persons with a propensity for violence can slip through, especially in the high turnover retail environment. It is more likely that the front-line supervisor will afford the retail company its best chance to identify a problem case. Supervisors need to be trained to read the warning signs that may indicate a worker is building toward an outburst. Tolerating the quirks and idiosyncrasies of workers on the job was vogue for a while, with self-expression being touted as a positive factor in productivity. But odd behavior may be more than a source of quiet bemusement for supervisors. The key for managers is to establish a relationship that lets the supervisor get close enough to workers so that they can notice unusual changes in normal behavior.

Without a frame of reference for supervisors to determine what is normal behavior for specific employees, they are unable to observe the distinct and unexplained changes that take place when a worker is having difficulty managing stress. Probably the first characteristic that comes to the supervisor's attention is the worker's poor interpersonal relations with co-workers. This is sometimes pointed out to the manager by other workers, and complaints about co-worker behavior should not be dismissed without serious inquiry. The more subtle signs, absenteeism, fallen productivity, and a tendency to blame others for job-related problems, can come to light more easily once the manager is alerted to the employee's interpersonal difficulties.

These developments may lead to a confrontation between the supervisor and the employee. Certainly conduct detrimental to the operation needs to be formally addressed, especially if an employee's behavior is disruptive or threatening to other employees. But the confrontation must be managed carefully by the supervisor, so as not to be the catalyst for a violent episode. In the event mediation has been ineffective and the termination of this worker is deemed necessary, the supervisor should be prepared to take some precautionary steps prior to the exit interview.

The termination should take place at the close of the last working day. Security personnel should be alerted beforehand, and at least "be in the wings," if not present. The office and desk area should be cleared of any objects that could be thrown around or grabbed and used as a weapon. If he wants to smash your lamp, he will; but put the scissors away.

As tactfully as possible, the manager should release the employee, minimizing the involvement of others in the decision while emphasizing the employee was neither happy nor productive in his job, and that he is better suited to a work environment that matches better to his skills. In short, it should be made clear that the employee will be better off elsewhere, away from the stress and demands of this situation.

Be wary in the exit interview of body language and indications associated with an outburst, the heavy breathing, clenched fists and gritted teeth. Try to arrange the seating positions so that the employee does not feel boxed-in, but make sure you can get to the door or summon help. Prepare in advance all separation paperwork, but do not press that he complete every document if you sense the tension rising. Try to ensure that no legitimate reason remains for him to return to the job site. An escort to his locker or desk, and then from the building is advised. Note, too, the description and tag number of his vehicle. Advise security personnel or the receptionist that this individual is to be restricted from the building, and discreetly notify persons involved in the termination, especially co-workers who may have come forward with complaints, that it has been effected.

Pre-employment screening, especially contact with previous employers and references, is a logical first step in reducing exposure. Drug testing may also be a viable tool in weeding out substance abusers who often surface in the profile for employee violence. You may also learn of an applicant's reliance on prescription medication in the drug testing process, and become alerted to candidates being treated for depression or other behavioral deficiency. These steps may help insulate a company from liability for negligent hiring should an incident result that could have been prevented by diligent applicant screening.

Plant security should incorporate uniformed guards who control access and can respond to emergencies in the work area. Panic buttons in the offices of key executives and the reception areas, to summon assistance in the event of an incident, should be available. A plan to deal with an employee's report of stalking, by an old boyfriend, a customer, or a present/former employee with an unhealthy affinity for her, should be at the ready. Logical steps to be taken in this event involve "invisibilizing" the employee: screening her calls, changing her extension, removing her name from the directory, varying her schedule, and providing escorts to and from the parking lot. The company should insist and assist the employee in notifying the police of any threats or unwanted coercive advances that they may receive. If management demonstrates they have a plan, more employees will be encouraged to come forward and report unusual activity or events. Workers will not feel embarrassed to share personal information with the employer when they believe the matter will be handled in a confidential, professional manner.

Companies must also insure that they have an unequivocal policy in place regarding firearms. No employee should be permitted to bring a gun or other lethal weapon into the building. This regulation should be clearly stated in the employee handbook, and prospective employees should be questioned about their willingness to comply with the rule.

As badly as the security industry would want to provide a profile of individuals associated with violence in the workplace for consumption in the private sector, such data is inconclusive aside from the general characteristics alluded to in this chapter. They are summarized below:

- Short tempered with a history of violent behavior
- Difficulty sustaining interpersonal relationships; a loner
- Tends to purposely intimidate others
- Considered a troublemaker; history of grievances
- Disgruntled with the job (or life in general)
- Uncomfortable with constructive criticism; overly defensive
- Familiarity/affinity for guns, weapons
- Drug or alcohol abuse likely
- Demonstrated psychological problems, e.g., depression, paranoia

Employers need to be particularly mindful of developments on the job that elevate stress levels, especially layoffs and downsizing, and threaten the status quo among persons whose self-image is crucially associated with their job. The damage done to this person in a plant closing is far more reaching than would be generally anticipated for the employee population at large.

The last lesson that can be learned from this discussion is the most telling of all. More often than not, a person who commits violence in the workplace has stated they would resort to violence on prior occasions. Supervisors must be sensitized to take threats seriously, and not dismiss verbal outbursts which promise bodily harm as "blowing off steam" or venting. A person who claims they will "get even," or intimates that "somebody is going to pay," especially those who specify individuals such as "the boss," have been known to carry out those threats in very short order. Management intervention in these instances should be swift and certain.

Section **IV**

Security Operations

Overview

This section provides the reader with the nuts-and-bolts for the procedural development of security policies. Security policies differ from those of loss prevention as they tend to focus more on the quasi-police function inherent in the business of asset protection.

It is important to point out that some of the security subjects explained in this section result from instances where the methods to prevent losses were unsuccessful, and focus more on the aftermath of failed prevention: apprehension and prosecution, which are areas of the business retailers should be involved in as a last resort.

These topics involve areas of expertise that are unique to security professionals, and as such, represent potential for exposure to liability when practiced by laypersons. Where no such resident expert exists in-house, companies should seek guidance from the law enforcement and legal communities when developing procedural guidelines for use in the field.

Retail security consultants, trained in the nuances of criminal law application in the private sector, would also be a resource worthy of consideration. In addition to procedural development, they can offer training for your personnel in the field, which is valuable certification should this issue come into question in court proceedings.

Other security-related contingencies a company must be prepared to address include sabotage, extortion, bomb threats, etc., and these are explained in the context of procedural response through prompt notification from the field, and the intervention of the company's crisis management team.

Incident Reports

17

Documentation of loss prevention events has long been a mainstay of shortage program management. A company's ability to respond properly to conditions in the field are predicated upon timely information communicated in a concise format. Whether individual incidents are reviewed for immediate action, or situations of a particular category are analyzed for a comprehensive response, a consistent reporting format is necessary for complete information to reach the appropriate policy makers.

Loss prevention incidents encompass a myriad of events that need to be broken down for the absorption of specialized departments in a retail business. Disseminating this information along the corporate ladder requires a system that classifies incidents by type, then routes them to the effected internal departments tasked with managing them.

Ineffective incident reporting has been at the crux of many situations that could have been handled better by the company had they been afforded the opportunity to do so at an earlier juncture. For instance, the customer accident that went unreported because the customer seemed uninjured later surfaces as a six-figure negligence action. Timely notification and intervention by management may have been able to mediate this situation to a more favorable outcome. This chapter will help retailers design and implement an incident reporting structure that can effectively keep upper management abreast of field activity. Two formats will be offered: the conventional written report copied to the home office, and an automated on-line database using a modification to the POS.

Incidents relevant to the LP program include mostly events that describe shortage-related issues: theft of merchandise, apprehension of shoplifters, dismissal of dishonest employees, and details of criminal activity such as robbery, burglary, and fraud. As such, the incident report must be designed to answer the basic investigatory questions of who, what, when, where, (how and why are helpful, if known). All events that involve contact with the police warrant the generation of an incident report, even if no arrest is made. Any time a report to the police is made concerning the theft of merchandise, incidents involving bad checks or stolen credit cards, damage to the building, after hour alarm response, etc., requires an internal incident report to document the notification and record the corresponding police department report number referencing the incident.

For the purposes of reporting missing merchandise, it is important to separate verifiable incidents from discovered instances of known shortage. If the shortage is the result of an event where a theft occurred, and store management can identify the circumstances of that event, an incident report should be completed. For example:

Complete Heading: Date, Time, Store, Reported by, etc.

Two males entered the store and grabbed an arm load of jackets from the rack and ran outside. They got into a waiting car, dark colored sedan, tag number 45- --G, and sped off. The approximate loss is seven pieces of SKU 00112233, valued at $125 each. Police notified, complaint number 9999, officer Jones. Alerted Stores 05 and 06 of descriptions as follows:

This represents a verifiable incident of theft, one that needs to be documented in the event that (1) the Police someday catch these two pulling a similar heist and wish to tie them to this crime, (2) the buying line/inventory control wishes to replenish the items stolen, or (3) LP can measure the external theft activity of verifiable losses to shoplifting in relation to the shortage results at this location.

Contrast this incident to a discovered instance of presumed theft, and it becomes clear why the two should be reported separately:

Complete Heading: Store, Date, Time, Reported by, etc.

"While cleaning out the racks, I found six hangers and six EAS tags hidden in the center of the carousel."

While this event is indicative of shoplifting activity, and therefore noteworthy, it cannot provide the circumstances of the theft, i.e., date and time, suspects, product taken, etc., which is useful to police, inventory control, and LP in formulating a response to the event. Nonetheless, discovered instances of presumed theft should be tallied at the store level, and perhaps summarized weekly or monthly for review by the regional manager and LP. Another commonplace shortage issue which finds its way into incident reports, but should be recorded separately, are instances of short-shipments.

Receiving discrepancies need to be documented for internal follow-up, but the incident report is not the best vehicle for this program. A discrepancy report for dissemination among inventory control, distribution, and LP would better facilitate the remedy to such an event, and would help identify its cause as clerical error or theft at the warehouse.

Separating these events into categories, i.e., incidents of known theft, instances of presumed theft, and documented shipping discrepancies, allows LP to evaluate three sources of information when considering the shortage results over an inventory period.This permits the shortage program for a particular location to be fine-tuned over the next inventory period allocating resources proportionate to the prevailing shortage factors. If the incident reports document few shoplifting apprehensions in relation to comparable stores with comparable performance, but the instances of presumed theft far exceed the norm, then it can be concluded that undetected shoplifting is accounting for much of the disparity. The initial focus for improvement should center on employee awareness and training to better prevent the shoplifting activity that is evident, but undetected; or perhaps the allocation of additional resources, i.e., staffing, EAS, and CCTV would have a favorable impact.

LP professionals have often determined inflated reports of missing merchandise (i.e., the frequent discovery of empty packaging, defeated EAS tags, etc.), absent a sufficient number of incident reports detailing known activity, to be indicative of internal dishonesty, i.e., employees generating phantom theft reports to offset the discovery of product lost to their criminal activity.

The point is, without a system to manage the information from the field, management has few clues to draw upon to effect corrective action. No retailer wants to assume an investment in EAS or cameras may help the situation based on a store manager's assessment that *"we get a lot of shoplifting here".* Accountability requires that such a case be proven, and that justification be presented explaining why traditional means, successful elsewhere in the organization, are ineffective at this location. A history of incidents that support this contention lend credence to both the conclusions drawn, and the remedial steps initiated to improve performance.

In addition to the benefits that incident reports provide in shaping LP strategy, they must also serve to document the company's perspective of events that may lead to future litigation. This is especially true in cases where customers have been detained or prosecuted for shoplifting. Since criminal cases are dispositioned in an irregular manner, an incident report serves as the cover sheet for a case file which includes a summary of the event, witness statements, and other documentation deemed evidentiary to the case. All too often, retailers have otherwise sound cases dismissed in court because the proper documentation is not available by the time the matter is heard. Reconstructing the event, who saw what, is difficult after the fact no matter how unforgettable the matter seemed at the time. Employee turnover results in losing contact with key witnesses over time, and incomplete case files produce few convictions.

An incident report involving an apprehension should be forwarded to the home office where a duplicate file can be opened and remain active until the case is dispositioned. The record keeper can be tasked with obtaining copies of all supporting statements and communication with the courts.

Having written reports produced in a format which lends itself to data entry can computerize apprehension activity for future analysis, and will expedite the retrieval and status updates on matters as they come to court. Collating pertinent information on shoplifters enables a company to build profiles of shoplifters most often apprehended in stores, the kinds of merchandise most often found in the possession of shoplifters, and patterns by day of week and time of day. Such information may point out exposures inherent in the way goods are displayed or deficiencies in staffing schedules.

Database entry of apprehensions can permit cross-referencing with other indices of adverse information, such as frequent refunders or bad check operators known to the company. Incident reports should also be the mechanism for reporting customer accidents, employee injuries, or other situations which need to come to the attention of the company's insurance carrier. Many companies have supplemented the written report of these incidents with a telephone hotline which insures management of rapid notification. However, the permanent record — the case file documenting the circumstances, persons involved, and action taken — all begins with the incident report. These events should be available for data entry as well, as instances of general liability can have a pattern of their own to highlight commonalties of customer or worker injury for management to address in safety training.

Designing the format for written incident reports should involve input from your legal and insurance representatives, as certain phraseology has preferred connotations for the practitioners of general liability cases. Requirements for supporting documentation, witness statements, photos, training policies, etc., should be clearly defined in the procedural guidelines for incident reporting.

One innovation which may be useful in improving both the quality and timeliness of incident report information would be to design the report to interface with the POS system. Instead of incident report forms, which must be copied, disseminated, and filed centrally, a software enhancement to the POS system could permit electronic communication of incidents to the addressed end-users at the home office.

A generic form could be reproduced on the POS screen and accessed by way of select function. Within that function, alternate categories could be displayed with modifications made to the form that accommodates specific incidents. Information is entered using the keyboard, and directed to the electronic address of the appropriate departments. An illustration of such a program follows:

F7   Enter →   Incident Report

Alt 1 Enter →   Customer Accident
                 Distribution: regional office, legal, insurance carrier

Alt 2 Enter →   Employee Injury
                 Distribution: regional office, human resources

Alt 3 Enter →   Shoplifter Apprehension
                 Distribution: loss prevention

Alt 4 Enter →   Known Theft
                 Distribution: loss prevention, inventory control

Alt 5 Enter →   Shipping Discrepancy
                 Distribution: warehouse, inventory control, loss prevention

Alt 6 Enter →   Unusual Event
                 Enter distribution:

Alt 7 Enter →   Other
                 Enter distribution

The sophistication with which such information is communicated is incidental to the necessity that it be communicated. Companies with the resources to automate such a process enhance their controls when they do so, and make the process less cumbersome. But no company can afford to neglect this process without creating a needless exposure to the bottom line.

Apprehension Criteria  18

Store management personnel, the foremost apprehendors of bad guys in a retail environment that is not serviced by on-site security employees, all seem to ask the same question: *"when is it okay to arrest somebody?"*

In practice, a merchant does not really arrest anyone; they detain a subject until the police arrive (technically, a citizen's arrest), and it is the responding police officer who actually effects the formal arrest based on the complaint of the merchant. But since it is the lawful agent of the retailer who initiates the process, unambiguous guidelines should be known to all store personnel who potentially would be called upon to make a lawful detention of another person.

The lawful detention is an act which inhibits the rights of another person to go, either by word or deed. Any citizen who witnesses a criminal act committed by another has the right to lawfully detain the person committing the offense. Retail store personnel generally find themselves in the position to make lawful detentions relating to the crime of larceny and its various forms. Larceny is the taking of another's property without permission, with the intent of depriving the rightful owner of its use and value. There are varying degrees of larceny, based predominantly on the value of the item(s) taken.

Different jurisdictions establish a fixed dollar-limit separating the degrees of larceny between petty larceny, a misdemeanor offense, and grand larceny, a felony offense. The difference is significant for the person charged, as the judicial process is far more exacting in felony cases. Larceny cases include most shoplifting events, but the circumstances of the theft could compound the crime, escalating the severity of the charges.

For instance, a larceny committed with the use or threat of force becomes a robbery; a larceny committed in conjunction with unlawful entry becomes a burglary; a larceny involving a fraudulent instrument (stolen credit card, bad check), can fall under the crimes of fraud; and systematic theft by employees may be governed under the statutes of embezzlement.

For the purposes of this chapter, and to answer the most sought after questions of when and how to apprehend someone, we will stay mainly with the shoplifting situations most often encountered by store management personnel. To preface this discussion, we should point out that apprehensions are the least favorable outcome to a shoplifting scenario because they place employees in harm's way and they call upon them to take actions for which they are generally unprepared, at least from the point of view of job description and formal training. Apprehensions also represent an occasion of failed prevention, *i.e.,* some element of your loss prevention efforts was ineffective; a person believed they could steal your merchandise and get away with it. How did that person make that assessment?

But since we acknowledge prevention is not preclusion, a determined thief will test the training and resolve of store personnel to safeguard merchandise by shoplifting. When that act is detected by a lawful agent of the merchant, a lawful detention should follow. The retailer has to be certain that their store representative is thoroughly aware of the elements of the crime of larceny. A police officer may make arrests based on "probable cause" and even "information furnished by another." The citizen's arrest has little latitude in this regard. A citizen must observe the criminal act in order to initiate a lawful detention.

To be rightfully accused and lawfully detained for shoplifting, a person must engage in conduct consistent with demonstrating both the intent and action of depriving the owner of his property. A person must be deemed to have knowingly and willfully taken the property of another. In a retail environment, leaving the store with merchandise for which one has not paid is consistent with the act of shoplifting; but other conduct, suggesting intent, would have to be observed by the merchant in order to prove the crime of larceny. For instance, a woman with a stroller leaves a discount store after buying several items. Store employees confront her in the parking lot and produce a pack of batteries from the foot of the stroller for which no money was paid. Was the item shoplifted, or did it inadvertently slip from the rack at checkout into the stroller? Without observing how the batteries got into the stroller, the store representatives cannot conclude with certainty the item was stolen because the element of intent cannot be truthfully attested to. Does the store have every right to stop the woman and inquire about the matter? Absolutely. Can they request the customer purchase the item or surrender it? Yes. Are they within their rights to call the police and have the woman arrested? Probably. Should they do that? Probably not.

A man enters the checkout at the supermarket and empties the contents of his basket onto the conveyor. The clerk rings up the sale and bags the items, which are placed into the customer's cart which he wheels out to the parking lot. The man is then confronted by store employees who point out a case of beer on the bottom rack of the cart which was not placed on the conveyor for purchase. Was the beer shoplifted or overlooked? It has certainly left the store without payment, and the owner would have been deprived of its use and value, but is it prudent to summon the police and press criminal charges, or should the customer be offered an opportunity to pay for the merchandise? The answer may be apparent to you, but how apparent do you make it your employees?

Each of these examples points out the reason why the law stipulates a person must demonstrate the intent to steal property before such an offense can be lodged. Merely having possession of someone else's property, through some unknown sequence of events, is different than willfully taking owner-ship of someone else's property, in the eyes of the law. Fortunately, there are some general parameters merchants can use which are recognized by the courts as actions demonstrative of intent to steal. Knowing it is unreasonable to require one person to know the thoughts and intentions of another person, certain observable conduct is attributable to establishing intent for the purposes of proving larceny. In a retail environment, a person demonstrates intent to shoplift when they engage in conduct inclusive of one or all of the following activities:

1. **Alters merchandise to obfuscate ownership:** this entails removing identifying tickets, tags, labels, etc., that identifies merchandise as property of the retailer. Shoplifters often engage in this practice to make items appear as their own, such as gloves, wallets, etc. Such actions lend credence to an assertion a person intended to shoplift.

2. **Defeat protective devices:** to disable safeguards on merchandise pro-vided by the retailer to inhibit its unlawful removal, such as showcase locks, apparel cables, alarm devices, and electronic article surveillance (EAS) tags. Such actions lend credence to an assertion a person intended to shoplift.

3. **Concealment:** when a person places merchandise in a place hidden from view, or in amongst his own possessions. This is normally observed when a shoplifter places merchandise inside his briefcase, tote bag, overcoat, etc. Such actions lend credence to an assertion a person intended to shoplift.

4. **By-passes an opportunity to pay:** demonstrates that if a person wished to make a legitimate purchase, the opportunity to do so was available, and the person did not. Effectively counters the argument: *"but I was going to pay for it."*

5. **Leaves the building:** obviously makes the issue a fait accompli, pro-viding irrefutable observation of how the unpaid for merchandise came into the subject's possession was made.

In the paragraph immediately preceding the five points listed above, it was stated that a person's conduct inclusive of one or all of these activities went to the matter of intent. In practice, we should realize that only observation of multiple factors can really determine the case for intent. To illustrate, observe the customer who selected a tie from your rack, removed the store identifying fixture clip, knotted the tie around his collar and slipped the price ticket to the inside flap; is this man altering merchandise to obfuscate ownership, or is he trying it on in a reasonable manner?

Is the man putting the wallet in his hip pocket concealing it, or merely testing the bulge it makes in his pants before buying it? Is the person who tries on a down vest, then puts their coat over it and is now leaving the department, attempting to steal the concealed vest, or is he looking for a full-length mirror?

Is the customer wheeling a cart of unpaid merchandise out of your building, bypassing a whole row of checkout lanes, stealing that product, or making his way over to your Garden Center annex?

Each of these cases represents the dilemma of rigidly applying the characteristics of criminal intent in a retail environment fraught with the shopping habits and idiosyncrasies of legitimate patrons. That is why interdiction of a potential shoplifting situation by a trained employee is encouraged.

Go over to the man with the tie and ask if he would like to be shown a shirt that goes with it. Ask the customer with the vest under his coat if he would like to use a fitting room. Tell the person wheeling the cart out of the store with items that need to be purchased before visiting the annex, that you will gladly hold his selections until he returns. Do not lie in wait hoping the person leaves the store with your merchandise so you can nab him. It is better to approach, deter, and prevent instead.

Inevitably, store managers will have to deal with a situation for which apprehension is the only alternative to effect the recovery of the stolen merchandise. In these cases, the following guidelines should be helpful in knowing when and how to make the approach:

See the entire operation.   In order to know the merchandise in question is stolen, you have to know the customer came in without it, selected it from your inventory, demonstrated intent to steal it by altering the product (defeating security devices or concealing it), and is now attempting to exit your store without paying for it. You must have personally witnessed this incriminating activity in order to later testify to it in court. Uncertainty about any of these elements should make you reevaluate the appropriateness of the stop.

Know the merchandise is still in the customer's possession.   In order to know the customer still has the stolen property at the time of the stop, you must have been able to maintain uninterrupted observation of the individual from the time of the theft to the time of the stop. This is tricky, because seeing the theft alone is not enough to warrant a stop and a search. A shoplifter may have discerned that you have seen them steal, and put the merchandise back, or "ditched it," prior to your approach. The amateur detective may miss this sleight-of-hand maneuver, and would be left with an untenable situation at the door should he fail to detect the shoplifter has dumped the goods.

Use good judgment as to the value of the apprehension.   A lady eats three grapes from the produce section of the grocery: she has deprived the owner of its use and value, and although a legitimate case can be made on behalf of the grocer, is there good sense in pressing on with an apprehension? Even if it is an old lady? In a wheelchair? With a seeing eye dog? There are many, many instances that are not so clear cut in determining whether there is value to an apprehension. Each apprehension encounter represents enormous exposure to civil liability, as well as potential legal fees, court costs, and time off the job for employee witnesses to give testimony. Make sure the decision of whether or not an apprehension has value is tempered by what actions are in the best interests of the company, and whether the goal and outcome of this apprehension is consistent with the overall thrust of your loss prevention program.

Plan ahead.   Knowing an apprehension is imminent, you should alert a coworker to witness the stop and preliminary discussion. Expect to make the stop inside the store at the exit, just before the subject leaves. Waiting for them to leave the store does not make your case that much stronger, and exposes the employee to assault as the shoplifter may be more likely to break and flee once outside.

Identify yourself as a store employee immediately.   Make sure the shoplifter knows you are a lawful agent of the retail establishment. Should a scuffle ensue, you are in a better position to defend your actions if you can testify there was no ambiguity as to your identity (a shoplifter charged with assault will say they believed you to be a mugger trying to steal their purse when they punched you in the nose).

Know what to say.   The initial contact is the most tense for both parties. Be professional, but firm, in your assertion that the unpaid merchandise in the possession of the subject must be returned at once. This eliminates the need for provocative words like "stole," "thief," and "I gotcha! You're going to jail!" Unnecessary, inflammatory remarks escalate the risk of altercation and do little to foster a civilized detention atmosphere as you await police response. When faced with the preliminary denial by the shoplifter, be certain you know exactly what items are concealed where, so you can respond to the denial with confidence: *"I'm talking about the red blouse in your green bag that you took off the round rack by the fitting room."* This degree of certainty can work to your advantage, as it can deflate the shoplifter's notion that you can be persuaded you have made a mistake, or that vocal, indignant protestation may carry the day. Some shoplifters, when faced with a definitive account of their crime and a professional level of resolve on your part, resign themselves that they have been indeed caught, and become cooperative in the hopes you will go easy on them. Conversely, not knowing what to say, and hedging on the accusation, emboldens the shoplifter to try intimidation in the hopes of getting you to back down, and you wind up debating the merits of the case in a circus atmosphere.

Recover at least one item of stolen property immediately.   This is essential in the cases where you must escort the subject off the selling floor and into an office area. Savvy shoplifters have been known to "ditch" the stolen product en route to the office. They had it when you stopped them, but when the curtain goes up on searching their bag, it's no longer there. Uninterrupted observation means uninterrupted observation. You cannot allow the continuity of your surveillance to be broken at any time while the subject is still in possession of the merchandise they are being detained for taking. The best tactic, therefore, is for you to take possession of at least some, if not all, of the booty. This way there can be no surprises in the office when their bag is searched, and if they break and run, at least you have recovered the merchandise.

Now that you have the subject in custody, what are you to do with her? If you are a male manager, and she a female subject, you do not want to be behind closed doors in an isolated office room. Immediately involve a female employee in the detention process, and absent one, conduct the interview on the selling floor in the rear of the store. You would like next to get a clear understanding of what was taken and why (without appearing uncertain yourself) to make doubly-sure you are making a lawful detention. If she says she took the blouse because she wanted it for a party tonight, but could not afford it, then that is an admission of theft you can later testify to in addition to your observations of the fact.

If, on the other hand, she says the blouse is hers, that she purchased it yesterday, the receipt is in the car, that she brought it in to match up a skirt she was looking to buy, and that she had every right to fold it back up and put it in her bag; then you may want to consider your position a little more carefully. The subject has offered a plausible explanation for what appeared to be a theft, and despite your unwavering observation of her removing that blouse from the rack, not her own bag, it would be in your best interest to see how far her story goes. Produce sales records from the date in question to determine if this customer indeed purchased the item at your store as stated. Escort her to her car and permit her the opportunity to produce a receipt. If it is a bluff, then you will discover it soon enough. If, in fact, there is a receipt and a believable story to go with it, you will learn that you either made an egregious error, or you were set up good by a pro. Either way, it facilitates damage control to not compound your potential false arrest situation with what may turn out to be a clearly inappropriate (malicious?) prosecution.

Retailers should have the chain of command at-the-ready for a store manager who needs guidance on how to proceed in these circumstances. Assuming this is a routine shoplifting situation, with no wild cards in the deck, the store manager may want to obtain information for an incident report which should be completed at the earliest opportunity. Asking the shoplifter for identification is appropriate, but allowing a shoplifter to go through a purse or jacket pockets could produce a weapon. Company policy on pat-downs and searches should be clear to store line management, just as policy on prosecution criteria should be.

Your store manager should know exactly what the outcome of this encounter is going to be. Store managers should know whether they have the discretion to release the person following an admonition never to return to the store again; or if the manager is duty-bound to initiate a prosecution in all cases where criteria has been satisfied. In this example, criteria is amply satisfied: uninterrupted observation of theft, recovery of stolen merchandise, and an admissible verbal confession; in all, it is a winnable case.

To prolong the detention period for the purposes of interviewing the subject, gaining written admissions, learning the frequency of her thefts in your store, seeking restitution, etc., is no business for employees other than loss prevention professionals on the scene, trained in interview techniques and capable of gauging the impact this person has had on the store's inventory performance.

If your policy is to prosecute, then call the police immediately. The response time will provide ample awkward moments for chit-chat. If your policy is to prosecute only significant cases or apprehensions involving repeat offenders, and minor incidents are adjudicated by the store manager with a warning and the shoplifter's promise never to return, then verify the person's identity and wrap it up expeditiously. There are too many variables that can come up in a detention environment that your manager may not be prepared to deal with properly.

Company policy should be written and disseminated with respect to known contingencies that may be encountered; managers must know how the company wants them to respond with respect to:

- Apprehension of juveniles: Do we call the cops? Do we call the parents? What if they look older? What if they are 7 years old?
- Apprehension of accomplices: Do we detain them too? "They were all in on it," do we prosecute them all?
- Contraband: What if we find a weapon? Drugs? If we let them go, do we give it back?
- What do I say if they want to make a phone call? If they want to use the restroom? If they say they need to take medication? That they left a toddler unattended in the mall food court and have to retrieve him?

Store managers, in the absence of staff security personnel, empowered as lawful agents to make detentions, may encounter incidents that are beyond the reasonable scope of their job description. It is therefore incumbent upon senior management to anticipate situations for them, and to provide written direction to address these concerns. The liability realities, both to your company and employees, make this an essential obligation of corporate to its agents in the field. Some suggestions on policy direction with respect to the contingency events enumerated above include:

Apprehension of juveniles.   Some states/jurisdictions have mandated that specific notifications be made in the event of the detention of a juvenile. In all cases, where the juvenile has been placed in custody at the store, the police should be called. The manager's discretion with the juvenile should end when he decides to detain him in a private area, as opposed to taking the merchandise back and kicking the kid out with a stern warning. Although police and merchants are reluctant to pursue prosecution of juveniles (because the family court experience is an onerous one for complainants), have the police respond and permit them the latitude of taking action they deem appropriate: notifying parents, transporting the juvenile, and awaiting parental pick-up.

Apprehension of accomplices.   Knowing a person "acted in concert" in the commission of a crime, and proving those actions "aided and abetted" the crime are two different matters with respect to apprehensions in a retail setting. Usually, "accomplices" are known to be in the company of the shoplifter and provide distraction, cover, or look-out functions that facilitate the theft. To prosecute the accomplice for aiding and abetting the shoplifter would require you to prove the unlawful intent of those actions, a subjective assessment since it cannot be proven the accomplice was to benefit from the crime (remember it is the shoplifter who has unlawfully taken the item).

On the other hand, some prosecutions of the subject who carried out the unpaid for merchandise, i.e., the person found in possession of the stolen property, would be incomplete without the person who acted in concert to the theft being so charged. To illustrate, suppose subject A loads a bag full of merchandise, then hands it to subject B who then walks out the door with it and is subsequently apprehended by store personnel for shoplifting. Subject B could claim he had no knowledge (therefore no intent) that the bag handed him by his friend contained stolen merchandise. Store personnel would be hard pressed to testify subject B was in on it the whole time, because they never observed subject B handling the merchandise in the store. But store personnel may be reluctant to detain subject A because he has no stolen merchandise in his possession. The law would hold in this situation that both subjects A and B are equally culpable for shoplifting because they acted in concert to commit the theft. The actions of one facilitated the actions of the other, and the unlawful acts would be considered to have happened in concert.

With respect to the requests of detained persons to use the telephone or the restroom, company policy has to ensure that lawful detentions are effected in a reasonable manner. In cases where you intend to prosecute and the police have been summoned, declining these requests temporarily in anticipation of a police officer coming to take charge of the scene is reasonable, so ask them to wait. You are not refusing the request, just delaying it until appropriate personnel arrive. However, even in this circumstance, permitting a person no alternative but to soil themselves would be imprudent, as the manner of detention would not be looked upon favorably by a civil court (nor the responding police officer for that matter).

Requests to take medication should be handled judiciously, as you do not want to be the cause of insulin shock (for medicinal deprivation) or narcotic overdose (for permitting the subject to swallow 30 valium). The best bet is to call the police back, inform the police a subject in custody awaiting transport is requesting to be allowed medication, inform the police of the drug name and dosage being requested, and follow their instruction, documenting the conversation in your incident report. Remember, the police may not be all that receptive to your dragging them into a matter of private custody, but they do not want their responding officer walking in to an addict high on angel dust either.

In cases where you are not planning to prosecute, but need to complete paperwork in the subject's presence, you should accede to reasonable requests, or expedite the process so the subject can be on her way quickly and can utilize public phones and restrooms in a reasonable time.

With respect to contraband recovered incidental to a proper search, such items should be turned over to the responding police officer in cases being prosecuted. Where you do not plan to prosecute the matter of theft, but certainly do not wish to be the custodian of a loaded gun or a gram of cocaine, notify the police you detained a person suspected of shoplifting, and have recovered contraband you wish to turn over to the authorites. In cases where prosecution has been initiated, and the subject in custody explains they have a toddler waiting in the schoolyard for a pick-up or out in the mall, and the subject requests you allow them to retrieve the child, you should notify the police immediately of this development, and follow their instructions. Where no prosecution is contemplated and your intentions are to release the subject, do so without delay.

As this chapter has tried to illustrate, apprehensions are a risky business with complex variables your store manager has to manage. The value of an apprehension lies in the recovery of your merchandise and ascertaining the identity of the shoplifter. To proceed with the prosecution is worthwhile as far as a punitive measure for the shoplifter and the potential benefits of deterring future thefts by this person, and perhaps by his associates. The downside is a bungled detention, resulting in injury to an employee, the detainee, or a lawsuit for conducting the detention in an unreasonable manner. Since store managers are not security professionals, the chances for mishap should not be minimized when disseminating procedural guidelines for in-house apprehension and detention.

Prosecution Criteria

19

Company policy-makers generally believe an aggressive prosecution policy to be a cornerstone of a strong loss prevention program. Taking a tough stand against theft sets a tone designed to deter persons from stealing because it escalates the perception of risk. Persons caught shoplifting who are prosecuted to the fullest extent of the law are less likely to return and steal again. Word will spread among the criminal element that your store means business, and they best ply their trade elsewhere.

Employees, too, will be hesitant to skim profits and participate in schemes to defraud the company. There is nothing like seeing a co-worker marched out the front door in handcuffs into a waiting patrol car to keep the honest workers honest. 100% prosecution: no breaks, no quarter.

These principles make terrific oratory in training classes, motivational seminars and new-hire orientation. In practice, however, the loss prevention community is somewhat divided about this approach. The allure of the prosecution has lost some of its luster, and progressive executives are weighing the assets and liabilities of such a blanket policy. It has come to the attention of some retailers that lockstep prosecution has become a path of diminishing returns in some cases. The capacity of the criminal justice system, especially those in the inner-cities, to mete out significant penalties to offenders convicted of crimes against property has declined. When the victim of the property crime is a corporation, the sanctions seem to be further reduced.

This is not to say that justice will not be done in all cases of retail crime: robbery, burglary, embezzlement, collusive fraud, sizable cash defalcation, and other major cases of considerable loss are investigated and adjudicated as best as the resources of the police and courts will permit. It is the low-priority cases that clog court calendars: the petty shoplifter, or the employee taking lunch money from the register, that become fodder for expeditious disposition and suspended sentences.

The effects of "turnstile justice" so often alluded to in the media has not been lost on the criminal community. Petty criminals have become desensitized to the trauma of arrest. Kids who run in gangs wear their rap sheet as a badge of honor. Career criminals are not deterred from crime as easily by the prospect of being returned to prison. Organized rings of illegal aliens are unleashed at malls with fake credit cards and metal-lined booster bags, making huge hauls with impunity; American jails often represent a step up in living conditions. And professional persons engaging in white collar crime realize their nonviolent malfeasance, coupled with their first-offender status, virtually assures them of one "free ride" through the system.

At the same time, compassion and courtesy for the victim of property crimes has waned: a person who reports their car stolen is told they are lucky they were not in it; the woman who reports her purse stolen is informed she is lucky she was not raped; the merchant who reports a robbery is consoled that he is lucky he was not killed. These factors, more ruthless criminals and less charitable authorities, suggest companies should revisit their prosecution policies.

The retailer should ask two questions: am I getting the return I anticipated from my investment of incurred time and expense (and exposure to liability) as measured by fewer apprehensions and improved shortage performance? And, are the presumptions we made when we established our prosecution policy still valid? To answer the first question, there should be a correlation between the number of apprehensions made and the percent of those apprehensions which are prosecuted; for prosecution to be having the desired deterrent effect, apprehensions should decline as prosecutions increase. If theft, both customer and employee, is believed to be a significant factor in a store's shortage performance, and prosecution is perceived to be a driving factor in reducing theft, then a reduction in shortage can be attributed to an increase in prosecution.

If, on the other hand, you discover apprehensions increase each year, and the prosecution percentage has remained consistently high (per policy), then you may conclude little deterrent effect has been gained. Similarly, if no improvement to a store's shrink performance is evident, you may surmise that no reduction in theft activity has been realized through vigorous prosecution; or that factors other than theft are contributing more to inventory loss than first believed.

The second question, that of perhaps the perceived benefits of aggressive prosecution becoming outmoded, requires a quick "reality check" between the home office policy mavens and the store line foot soldiers. What did you think happened when the police were summoned to take custody of a 14-year-old shoplifter when the benefits of a rigid prosecution mandate was touted to stores? Did you imagine he would be taken to the station house and issued a juvenile delinquent card? That he would be turned over to a scowling father who would march him to the shed for corporal punishment? That he would be whisked off to a reform school for wayward boys? That he would have a criminal record that would follow him his whole life? If your prosecution policy is conceived with these notions, canvas some store managers to verify these are not the musings of a time gone by.

If your company has the luxury to do so, order two studies be done. First, compile the payroll hours lost to the detention and prosecution of shoplifters. Include the "down-time" of management and staff engaged in custody, trips to the police station, and court appearances. Consider the administrative costs to open and update case files, the clerical expense to maintain them, and factor in supply and travel costs. Next, have your legal counsel tally billable hours attributed to defending litigation emanating from matters of detention or prosecution, as well as time spent providing guidance to your field executives in their pursuit of criminal cases. Last, have your insurance carrier provide amounts paid out or escrowed to settle lawsuits brought as a direct result of detention and arrest.

The second study ordered would be a breakdown of dispositioned criminal cases successfully concluded in the field. The nature of the offense, the progression of court dates, the sentences passed, and the disposition of evidence (you will be surprised to see how much of your "best-seller" merchandise winds up in the clearance rack following its hiatus in the evidence locker) should be detailed for your review.

These studies should enable you to determine if a blanket prosecution policy is working for your company. If the results are disconcerting, you may want to revise your strategy and redirect some of the resources into staffing, prevention equipment, and training, while pursuing a policy of selective prosecution. Selective prosecution involves two criteria: you prosecute only winnable cases, and you prosecute when it is in the best interests of the company to do so. A winnable case, as defined in the previous chapter, requires the uninterrupted observation of the theft by a lawful agent of the company and the recovery of stolen merchandise. An admission to the theft, even a verbal one, is desirable, but not critical. The uninterrupted observation permits the lawful agent of the company to testify in court that another person knowingly and willfully attempted to deprive the owner of the use and value of property. The recovery of said property is offered as evidence to substantiate the charge. Being able to attest to or produce an admission by the defendant is always helpful. Lacking these elements makes for a tenuous case and does not meet the criteria for a winnable case. You may win hundreds of tenuous cases that are presented for prosecution, but you could lose one. The one you lose could have serious ramifications if pursued as a lawsuit against your company in a civil action. There is little if to it; it will be pursued as a civil action.

This is not to suggest by any means you will win all your winnable cases. You could lose a couple of them, too. Either the defendant tells a plausible story and the judge/jury for some reason believes them over your employee witness, or your chain of evidence is bungled, or the prosecutor's office drops the ball in notifying you of court dates, or the defendant is in a position to pull strings or bring resources to bear you had not anticipated. These are the variables retailers must contend with when they stray into an arena outside their area of expertise. A retailer's province is shrewd buying decisions, innovative sales promotion, novel merchandise presentation, attentive customer service, and astute expense management, not depositions, interrogatories, and blistering cross examination.

Winnable cases are often predicated on the resources of the defendant. When assessing the merits of a case, to assume a level playing field once your case comes to court may be naive. A defendant of considerable resource, and a lot to lose if convicted, could mount a substantial defense that belies the facts of the case as in the O.J. Simpson trial. The rules of engagement may not line up on the side of truth all the time. You should size up your potential opponent: is he a nobody who is going to go through the system uncontested, cop a plea, and go away? (very winnable). Or is this a person of considerable wealth and influence who will overwhelm the prosecution with a top-notch attorney, character references, and expert witnesses? (suddenly tenuous). In a perfect world, such matters would be irrelevant: the truth would prevail. But more often than not, money prevails. Be mindful of such inequities when evaluating cases for prosecution.

The second criteria, that of prosecutions being in the best interests of the company, serves as an addendum to the winnable case prerequisite. To put the best interests of the company in perspective, you would have to consider whether it is more beneficial to the organization to barter for something of value in exchange for clemency. Do you prosecute the daughter of the Chief of Police in a small town simply because the incident meets the criteria of a winnable case? Should not clemency for this shoplifter be weighed against the good will that may be generated by foregoing a prosecution? Is not the best interest of the company served by a benevolent, rather than adversarial, relationship with the police? In a perfect world, a company should not have to compromise its principles and employ a double standard to accommodate a person's standing in the community, but business is business.

Suppose a store manager steals a deposit, say $15,000 from a holiday weekend, and through your determined investigation, he finally admits to the crime and offers to return the money if you will not prosecute. Your first instinct may be a resounding no deal, or you may entertain the idea of entering into an agreement you are fully prepared to renege on, once you get your money back. After all, a promise to a thief is not really a promise, and the gloves come off when a trusted employee takes you for big bucks.

Let's put our selective prosecution criteria to the test. We will assume the investigation was on the level, the document trail was conclusive as to means and opportunity, the manager's story unraveled, he broke down in the interview, fessed-up, and gave a written statement of admission to the investigator. All told, it is a winnable case. It is undeniable that somehow restoring the $15,000 to the company coffer is in the company's best interest. But there are the matters of policy, precedent, and perception to be reconciled. Policy, with respect to a winnable case, is satisfied. The best interests of the company are yet to be determined. Precedent has to be looked at, especially if you prosecuted a part time clerk last week for taking $5 from the register. You should not have your practices appear capricious, or worse, discriminatory. And how will this matter play to the employee population and their perception of your even-handed and consistent application of the rules to all?

If you proceed with the prosecution, for all the right reasons, you should be prepared to write off the $15,000. The district attorney might get it back for you in a plea bargain arrangement, or the court could order restitution in consideration of a probation agreement, but you cannot count on so favorable a result. Once the prosecution is initiated, your control of the outcome is handed off to proxies: the district attorney, the judge, and the defendant's attorney. The tenacity with which they will fight for your money is dependent upon many factors: the case load, the docket, and the merits of the case.

By the time the case comes up, if the defendant even appears, he could plead guilty to a reduced charge, claim he spent the money on drug rehab, pay a fine, skip out on his community service, and default on his restitution agreement to you of $10 a week. Or, in other jurisdictions, with a bulldog prosecutor and a hanging judge, he could do six months in county jail if he pays back the money; two years upstate if he does not. Since the disparity between jurisdictions, judges, and juries is significant, that matter of prosecution comes down to a business decision. Can we afford to lose the $15,000 if we gamble on the courts? If you can, then the best interests of the company are served by prosecuting. The intrinsic value in terms of company integrity, insistence on accountability, equal treatment for all, and steadfast resolve will provide ample shortage program mileage. If a loss of significant magnitude will erode any profit contribution by this location in the fiscal year, and such a shortfall is damaging to the organization as a whole, recovering the loss is in the best interest of the company. A tough business decision, yes, but one that needs to be made by those with fiduciary responsibility, not by a unilateral prosecution policy.

Some general guidelines for prosecuting winnable cases that are in the best interest of the company include most cases of employee theft where the deterrent value is more pronounced than any restitution arrangement may yield; cases of shoplifters known to be repeat offenders; persons who threaten, stalk, or assault employees; and fraud operators who are known to have passed bad checks or obtained product through the use of stolen credit cards on past occasions.

Two areas of concern should be touched on in conclusion. From time to time your store may get a call from the police department that merchandise believed stolen from your store has been recovered by virtue of an arrest initiated by another retailer. The officer will request one of your employees to come to the police station and identify the merchandise as belonging to your store. On the surface, this seems like a good deal: product you never knew was stolen is being returned courtesy of another merchant's vigilance.

There may be a catch: the police may want your representative to identify the merchandise as stolen from your store in order to add another count of shoplifting to the original complaint. This is a common practice, and a troublesome situation for the store manager. The police expect you to be grateful your merchandise was recovered. They become perplexed and maybe a little perturbed if your representative hesitates to follow their instruction.

When your employee states he can't really attest to the shoplifting because he is unable to identify the defendant, or even establish the date and time of the theft, the police may want to amend the charge to possession of stolen property. This, too, presents a dilemma because you can not, for certain, establish that the merchandise was stolen. Your reticence to press charges is vexing to the police, especially when the defendant has admitted to stealing it! They will not take kindly to your explanation of the rules of evidence as you understand them, particularly in a case made by a police officer.

You may think trusting the police and following their direction, believing they can make the charge stick, demonstrates a spirit of civic cooperation and cannot turn out too badly. But it can turn out badly, if the defendant is a person of resource whose attorney bullies the other retailer into dropping the shoplifting charges in exchange for a "hold-harmless" agreement and waiver of liability. Now the only charges the defendant is facing are the ones you brought, with no observation, no witness, and no proof. That case will get dismissed in a flash and your company (and probably the employee who signed the complaint) will be slapped with a malicious prosecution lawsuit. Also, the cop who told your store manager *don't worry, just sign it* will be indemnified from liability (by virtue of his police officer status) and will console your employee by reminding him, *"hey, that's what they got insurance for."*

The other point to be mindful of when involved in prosecutions are the occasions where cases are dismissed by the courts. It is not really anything you did, or failed to do. You just receive a notice that your case, ABC Company vs. Jesse James was "dismissed." Sometimes, the district attorney will request a case not be heard "in the interests of justice." Other times, you may not be notified to appear and the case is dismissed for lack of a complainant.

These are not cases that are lost as much as they are cases that are not won. Should a trial result in an acquittal, the defendant is found not guilty. He is then in a strong position to pursue civil redress against the complainant. But if a case is dismissed, there is no verdict. You are not immune from a lawsuit, but you have the protections of the merchant's statute, and your testimony at a civil trial is just as valid as it would be in a criminal trial. It is just that you do not want to be in that position; the stakes are too high.

One of the ways you can insulate yourself from the fallout of a dismissed case is to instruct the D.A. or the court to petition for a "hold-harmless" stipulation as part of the court record anytime a case where your company is the named complainant is contemplated for dismissal. This is more substantial than a blanket waiver of liability often imposed when cases are dismissed "in the interests of justice," and would be a real impediment to a defendant's chances of filing a future suit against your company. The most effective way to avoid these situations, however, is to monitor developments in your pending cases very closely, establishing strong links with the prosecutor's office and the courts.

In summary, selective prosecution is a useful tool in your arsenal of loss prevention resources. Like so many other aspects of your shortage program, clear policy, sound judgment, and trained personnel make the difference.

Criminal Trespass 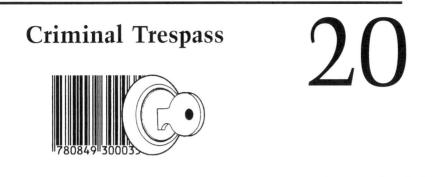20

Store management personnel often encounter situations where an undesirable has entered the store and is conducting himself in manner that unnerves employees. This can be the case of an intoxicated person; a disoriented person; a street person whose hygiene is offensive; loud, boisterous persons; a person who either has, or has attempted to, shoplift on previous occasions; or a group of young people that become disruptive.

What to do about this has been a gray area in retail management for a long time. A long-held tactic has been to ignore the individual and hope he eventually leaves. This notion was reinforced by a sense of helplessness that there really was not anything you could do about it. But inaction began to take its toll: offensive people would drive away paying customers, shoplifters would ultimately seize an opportunity to steal merchandise, and rowdy juveniles would carry on until they were approached by store employees, an outcome that too often only exacerbated the problem.

Seeking relief, loss prevention professionals canvassed penal code statutes defining harassment, criminal mischief, and disorderly conduct. The terms and definitions of these offenses, however, were difficult to apply uniformly due to the potential for subjective interpretation by anxious managers. Criminal law requires that a person not only commit an unlawful act to break the law, but oftentimes it must be proven that the person intended to commit the unlawful act as well.

A disgruntled customer swearing and gesturing at a store manager who refuses to give him a refund may indeed be committing the criminal act of harassment, but proving this was his intent is another matter. A group of unruly boys running in the aisles, despite your admonitions to stop, knock over a fixture causing merchandise to be smashed may have crossed over the line into criminal mischief, but proving this was their intent in order to effect their arrest, may be difficult. An unbalanced street person standing in the center of the selling floor reciting Psalm 23 at the top of his lungs may be committing disorderly conduct, but the question of intent in this case would hamper successful prosecution.

But something needed to be done for the merchant to address these incidents, many of which were becoming more prevalent as social restraints and respect for authority eroded over the years. Gradually, applications of the criminal trespass statutes came to the attention of the private sector. By definition, the misdemeanor crime of criminal trespass is committed when a person enters and remains on premises unlawfully. A person enters and remains unlawfully on a premises when his right and privilege to do so has been revoked by a lawful agent of the premises. This revocation of license and privilege to enter and remain must have been lawfully issued prior to the event at hand.

Put in context of a retail establishment, a disruptive person could be asked by a member of management (the lawful agent) to cease and desist his disruptive behavior. Refusal to comply could result in the lawful agent revoking the person's license and privilege to enter and remain on the premises (issuance of the lawful order to vacate the premises). Refusal to obey the lawful order by the lawful agent to vacate the premises constitutes the elements of the crime of criminal trespass.

The store manager is now in the position to call the police to effect the arrest of the disruptive person. Prior to the advent of applying criminal trespass statutes to these situations, the police would query the manager before responding to the scene as to whether or not the store was prepared to press charges. Given the previously mentioned complexities of intent with respect to disorderly conduct, the store manager was hesitant to affirm that charges would be pressed. This enabled the police to decline participation in what they wanted to consider your problem.

Once the lawful order to vacate the premises has been issued, known as an admonishment, the subject has been informed it is unlawful for him to remain. His election to disregard this order and remain in spite of it fulfills the element of intent to commit criminal trespass. The gray area has become black and white. Fulfilling your lawful obligations to proceed against an undesirable person is but the first part in achieving your objective. The second phase is persuading the police to recognize the validity of your admonishment, and inducing them to take appropriate action on your behalf. This requires tact and forethought on your part because your real purpose is to have the person forcibly removed and warned not to return, not to actually proceed with criminal charges. This is because the police would prefer not to have to process this type of complaint; your store manager belongs in the store not at the police station (and later, in court); and the unruly patron does not want to be arrested, but does not want to back down either.

Invoking criminal trespass statutes properly can facilitate the desired outcome if handled correctly. It is a matter of reasonable negotiation, face-saving diplomacy, and restraint on all sides. A preprinted notice, explaining the admonition on company letterhead, should be available to the store manager for him to issue to the offending party. This document can be shown to the responding police officer demonstrating the merchant's good faith in attempting to resolve the matter without assistance from the police department. The inference is that only the unreasonable recalcitrance of the unruly patron necessitated police involvement, not the inability of the merchant to manage his business.

Let's assume your manager approached someone who was attempting to shoplift an item. A theft did not actually occur, but was interdicted by the manager's approach (as recommended in Chapter 8), and the subject became loud and abusive to the manager, claiming your employee unjustly accused him of stealing. The manager explained this was not his intent at all, and that the patron will have to control himself or leave. The subject derides the manager and rails of the discriminatory policies of your company, insisting he will remain, and uses words and body language suggestive of a physical confrontation if he is not left alone.

The manager should leave, return with another employee witness, and hand the person the pre-printed admonition. The manager should explain that he wants the person to leave, and that the police will be summoned, if necessary, to effect his removal. The patron's response will range from crumpling the paper up and throwing it on the floor (or in the manager's face), and asserting his right to remain, to stomping out of the store amid a flurry of expletives (and perhaps tipping over a fixture near the door). Although not the best scenario, the patron has left, and order can soon be restored.

The manager should then complete an incident report, detailing the time and date of the admonition, the employee witness, and a brief description of the event and subject. This is enormously helpful should the person return on another occasion and the manager wishes to exclude the subject from the premises based on the previous encounter. If, on the other hand, the offending party adamantly refuses to leave, and challenges the manager to call the police, the manager and the employee witness should walk away, and call the police:

MGR: *"Hello. I have a problem at the ABC Store on highway 123. There's a guy here who is being disruptive and abusive and will not leave. He has upset my employees and my customers have walked out. I want him removed."*

PD: *"We can't come over unless you are going to press charges."*

MGR: *"I'm willing to press charges. Please come right away, I think he's dangerous."*

All the elements for police dispatch have been fulfilled. Await the responding police unit near the front of the store and do not approach the subject again. If he attempts to re-engage you or your employees, simply suggest he should leave, and move away. When the police arrive, you should expect the incident to unfold along these general lines:

PD: "*What's the problem here?*"

MGR: "*This guy is causing a lot of trouble and refuses to leave. I don't want his business and I want you to make him leave.*"

PD: "*What did he do?*"

SUBJ: "*I didn't do nothing. This* (expletive) *accused me of stealing. I didn't take nothing. (*Turns his pockets inside out*). They discriminate against my kind here, always saying we're stealing.*"

PD: "*Is that true?*"

MGR: "*No. I didn't accuse him of stealing. He removed the wrapper from this item and I told him he would have to pay for it or leave. I can't sell it now. I'll have to return it to the manufacturer. When I told him that he said I was accusing him of stealing and he became abusive.*"

PD: "*That wrapper was on the floor. I never took it off the item. He's just looking to harass me.*"

MGR: "*I just want him to leave and not come back. I gave him this admonition* (show it to the officer) *but he threw it on the floor.*"

PD: "*Did you do that?*"

SUBJ: "*Yeah. I don't have to read no paper from him.*"

MGR: "*Look, I'm just trying to run a business here. The guy damaged my product, won't pay for it and won't leave. This is private property and I want him off. If he won't listen to you, then what am I supposed to do?*"

This *"won't"* comment is pivotal in the discussion. The police officer is properly baited to demonstrate to you that indeed, this person will respond to the authority of a cop.

PD: "*Look pal, this is going nowhere. Why don't you just move along before you make more trouble for yourself.*"

SUBJ: "*Why you taking his side? This place is open to the public and I can be here if I want.*"

PD: "*No, you can't. This is his store. Why would you want to shop here if you're treated so poorly, anyway? You just want to make trouble for him, and now for me, and pretty soon, big trouble for yourself. I'm telling you to leave, and that is a lawful order. I can arrest you if you disobey it.*"

SUBJ: *"Arrest me? But I ain't done nothing!"*

PD: *"Last chance, bud. Start walking or I'll put the cuffs on you, and then I'm taking you in."*

In most cases, the subject will start moving out. Wait for the person to take his parting shot, usually a disparaging remark or threat, then seize that moment to say to the officer: *"he's going to come back right after you leave."* This ploy suggests the officer's resolution may be inadequate in your eyes, prompting the cop to get in the last word to the subject: *"that is enough lip out of you, buster. And stay out of this store for good. If I have to come back here and deal with you again, you'll be in for real trouble."*

Make sure the officer knows you are appreciative of his time and expertise. Ask if you handled the situation properly, and request any advice he may have for dealing with these events in the future. Usually, the officer will tell you that you did all you could, and if it happens again, call the police, just like you did. He'll remind you that is what they're there for. Always complete an incident report following any police response to your store, detailing the event and the identity of the responding officer. Should this unwanted patron return another day, and you wish to exclude him again, reference this event on the phone with the police, saying the subject was formally excluded by an officer on a given date, and still refuses to leave.

In the event the unwanted person returns on another day, you have several options to keep in mind. The first, is to do nothing. Assuming the subject is in a better frame of mind, he may not offer any trouble; just goes about his business without accosting you or attempting to shoplift. You may choose not to provoke the individual with a confrontation on this occasion, although you are within your rights to reissue the lawful order to leave, based on the previous exclusion. Knowing this person has tried to shoplift in the past, you will have to keep a wary eye on him this time as well. This may be part of a ruse to keep you occupied so a cohort can shoplift, or perhaps this person has indeed been sufficiently deterred from the practice in your store. Regardless, having to discreetly observe the person in the store could instigate another brouhaha once he senses your ever-present, gaze upon him.

If you choose to permit him to stay, your actions could be interpreted as a tacit rescission of the previous lawful order. You cannot exclude someone from your premises in March, then allow him to enter and remain in April and May, then expect to be able to exclude him without cause in June. Once you have permitted the person entry, his rights and privileges are implicitly restored. This is especially for the case where the customer approaches you and apologizes for things getting out of hand the last time, seeking the restoration of shopping privileges. Should a lawful agent acquiesce to this proffer of good faith by the customer, then the previous exclusion is formally rescinded. The patron would have to furnish just cause through subsequent (not previous) misconduct in order for you to exclude him in the future.

Rescinding the admonition is not advisable for two reasons: first, another shift manager unaware that the subject's privilege has been restored could confront him aggressively, ordering him from the premises. This would no longer be a lawful order, since he has not entered and remained unlawfully because the ban was lifted. Second, in the event you required police assistance in ejecting him at some future time, you do not want the subject to complicate the dialog by explaining to the responding officer that he straightened the problem out with another manager, and that he has been welcomed back to the store. This development would not be appreciated by the responding officer, and future assistance could be jeopardized.

Remember that the criminal trespass statute is a precision tool. It cannot be applied capriciously, and punitive application of the trespass admonition will not pass the scrutiny of reasonable conduct. Only management personnel trained in the nuances of its intent should be allowed to act in the capacity of lawful agent for your company.

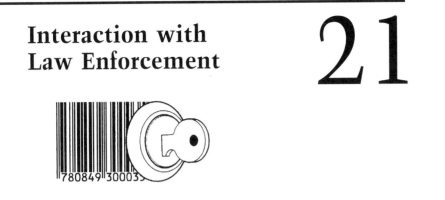

Interaction with Law Enforcement

21

It wasn't so long ago that the subject matter in this chapter was irrelevant to a business person operating a retail concern. You never used to "interact with law enforcement;" you merely "called the cops."

Today, protecting property is very much left up to the owner, especially if the owner is a business. The police will be very accommodating in instructing merchants on crime prevention, and they will respond to reported crimes in and around your premises, but they cannot protect your property for you. That task belongs to you.

The realities of crime in America is well documented in the media, well debated in the Congress, and well known to retailers coping with an epidemic of theft. Police are undermanned, under supported, and under siege from the very public it protects. Courts are overwhelmed, overbooked, and over-rated to dispense justice. Prisons are ineffective, inefficient, and infamous for achieving neither punishment nor reform. The law enforcement community can only close ranks, weather the storm, and watch their backs. The alternative, to publicly decree an inability to protect citizens from harm, is unthinkable; the last vestiges of law and order would dissipate into vigilante justice and anarchy.

Into this mix we have the retailer, generating a fair share of the jobs and commerce that fuels the economy which sustains the society. The private sector has legitimate concerns regarding the apparent inability of law enforcement to provide a safe environment for business to flourish. Like most successful enterprises, retailers wish to reinvest profits into their business. They want to expand their stores, modernize their equipment, upgrade their fixturing, diversify their product line, all of which are capital investments that stimulate growth.

Instead, capital expenditures once earmarked for such purposes are siphoned off, redirected into unproductive overhead for security; the term necessary evil is often used to describe it. A good example is the expense structure of an inner-city store located in a high crime area. This is still a viable market for the company, and its presence in the neighborhood has been well-established, servicing the needs of the residents for many years. Because of customer density and the flight of competitors to suburban mega-malls, sales volume has always met or exceeded plan. Stacked against comparable store results in the rest of the company, it would be a primary profit center, except for two expense factors: shrink and security cost.

The store's payroll load is higher because selling floor coverage has to be supplemented on nights and weekends to deter shoplifters. The storefront was supposed to be remodeled to brighten its appearance and draw attention to its show windows, but those funds were allocated for motorized roll-down steel shutters. New track-lighting was to be installed to highlight merchandise displays, but instead of chic spots and high-hats, the ceiling is accessorized with mirrored domes concealing surveillance cameras. The fixturing is long overdue for upgrading, but they would have to be nailed to the counter and fitted with lockable brackets and electronic cable boxes, so there's no real advantage to replacing the old ones.

The aftermath of the two burglaries resulted in costs beyond the losses of inventory. A new industrial safe imbedded in the concrete floor was necessary, as were additional alarm devices (although their value is suspect as long as the police take an hour to respond), and the new burglar bars on the back door seems to have only raised tensions with the fire marshal.

The real drain is the on-going expense of guard service from open to close. After the robbery, the employees did not feel safe anymore. The guard was supposed to be a stop-gap measure until the employees settled down, but every time the subject of scaling back the coverage is discussed, the staff becomes adamant about safety. The invoices for the armored car service keep rolling in, but after the close call the manager had in the parking lot on his way to make the deposit, nobody wants to go to the bank anymore.

Each inventory, the shrink results deteriorate, and with sales barely remaining flat due to the cut back in operating hours from 10 p.m. to 9 p.m., the losses eat into the margin more and more each year. Cash shortage keeps climbing, bad checks are proliferating, the employees seem indifferent to the losses (several of them have been caught stealing), the good managers refuse to be reassigned here, and the ones in place want out.

Eventually, management will have to decide how long this location can remain viable. It is unfortunate that downtown landmark stores have closed or relocated. Employees are displaced, the city is deprived of revenue, the community loses yet another mainstream retailer, and the company forfeits an otherwise thriving location, but for the costs of shrink and security.

The fate of this site will often turn on the company's relationship with law enforcement. The nature of police response to crime in and around the premises can be a determining factor. What retailers need to communicate to law enforcement is a strategy for addressing the issues that are within their mutual control. The business community cannot expect the police to prevent and solve all the crimes which will occur. Instead, the police and the retailer would be better off fashioning the rules of engagement which govern both communication and response.

The keys are for the retailer to articulate what their expectations of police assistance consist of, and for the police to correct those expectations and propose alternatives which can be delivered.

For instance, suppose the expectation of the retailer is a patrol car to be circling the strip center parking lot because there is ample evidence of prevalent criminal activity. The retailer's perception is: if it is your job to serve and protect, you should be where the crime is.

The police will be reluctant to commit resources it cannot sustain and do not want to be vilified later for breaking promises. This is an unrealistic expectation, and should be stated as such. However, the police can suggest the tenants lobby mall management to provide a security patrol, and agree to support that effort with training, communication, intelligence information, and rapid response when summoned. This conveys a constructive attitude from the police and builds a partnership of cooperation. Too often, unrealistic expectations presented to the police are dismissed out-of-hand, fostering resentment and a sense of isolation for the merchant. Should that sentiment be carried back to the home office, the days are numbered for that location.

Instead, police should nurture their relationship with the business community, reassuring retailers that their concerns matter, and that the police will make whatever presence they can muster more visible. Retailers must make the police understand that employees will do their part to safeguard merchandise if they have a sense of security and confidence they can rely on police support. The police may want to rethink their deployment and encourage officers to stop in to merchant's shops along the strip and chat briefly with employees. If they are to spend 20 minutes at a strip center, they would get much more mileage out of unannounced drop-bys into retail locations than they would cooped in their patrol car observing the parking lot.

Address the specific concerns of employees with police department representatives, especially when workers call to report suspicious persons. The retailer's expectation is that the crime prevention doctrine espoused by the police means they will respond once alerted to the possibility that a crime is about to occur. The retailer is disheartened to learn the police will not respond to "suspicions," only to crimes in progress or after-the-fact reports of actual loss.

The police exacerbate this chagrin in the private sector with inconsiderate replies to these calls, failing to appreciate that the clerk calling (1) believes she is practicing the prevention techniques endorsed by the police, (2) may be fearful of the persons she is suspicious of, and (3) feels powerless once rejected by the police. If the subject she is suspicious of later takes out a gun and robs the store, she will no doubt tell the responding officers she thought he was up to no good all along. They will likely admonish her that she should have called them when she became suspicious. The mutual frustration between the cops who want to respond but cannot, and the clerk who is seething at the irony of this exchange, creates a loss of faith.

The retailer's expectations should be modified by the police, and police dispatchers cognizant of their inability to meet the demands of the caller should be trained to refine their responses:

Poor Response: *"What has he done? Well if he's not doing anything, what do you expect us to do? Oh, he might do something? Then call us back if he does."*

Constructive Response: *"I don't have a car I can send over right now. Tell me what he is doing. Is he alone? What does he look like? Is there a car outside with the engine running? Have you asked if he needs help? Why don't I stay on the phone while you ask him, then tell me what he says? Are you alone in the store? Is your manager there? Does the mall have security guards you can call for now?"*

This is not to suggest that police undergo specific sensitivity training designed exclusively for nervous sales clerks. Rather, somewhere in between these two responses lies a helpful reply that assures the caller without taxing the police resources. Retailers must convey to the police that regardless of how factually correct their response to such a call may be, it must be presented in a way that does not alienate store employees. Once the staff feels cut off from police support, the active involvement with which they would normally perform their LP role is diminished significantly.

Professionalism and tact is another area police need to exhibit when responding to a legitimate call at a retail establishment. Retailers do produce their share of what can only be termed "nuisance calls" by police. Yet to many store managers, the detention of a shoplifter while waiting for the police to arrive is a stressful situation. As generally law-abiding citizens, store personnel may have little or no other contact with the law enforcement community in their private lives, so the judgments they form about police often result from the exposure they get from observing police conduct at the store.

For officers to show their indifference and impatience over responding to a call to arrest a 13-year-old kid who tried to steal a pair of sneakers sends the wrong message. The store manager is naturally excited about catching a shoplifter, and has expectations that the police will actually congratulate him on preventing a crime. When the officers show up with a ho-hum attitude, and then proceed to debate the merits of the case in the presence of the shoplifter, hoping to dissuade the manager from pursuing prosecution because "he's a juvenile and nothing's going to happen to him anyway," is harmful to the merchant-police relationship. Worse, the cynicism which often pervades the ranks of police is passed along to lay people, dampening their enthusiasm and faith in the system.

Corporate representatives often have mixed reviews from encounters with police as well, especially when attempting to elicit cooperation in a joint investigation of substantial loss. When the "mysterious disappearance" of a deposit from the safe is reported to the home office, executives there have expectations that the police will aggressively pursue the investigation. Thousands of dollars are gone, the suspect pool is narrowed since few people know the combination and have the opportunity, the matter has been duly reported, and the police should have little problem getting the culprit to confess. After all, the police are professionals, the thief is an amateur; the cops should be able to interrogate, polygraph, and otherwise strong-arm their way to a successful arrest.

Once the matter is reported, the police assign the case to the detective division where it takes a number in the detective's caseload. The retailer, anticipating instant gratification, wants to know how quickly the police will solve the case, what's been done, who the leading suspects are. When will you begin interrogating the staff? Why don't you polygraph everybody? Do you plan to dust for fingerprints? These meddling questions irritate the police, as they have no plans to do anything different from what they normally do…get to it when they get to it.

Senior management, accustomed to issuing directives and seeing results, does not come away with a positive impression when the police seemingly "blow off" what is a priority to the company. Sometimes such treatment results in the company reevaluating the viability of business in this market earlier than they would have, where a positive, accommodating response by police could forestall a store closure.

With the investigation stalled, the company dispatches its loss prevention professional to the scene, mandating that he somehow "coordinate" the investigation with police. The LP investigator has expectations of his own, beginning with the police returning his phone calls. Suddenly, the investigating detectives are on the night shift, or in court, or off until Thursday. Appointments are broken, calls go unreturned, and the urgency of the case dissipates.

Leads that the investigator feels should be followed up on by the police grow cold.

Meanwhile, the retailer must decide if employees on suspension pending the outcome of the investigation should be brought back, or if key suspects want to resign because they are "no longer comfortable" working in the store under a cloud of suspicion. Perceiving a lack of interest by the police, the guilty employee becomes emboldened, accusing the company of unfair labor practices or discrimination in a "witch hunt."

In the event a major loss is reported and it becomes clear the police will be brought in, retailers need to express the expectations they have, and the police should explain what they realistically can do. The company should offer its LP resources to handle many of the time-consuming details that occupy much of the police time they could otherwise devote to the case. A game plan can be proposed that coordinates resources and shares the burden.

The company LP investigator will: (1) conduct preliminary interviews with employees involved, and submit written statements to the investigating officers, (2) order up a credit check report on involved employees (where possible) and submit findings, (3) provide verified information on name, address, date of birth, previous address, and social security number from employment records for police to initiate criminal checks, (4) schedule employees for police interviews, arranging for transportation as necessary, (5) review past instances of cash shortages; and audit employee-specific trans-action histories and POS exceptions for indications that may help narrow suspect pool, and (6) provide pager numbers to police to facilitate their communication with company representatives.

Given this kind of proactive assistance, the police should: (1) agree to run the criminal background checks and report the results to the LP inves-tigator in a timely manner, (2) pursue the leads developed by the LP inves-tigator's interviews quickly, before alibis and explanations can be solidified, and (3) conduct employee interviews on schedule, realizing the labor rela-tions implications of sustained suspension or restricted duty assignment.

For this type of case, and with the coordinated effort described above, the case should be satisfactorily concluded. Even absent an arrest, the inves-tigation will yield enough circumstantial evidence against a prime suspect to move against him on procedural grounds for termination. Once the matter is resolved, especially when the losses are recovered, the company should write letters of commendation to the investigating officers, copying the unit commander and chief of police.

In discussing the "rules of engagement" with police officials, the retailer should demonstrate that they are willing to provide training and equipment to their stores to assist employees in preventing crime. Point out how fre-quently situations are resolved in-house without police assistance, and that frivolous calls for police response is discouraged. Bring a letter from your alarm company which certifies the operational readiness of your alarm system. Explain your testing and maintenance procedures that have drastically reduced false alarm incidents, and discuss how your program strives to be self-sufficient.

When an incident indicative of shabby police response comes to your attention, designate a corporate executive (not the store manager; he has to live there) to make an inquiry with the police department. Don't be accusatory or judgmental: hear their side. Make no formal complaint over a trivial matter, agreeing instead to overlook a misunderstanding, and express confidence that it will be handled better next time.

Keep mall management abreast of security concerns, and open a dialog with other tenants. The local Chamber of Commerce has also been known to rattle a few cages in the upper echelon of city government when the business community becomes restless with city services.

A strong tenant association is a linchpin to improved police response. Through it, the retailer can avail itself of many programs for the businesses, offered free of charge from various law enforcement agencies. Police departments usually have a community affairs officer who visits merchant associations and provides tips on crime prevention and trends. Even if it is nothing more than a pep talk, you show you are involved, you get a name, make valuable contacts, and eventually, a little more attention.

State and federal agencies offer programs too. The Secret Service will come and talk about counterfeit money. The Postal Inspector will come and talk about mail fraud (helpful if organized refunders are using blind mail drops to receive your checks). A representative from the district attorney's office may address a prominent merchant's association, offering guidelines on rules of arrest and the elements of a successful prosecution. The Fire Marshal will come and talk about safety and emergency readiness. Commercial banks have also been known to contribute their expertise to retail tenant groups on credit card fraud and spotting bad checks.

Another consideration for interaction with law enforcement extends to the prosecutor's office and the courts. When retailers prosecute an individual, much of the outcome rides on precise communication between the complainant (the merchant) and their advocate in court (the district attorney/solicitor's office). Once a prosecution is initiated, and throughout the time the case is pending, the retailer must establish a communications link with the court to remain apprised of developments.

Subpoenas for court appearances, preparation for testimony, and provisions for the custody of evidence should be worked out with the prosecuting attorney. Sometimes cases drag on so long that employees with eyewitness testimony move on, damaging the case for the prosecution unless an affidavit of the witness's statement is secured. At other times plea bargain arrangements are entered into on the retailer's behalf without consultation. The terms of these arrangements, especially when the court will consider a disposition known as "adjourned in contemplation of dismissal," or ACD, is of particular concern.

This outcome in effect removes the conviction from the defendant's record after a prescribed period of time lapses, provided there are no further arrests and convictions for other crimes. Essentially, it is a second chance to keep one's nose clean, most prevalent among first offenders. A caveat to any such agreement should be entered into the court record citing the defendant's agreement to "hold harmless" the complainant from future liability exposure resulting from the ultimate dismissal of charges. To be unaware of these developments by virtue of poor communication with the courts results in the state looking out for the welfare of your business.

Stores should implement a control log which tracks pending criminal cases they have initiated. Monthly contact with the prosecutor's office will help update case status, and will permit you to return merchandise held as evidence to the selling floor in a timely manner. Should the store manager learn any criminal proceeding was dismissed due to "failure to appear" or "in the interests of justice," notification to corporate counsel should be immediate.

Positive interaction with law enforcement, i.e., getting the services you require to stay in business, is best attained with mutual cooperation and an understanding of the retailer's expectations and ability of the police to deliver. Many retailers engage in practices that reward police response to their concerns. These range from sizable donations to police charities to merchandise discounts offered to police officers. Some of these practices, as well-intentioned as they may be, can be perceived incorrectly and occasionally cross the line of departmental guidelines governing police ethics and integrity.

Before endorsing any such program which provides a tangible benefit to the police officers performing their duty, check with the commanding officer for authorization. A roast turkey on Thanksgiving Day, or a spread of cold cuts on Christmas Eve, sent to the station house compliments of the ABC Company in appreciation of all the support is far more appropriate than a free television set to a cop who nabs your burglar.

Also, some police jurisdictions permit (urgently recommend?) that the retailer hire off duty police for special event guard coverage or traffic control. This is a precarious arrangement that should be approved at senior levels of the company. Even where such an expense may be overkill, stores like to comply with such a request because it fosters good will and shows the merchant is willing to support the police. The store gets quality security for the event, the cop makes a few bucks on the side, and the police may be more likely to do the store a good turn in the future.

That is where the arrangement crosses the line. If the store is made to feel compelled to participate (*"everybody else hires us for warehouse sales, what's your problem?"*) or if there is a veiled inference that traffic may not move as smoothly without the police directing it, or in the worst case, the insinuation that perhaps future police response may not be as forthcoming, comes dangerously close to the organized protection rackets practiced by the mob. Senior company officials must report such conduct to the highest police level.

Oftentimes, the police officers request to be paid in cash for their off-duty work. This is reasonable and quite understandable. The police officer is not an employee and cannot be accommodated by timely payroll checks. He is an independent contractor, but one hardly in the position to invoice the company and wait the prescribed 60-plus days for payment. Reimbursement out of petty cash, especially for one-shot events, is commonplace among retailers. It is also illegal as the company will probably not generate a withholding form or report the wages earned on a 10-99. That the company aids and abets income tax evasion by a member of law enforcement is not a matter you want reported to the IRS by a disgruntled employee.

Crisis Management

As is the case with most major industries, retailers have on occasion experienced a cataclysmic event which can plunge an organization into crisis. Many of these tragedies are natural disasters, such as earthquakes or widespread flooding, which disrupt the business operation and result in substantial loss of inventory and earnings. Since these events are largely unpredictable, and the degree of control an organization has in the aftermath is often predicated by the relief efforts of government agencies, the private sector's response should be a measured strategy designed to recover the operation and minimize property loss.

Emergency planning procedures, which anticipate disasters and instruct field management on the protocols of managing an array of crises, had been sufficient for restoring normal operations from the disruptions of severe weather, smoke and fire, water flow, power failure, and to some degree, criminal activity such as bomb threats, burglary, and vandalism.

Most Operations Policy Manuals contain provisions for notifiying the home office via chain-of-command, and authorize limited contact with the appropriate agencies to address the immediate concerns. The resources of the organization were marshaled to provide support personnel, contingency funds, and inventory replenishment. Insurance claims were prepared and filed, earnings' forecasts were amended, and efforts prioritized for a return to business as usual.

Until our changing times dictated otherwise, these were adequate precautions and reasonable responses. Not that the kinds of crises to be discussed in this chapter were unheard of a two decades ago, for they did occur from time to time. But because the frequency with which they were manifested among the retail community was so rare, the industry was slow to embrace sophisticated crisis management strategies, and to develop the in-house resources to properly administer a crisis management plan.

Today, you could convene a roundtable discussion of retail loss prevention professionals who have weathered crisis situations that render the profferred direction in the Emergency Procedures of the Operations Manual woefully obsolete: the abduction of a customer, the shooting death of an employee in a robbery, arson attempts, terrorist bombings, extortion demands, product tampering, stalkings and assaults, full-scale riots, and co-worker rampages.

Although the parameters of the crises retailers could potentially encounter have broadened over the years, the principle tenets of restoring the operation and minimizing the loss still hold. It is the methodology employed to reach that end that retailers need to refine in order to best anticipate and survive a crisis situation.

To illustrate the inner-workings of a crisis management plan, we will examine three separate crises that could befall a medium-sized retailer, and devise a model plan to manage each one. Each crisis will be managed from the home office to the field, and the specific responsibilities of the key players in the corporate structure will be assigned.

In establishing a Crisis Management Team, a company must recognize that the duties of such a committee require the participation of persons with both the authority and expertise to operate in the best interests of the company. The authority should emanate from a senior officer of the corporation, empowered to make unilateral decisions with respect to company resources and policy. The expertise flows from a cross-section of department heads, capable of implementing the directives of the Team Leader.

Crisis Management Team

Duties:

- Confirm and evaluate the nature of the crisis; initiate management response.
- Coordinate all contacts with internal operating units and external agencies.
- Provide recommendations to the Decision Maker regarding strategy and disposition of departmental resources.
- Implement the policy directives of the Decision Maker.
- Prepare lists and make arrangements to involve outside consultants and services as directed.
- Allocate company personnel, facilities and services as necessary.

Team Membership:

- **Decision Maker (CEO/COO):** determines course of action to be taken by the Crisis Management Team.
- **Team Leader (V.P. Operations):** coordinates team's activities to implement the directives of the Decision Maker.
- **Finance:** allocates funds, tracks expense, revises earnings forecast.
- **Legal:** assesses potential for corporate liability resulting from the crisis event and the response options presented to the Decision Maker.
- **Human Resources:** sees to the welfare of employees and their families, liaison with health and benefits providers, provides relevant personnel and employment records for reference purposes.
- **Risk Management:** coordinates activities of loss prevention/security and inventory control to safeguard assets and initiate insurance claims.
- **Public Relations:** reviews published accounts, designates company spokesperson, prepares press releases, and evaluates information to be disseminated to employee population.

Crisis One

The Midwest Regional Manager receives a call at 1 a.m. from the District Manager that an after-hours robbery went bad at a suburban store. The assistant store manager and two clerks were forced back into the store as they were locking up. Two masked men kept them in the back room and had the manager open the safe. In the course of the robbery, the manager was shot and killed, one clerk was shot twice and is in critical condition, another clerk was unharmed. The gunmen left immediately.

Per procedure, the Regional Manager reaches the Crisis Management Team Leader. The Team Leader directs an update briefing from the District Manager at 2:30 a.m. at the Crisis Management Center, and dispatches the Regional Manager to the location (four hours away). He then activates the Crisis Management Team Plan for this contingency.

The Crisis Management Plan calls for the Team to assemble at the predesignated meeting facility. This facility is equipped with multiple phone lines (with caller ID where available), telephone recorders, pagers, copier, fax machine, TV, VCR, etc. By 2:30 a.m., the team members are in session and are awaiting the field update from the District Manager. Each member has a list of questions and instructions for the District Manager, pertaining to specific areas of concern.

Human Resources

Information Needed:

- Present status of family notifications
- Treatment facility and condition of wounded employee
- Identity of attending physician(s)

Preliminary Response:

- Brief and dispatch HR representative (Benefits Manager?) to the scene to coordinate family relief efforts
- Arrange counseling service for families and remaining staff

Loss Prevention/Security

Information Needed:

- Copy of Police Report
- Preliminary assessment by Police of crime (who, what, when, where, how, why)
- Statement of uninjured employee to Police
- Identity of investigating officer(s)

Preliminary Response:

- Brief and dispatch LP representative to the scene to liaison with Police and provide timely investigation updates
- Make contact with investigating officer
- Contact alarm company and initiate review of alarm reports
- Arrange for in-store guard service on standby basis

Finance

Information Needed:

- Amount of loss sustained

Preliminary Response:

- Allocate intermediate relief funds
- Forecast expense for medical care, funeral cost, investigation and outside services
- Determine negative impact to revenue for duration of suspended store operation
- Replenish safe fund
- Authorize reward posting if recommended by police

Operations

Information Needed:
- Determine level of compliance to closing procedures by closing staff
- Sequence of events leading to notification

Preliminary Response:
- Determine temporary options for re-staffing store
- Arrange cleaning crew on standby once crime scene is released
- Determine content of notification to employees not involved
- Arrange to suspend shipping schedule if necessary
- Arrange to contact mall management/landlord office

Legal

Information Needed:
- Employee files
- Copy of closing procedure
- Copy of instructions regarding robberies furnished to stores
- Documentation of employee training

Preliminary Response:
- Evaluate incident with respect to procedural direction and compliance to assess exposure for negligence in a wrongful death/wrongful injury action
- Determine the impact that enacting after-the-fact security measures or procedural revisions could have on potential litigation
- Determine appropriateness of third party conduct, i.e., police, emergency service, alarm company

Public Relations

Information Needed:
- Media inquiries/reports to date

Preliminary Response:
- Draft press release
- Appoint spokesperson
- Determine content of posted notice/communication to customers during period of suspended operation

The preliminary responses prepared by the members are designed to facilitate and expand the options presented to the decision maker. The decision maker may believe it to be in the best interests of the company to revive the operation at this location without delay. Hence, contingencies to clean up the aftermath, re-staff the store, replenish the safe, and open for business need to be underway. On the other hand, the decision maker may feel it is more beneficial to the operation in the long run to shut down, mourn the company losses, and focus the company's energies on capturing the perpetrators and supporting the employee families. Therefore, support personnel must be at the ready to assist in investigation, dependent care and counseling. Pre-planning by the crisis management team permits the decision maker latitude in the company's response.

Crisis Two

In an urban location, tensions between residents and the city have become strained following the aggressive break-up of a demonstration by police. Community leaders oppose the shutdown of a hospital the city has targeted for consolidation into another facility in a cost-cutting measure.

Residents complain the alternate facility is too far away and lacks the resources to provide adequate care. They further contend the loss of jobs and services is detrimental to the local economy, and criticize the move as evidence of institutionalized discrimination against the poor.

The turnout for a Saturday rally was greater than expected and the streets around the hospital became impassable. The police attempted to clear a lane for ambulance traffic, but the situation deteriorated when protesters thwarted their efforts. Reinforcements were called in, many arrests made, and a small contingent of demonstrators vandalized dozens of cars in the hospital parking lot before order was restored.

Community leaders blamed belligerent police tactics for the outbreak, and vowed to rally supporters to commit civil disobedience by immobilizing major traffic arteries in the community during the Monday evening rush hour. The event has become a lightning rod of media attention and public debate.

Following the Saturday disturbance, the store manager of a location close to the hospital has informed his District Manager of the incident. The store manager confides her employees were unsettled, many having family and friends among the demonstrators, and that the "word on the street" is Monday could be a tumultuous event. The district manager, aware that two other stores operate on the fringes of the possible cites for demonstration, informs the regional manager of the potential for civil unrest, and the regional manager places a call to the crisis management team leader.

Noting that this is a situation which calls for planning more than reaction, the Team Leader can conference call with select members of the Crisis Management Team, in effect a "yellow alert," and later update the Decision Maker with both the crisis scenario and the remedial plans. At 8 p.m., the conference call is underway, and the following precautionary steps are decided:

1. District Manager will attend an impromptu meeting of the merchant's association Sunday at 10 a.m. with police representatives. Solicit police recommendations based on their intelligence assessment. Identify the police contact person for information and/or hotline number for status updates through Monday. Report minutes of meeting with police in Sunday conference call, 1 p.m.
2. Operations will plan usual staffing coverages for Monday. Adjust shipping schedule if needed.
3. LP/Security will arrange guard coverage for uniformed presence (2) at "ground zero" location, and one officer in each of the two fringe stores, from noon Monday through close. Plan for armored car service to handle deposits through Wednesday.
4. Store Planning/Construction will arrange for laborers to deliver adequate plywood and materiel for boarding windows to all three locations by noon Monday. Install "burglar bar" hardware on fire exit door from back office to street. Determine necessity for supplementing stockroom door lockset with heavy duty deadbolt, and reinforcing stockroom door with wood panel.

The Team Leader then apprises the Decision Maker of the precautions taken, and agrees to update the Decision Maker after the Sunday 1 p.m. conference call. Overnight and mid-morning press coverage on the planned event has been considerable, with both sides resigned to a Monday showdown. The District Manager has been assured at the merchant's association meeting that adequate police will be in place to protect property, and the police urge storekeepers to take prudent precautions, but a shutdown of operations is unnecessary. The police have promised intelligence reports to the merchant's association, and will provide updates through a hotline number of any new developments.

The District Manager further reports that "the word on the street" as communicated by store employees predicts strong consequences if the mayor does not relent, and some workers have expressed concern about reporting to work for Monday's afternoon and closing shifts. The District Manager is unsure whether employees are frightened, or merely wish to participate in the event.

The Crisis Management Team agrees to a shutdown contingency in the event the situation Monday deteriorates to the point where employee safety is jeopardized. The intent will be to secure the building in an orderly fashion, yet ensure personnel have ample opportunity to depart the premises with transportation options.

LP/Security will arrange for overnight guard coverage in this eventuality, with a K-9 patrol team replacing one of the two guards scheduled for the primary location. The secondary locations will plan one guard overnight. In each case where the building is to be manned by an outside guard service, the perimeter alarm will be set with the interior motion disarmed, effectively ensuring the guard does not leave or admit unauthorized personnel. The guard company will make available response teams to report to the stores in the event of a break-in.

All store management personnel will be scheduled Monday to backfill staff personnel who may not show. Store managers will secure essential equipment and valued inventory in the reinforced stockrooms prior to departing. Emergency equipment at the stores is to be inventoried, and extra fire extinguishers, flash lights, and cellular phones will be delivered Monday as needed. Signs stating "closed for inventory" will be posted before departure. All interior lights are to be left on. Maintenance personnel and/or outside contractors will operate on standby alert.

The team leader has designated the evacuation plan as "Option B" and in lieu of new information from the police, has designated 2 p.m. Monday as the "H-Hour" for the Decision Maker to begin monitoring the situation for making the call when, and if, to go to Option B. In the event Option B is initiated, the evacuation plan calls for the employees being permitted to leave via their preferred route: making their own way home, or riding in a rented van that will take them to one of the two secondary locations that will be designated as a field communications center. Subsequent arrangements to see them safely home will be made from that location. The team leader has directed a briefing on the status of all plan contingencies be presented to the full crisis management team on Monday at 11 a.m. He then informs the decision maker of the enhanced response positions agreed to in the Sunday conference call.

What the crisis management plan for incidents of civil unrest demonstrates is that effective strategies can be initiated in anticipation of the event, without disruption to the business. Between the "first alert" Saturday evening, and the 1 p.m. conference call Sunday, a preliminary plan has been mapped out, then refined as the situation developed. Department heads have a full day (albeit a weekend day) prior to H-hour to effect the deployment of resources. The decision maker's role has been reduced to merely "calling the shot" due to the management skill of the team leader.

Crisis Three

> The Regional Manager for a medium-sized supermarket chain has received a call from one of his store managers who recounts receiving a letter in the morning mail. The letter is from an unidentified person who claims to be in possession of several cans of baby formula into which he has introduced cyanide poisoning. Unless $100,000 is paid, he will place the contaminated product on store shelves at undisclosed locations. The Regional Manager informs the Crisis Team Leader.

The Team Leader consults the Crisis Management Plan for this contingency. The Plan instructs the Team Leader to initiate a policy of information containment, to ensure persons with knowledge of the event do not disseminate it to third parties. This is essential for management to be afforded the opportunity to assess the threat. Otherwise, leaks and speculation will eventually reach a media outlet, and the company will forfeit some measure of control should they be compelled to issue a formal statement in response to an ill-timed inquiry from a news agency.

His second priority is to preserve the letter for evidence, and obtain a copy of it for use in threat assessment. The store manager should be instructed to place the letter and envelope in plastic bags and seal them. A handwritten copy of the letter, a verbatim transcript, should be made and faxed to the home office. Any distinguishing characteristics about the handwriting, stationery, postmark, etc., should be noted.

The Team should be convened without delay, and a senior LP/Security representative dispatched to the target location immediately to coordinate the strategic plans of the Decision Maker with the Regional Operations Manager. The Team's focus should next turn to threat assessment: an analysis of the facts at hand to determine whether this is a hoax which should be ignored, or a legitimate product extortion case that could degenerate into an episode of malicious product tampering.

Specialized consultants that offer profiles, handwriting analysis, specimen collection and testing, contacts with law enforcement and public health agencies, payment negotiation, and strategies for a positive perception in the media should be identified in The Plan for this emergency. The DM should opt for professional expertise in the assessment of this threat, while marshaling his committee to prepare for the exigency of premature divulgence in the media.

In analyzing the demand, the policy makers should be attuned to the level of professionalism demonstrated by the extortionist. Does his communication suggest an intimate knowledge of your operation? If so, this could indicate sophisticated reconnaissance, or it could be the work of a disgruntled employee. Is the targeted product susceptible to tampering by the means described? If so, the assessment has to be elevated. Has he threatened to notify the media himself to punish the company in the event demands are not met on a timely basis? If so, the element of coercion is added to the extortion, perhaps signaling your adversary will employ intimidating tactics to neutralize your defense, which is the mark of a pro. How has he approached the subjects of future communication and payment arrangements? A carefully thought out scenario where subsequent contacts afford no hope of detection, and the circumstances for payment delivery offer little chance of capture, illustrate the extortionist is resourceful beyond the logistics of just the tampering procedure. Professionals skilled in threat assessment will evaluate these factors and render an informed judgment as to which options work in the company's best interests.

In most cases, companies that keep a level head in the early stages following notification survive product extortion attempts with little impact on the operation. Discreet advisories to trusted contacts in the law enforcement community, and perhaps to the product manufacturer, are sufficient first steps in cases where no evidence of tampering can be connected to the extortion demand.

Should future communication with the extortioner result in the discovery of tampered product, and a clear danger to the public exists, then the response is modified accordingly. Considerations for product recall must be initiated with the product manufacturer. A disclosure to the media in conjunction with health department alerts to advise the public is warranted, and involvement in some sort of payment delivery orchestrated with the police would likely follow. Each of these contingencies has significant ramifications on the company's image, earnings, and stock performance. The company must be perceived as acting in good faith to protect the public, yet manage the crisis in such a way that resolution can be anticipated and confidence restored.

The three crises we have examined all demonstrate the value of a company having prepared for emergencies by designing specific response plans and having a communications network that affords management early warning to implement the strategic plans effectively. Designated executives responsible to perform specified roles facilitate the company's control of a situation, and enhance the prospects for a successful conclusion to the urgent problems that may arise.

Index

A

Accident investigations, 163
Accomplices, 230–231
Admonishments, 242–243, 246
Alarm systems, 27–47
  advantages and disadvantages, 176–180
  after-hour activity, 27–28
  alarm panel and keypad, 44
  alarm reports, 29–39
    arming and disarming of system,
      37–38
    CNF, 35
    event detail by store, 32–33
    incidents by region, 35–36
    inventory shortage investigations, 145
    next-day reporting, 29–30
    open and close reports, 36–37
    recap report, 31–32
    value of, 30
    work orders, 34–35
  buying vs. leasing equipment, 45
  cellular telephones, 44
  closed circuit television integrated systems,
    70–72
  contract issues, 45–46
  conversion programs, 41–47
  electronic access controls and, 15–16
  emergency exits, 18–19
  expenses, 41, 42–43
  field work orders, 40–41
  generic vs. customized, 27–28
  glass break detectors, 44
  hold-up button, 176–179
  for lock boxes and cables, 22–26
  magnetic contacts, 44
  motion detectors, 43–44
  opening and closing schedule, 46–47
  passcode authorization, 16–17, 38–39, 46
  selecting provider, 28–29
  service and maintenance agreements, 39
  telephone line resources, 44
  temperature variance detectors, 44
  testing, 40
  unscheduled entry, 47
Americans with Disability Act, 19
Application process, 119–120, 182, 211–212
Apprehension, 223–232
  for accomplices, 230–231
  by-passing opportunity to pay, 225
  concealment, 225
  defeating protective devices, 225
  intent, 224–226
  of juveniles, 230
  leaving premises, 225
  making approach, 226–229
  obfuscating ownership of merchandise,
    225
  police response, 250–251
  policies, 229–230
  reasonable requests, 231
  recovered contraband, 232
  terminology, 223
Armed guards, 81–82
Armed robberies, *see* Robberies
Armored cars, 190
Assault, 166
Audit programs, 97–106
  cash control, 98–100
  elements, 98
  goals, 98
  inventory shortage, 103–106
  merchandise standards, 102–103
  physical security, 98
  point of service exceptions, 101–102
  procedural reviews, 100–101
  procedures and policy implementation,
    97–98
  response to employee dishonesty, 125–126
  role, 85–86
  sales, 129–139
    discount activity, 134–135
    exception reports, 129–131
    in investigation, 144–146
    no sales, 135–136
    petty cash and paid-outs, 138

price look-ups, 136–137
refund transactions, 133–134
summary reports, 139
underground currency, 137–138
voided transactions, 131–133
Award programs, 83, 90–94, 126

B

Bank deposits
    deposit slips, 99
    liability issues, 182
    risks in, 181–182
    in security, 181
    timing, 182–185
Bouncing checks, 196–199
Burglaries, *see* Robberies

C

Cabinet locks, 5
Cabinets, 10–11, 20
Cables, for retail merchandise, 20–26
Cameras, *see* Closed circuit television
Card access systems, *see* Electronic
        access controls
Cars, 182
Cash control procedures, 98–100
Cash handling procedures, 180–186
    bank deposits, 181–185
    cash drops, 181
    cash on hand, 180
    checks and balances, 185–186
Cellular telephones, 44
Chamber of Commerce, 253
Change fund, 99
Check bouncing, 196–199
Civil demand, 201–204
Civil liability, 163–171
    employee investigations, 169–171
    employee vehicles, 182
    force and search and seizure, 168–170
    for*see*ability, 164–165
    incident reports, 169
    intentional torts, 166–167
    negligence, 164–165
    procedural enhancement, 164
    proximate cause, 165–166
    standard of reasonableness, 167–168
    surveillance and entrapment, 170–171
Civil recovery, 201–204
Civil unrest, 262–265
Closed circuit television, 63–74
    advantages and disadvantages, 174–176
    benefits, 64–65

cameras, 65–66, 67, 68, 69
elements of effective, 65
in employee surveillance, 63–64
equipment, 71
integrated systems, 66–72
legislative and privacy issues, 73–74,
        170–171
management issues, 72–73
programmable VCR, 71
in shoplifting prevention, 65–67
time lapse, 68–69
Closing schedule, alarm systems, 36–37,
        46–47
Clothing, lock boxes and cables, 20–26
Computers, electronic access controls and,
        17
Confidentiality in reward programs, 92, 93
Consultants, 215
Contraband recovery, 232
Contract issues
    alarm systems, 45–46
    guard force, 76–79
Controllers, role, 85–86
Corporate culture, in loss prevention,
        94–95
Coupons, 99–100, 134–135
Courts, 253–254, *see also* Prosecution
Crash-bars, 18–19
Credit cards, 199
Criminal trespass, 241–246
Crisis management, 257–266
    armed robbery, 259–262
    crisis management team, 258–259
    decision maker, 262, 263, 264, 265
    finance, 260
    human resources, 260
    legal issues, 261
    loss prevention/security, 260
    operations, 261
    poisoning of merchandise, 265–266
    policies, 257–258
    public relations, 261
    riot, 262–265
Criticism, 210

D

Daily sweep, 185–186
Deadbolts, 6, 9
Defamation, 166
Deposit slips, 99
Disabled persons, 19
Discount activity, 99–100, 134–135
Distribution center, 82, 103–106
Divorce, 123

Domestic problems, 211, 213
Downsizing, 207–210, 213
Drop safe, 178–179
Drug testing, 120, 212

E

Egress, electronic access controls and, 17–19
Electromechanical locks, 5
Electronic access control system, 15–19
    authorization for entry, 16–17, 38–39, 46
    egress, 17–18
    emergency exit, 17–19
    financial issues, 19
    integration with closed circuit television, 67–69
    vs. lobby guards, 15
    schedule of protection, 15–16
Electronic article surveillance (EAS), 49–61
    effectiveness, 55
    employee rewards, 90–91
    entranceway detector pedestal, 53, 54, 55
    false alarms, 52–55
    integration with closed circuit television, 66–67
    legal issues, 51–52
    maintenance, 59–60
    personnel issues, 54–56, 58–59
    in shoplifting prevention, 49–50, 57–58
    tagging innovations, 56–61
    technology, 50–51
Emergency exits
    crash-bars, 18–19
    electronic access controls and, 17–19
Employee authorization, electronic access controls, 16–17, 38–39, 46
Employee award programs
    awards, 126
    for guard force, 83
    for loss prevention, 90–94
        psychological issues, 91–92
Employee Polygraph Protection Act of 1988, 160–162
Employees
    audit of procedures, 100–101
    awareness programs, 87–95
        awards, 90–94
        corporate culture in loss prevention, 94–95
        employee theft, 89
        external theft, 89–90
        inventory control, 88–89
        risk management, 89
        trainees, 87–88
    dishonesty, 117–128
        background check, 119–120

    employee accountability, 120–121
    employer awareness of, 117–118
    monitoring employee finances, 121–124
    need and opportunity, 121
    perception of risk, 124–128
    response to, 124–128
    standard of integrity, 118–119
    electronic article surveillance, 55–56, 58–59
    interaction with guards, 80–81
    investigation and interview
        audit in, 145–146
        background research, 144–145
        dynamic of interview process, 147–150
        evidentiary statement, 150, 152–155
        goals, 143–144
        informational statement, 150, 159–160
        leads, 144
        legal issues, 169–170
        polygraph tests, 160–162
        preliminary, 145–146
        procedural violation statement, 150, 155–159
        restitution, 155
        setting environment, 146–147
        tactics for prolonged investigation, 146
        written statements, 150–152, 170
    safety and robberies, 173–191
    shoplifting prevention and, 109–115
    staffing and gender issues, 189–190
    vehicles, 182
    violence in the workplace
        domestic problems and, 211
        hiring practices, 212
        job developments and, 207–211
        predicting, 207–212
        psychological issues, 206–210
        risks to employees, 206–207
        security industry profile, 213
        terminating employee, 212
        threats, 213–214
Employee surveillance, 63–64, 67–70, 72–74
Entrapment, 170–171
Envy, in employee awards for loss prevention, 91–92
Evidentiary statement, 150, 152–155
Exception reports, *see* Point of service (POS) exceptions
Exit interview, 212
Extortion, 265–266

F

False arrest, 166
Family problems, 211, 213
Federal agencies, 253

Financial issues
 alarm systems, 41, 42–43
 crisis management, 259, 260
 daily sweep in checks and balances,
      185–186
 electronic access controls vs. lobby guards,
      19
 guard force, 76–78
 monitoring employee situation, 119–124
 prosecution decisions, 235, 237
 violence in the workplace, 205
Fire alarm systems, 17–19
Firearms policy, 213
Fire departments, locking mechanisms and,
      8
Fixtures, 1–2
Force, legal issues, 168–169
Forseeability, 164
401K plan, 123
Frauds, 193–199

G

Gender issues, 189–190
General Business Law, 167–168
Gift certificates, 99–100
Glass break detectors, 44
Guard force, *see* Security personnel
Gun policy, 213

H

Higher duty standards, 165–166
Hiring practices, 119–120, 182, 211–212
Hostility, 210
Human resources
 crisis management, 259
 investigations, 163
 monitoring employee finances, 122–124

I

Incident reports, 217–221
 criminal trespass, 243, 245
 database, 220
 design of, 217–218
 inventory shortage, 218–219
 legal issues, 169
 litigation, 219–220
 in loss prevention policy, 219
 POS system interface, 220–221
 theft, 218–219
Informational statement, 150, 159–160
Intent in apprehension, 224–226
Intentional torts, 166–167

Interior keyway, 6–10
Interior motion detectors, 33–34, 43–44
Internal Revenue Service, 92
Interviews, *see* Investigation and interview
Invasion of privacy, 167
Inventory
 audit, 103–106
 employee awareness programs, 88–89
 incident reports, 218–219
 investigation, 144–145
Investigation and interview, 143–162
 abuses, 169–170
 audit in, 145–146
 background research, 144–145
 dynamic of interview process, 147–150
 evidentiary statement, 150, 152–155
 goals, 143–144
 human resource investigations, 163
 informational statement, 150, 159–160
 leads, 144
 legal issues, 169–170
 polygraph tests, 160–162
 preliminary, 145–146
 procedural violation statement, 150,
      155–159
 restitution, 155
 safety programs, 163
 setting environment, 146–147
 tactics for prolonged investigation, 146
 written statements, 150–152, 170
Invoice, 104–105
IRS, 92

J

Jewelry
 locked showcases, 20
 scams, 195–196
Job description, 182
Juveniles
 apprehension, 230
 prosecution, 234–235

K

Key rec, 104–105
Keys, *see* Locking hardware

L

Larceny, 223, *see also* Robberies
Law enforcement
 apprehension and, 229, 231–232
 closed circuit television in investigations, 174
 criminal trespass, 243–245

hiring off-duty police, 254–255
incident reports, 217–218
prosecuters and courts, 253–254
prosecution criteria and, 238
relationship with police, 247–255
in robbery prevention, 190
state and federal agencies, 253
Layoffs, 207–210, 213
Leasing equipment for alarm systems, 45
Legal issues
    alarm systems, 45–46
    apprehension criteria, 223–232
    civil liability, 163–171
    civil recovery and civil demand, 201–204
    closed circuit television, 73–74
    criminal trespass, 241–246
    crisis management, 259, 261
    incident reports, 219–220
    polygraphs, 160–162
    prosecution criteria, 233–239
    written statements, 150–160, 170
Liability, 163–171, *see also* Civil liability
Lie detector test, 160–162
Loan applications, 122
Lobby guards, *see* Security personnel
Location withdrawal, 185–186
Lock boxes, for retail merchandise, 20–26
Locking hardware, 1, 3–26
    electronic access controls, 15–19
        authorization for entry, 16–17, 38–39,
            46
        egress, 17–18
        emergency exit, 17–19
        financial issues, 19
        vs. lobby guards, 15
        schedule of protection, 15–16
    keying scheme, 10–15
    lost keys, 6, 13
    mechanisms, 3–10
        alarm systems and, 6
        cores and cylinders, 4, 5–6, 9, 11–14
        deadbolts, 6, 9
        interior locksets, 10
        for multiple users, 4–5
        padlock repair and parts, 6, 8
        quality, 10
        for showcases, 20–21
        thumb-turn or keyway, 6–10
    point of sale stations, 173–174
    retail merchandise, 19–26
        lock boxes and cables, 20–26
        showcases, 20
    in robbery prevention, 190
Loss prevention programs
    audit programs, 97–106
    benefits, 86
    crisis management, 259, 260, 264
    employee awareness, 87–95
    employee dishonesty, 117–128
    integrating, 85–86
    sales audit, 129–139
    shoplifting, 107–115

M

Magnetic contacts, 44
Mail order businesses, 199
Malicious prosecution, 166
Malls
    bank deposits, 184
    law enforcement relationship, 253
Management information systems (MIS),
        POS exceptions, 129–131
Management issues
    closed circuit television, 72–74
    in employee awareness, 94–95
    guard force, 75–83
Manifest, 104–105
Master-key system, 4, 10–15
Medical issues, 123
Medication, 231
Merchant Statute, 167–168
Mission Statement, 118–119
Mortise locksets, 4
Motion detectors, 33–34, 43–44
Music business, tagging, 60

N

Negligence, 164–166
911 emergency system, 177
No sales, 135–136
NSF checks, 196–198

O

Opening schedule, alarm systems, 36–37,
        46–47
Operations, 261
Over and short log, 99

P

Packing slip, 104–105
Padlocks, 4
Panic exit devices, 5
Paranoia, 210
Passcode authorization, for alarm systems,
        16–17, 38–39, 46
Payroll management, alarm reports in, 36–27

Personal Safety Training, 189
Personnel, *see* Employee entries
Petty cash, audit, 99
Petty cash and paid-outs, 138
Physical security
  alarm systems, 27–47
    advantages and disadvantages, 176–180
    alarm reports, 29–38
    authorized passcodes, 16–17, 38–39, 46
    conversion program, 41–47
    field work orders, 40
    internal vs. industry expert, 27–28
    selecting provider, 28–29
    service and maintenance contracts,
      39–40
    testing, 40
  audit, 98
  closed circuit television, 63–74, 174–176
  defeating devices in apprehension, 225
  discipline and maintenance in, 2
  electronic article surveillance, 49–61
  guard force management, 75–83
  locking hardware, 3–26
    electronic access controls, 15–17
    emergency exits, 17–19
    keying scheme, 10–15
    mechanisms, 3–10
    retail merchandise, 19–26
  needs of business in, 1–2
  point of sale stations, 173–174
  retailers, 1–2
  task-related measures, 2
Point of service (POS) exceptions, 129–139
  discount activity, 134–135
  exception reports, 101–102, 126–127,
    129–131
  no sales, 135–136
  petty cash and paid-outs, 138
  price look-ups, 136–137
  refund transactions, 133–134
  summary reports, 139
  underground currency, 137–138
  voided transactions, 131–133
Point of service (POS) stations
  closed circuit television integrated systems,
    70–72
  incident report interface, 220–221
  physical security, 173–174
Police, *see* Law enforcement
Policies, legal issues, 167
Postal Inspector, 253
Price look-ups, 136–137
Privacy
  closed circuit television, 73–74
  legal issues, 167

Probationary periods, 120
Procedural violation statement, 150, 155–159
Productivity, of guard force, 82–83
Prosecution, 233–239
  best interests of company, 236–237
  case dismissals, 239
  courts and prosecutor's office, 253–254
  deterrent effect, 233–235
  employee dishonesty, 127–128
  financial issues, 235, 237
  police recovery of stolen merchandise, 238
  winnable cases, 235–236
Proximate cause, 165–166
Psychological issues
  in employee awards for loss prevention,
    91–92
  interviews, 147–149
  violence in the workplace, 206–210, 213
Psychological testing, 120
Public relations, 259, 261
Purchase journal, 104–105, 126
Purchase order, 104–105

R

Reasonableness, standard of, 167–168
Reasonable standards, 164
Receiver, 104–105
Receiving, *see* Shipping/receiving
Receptionists, 16
Refunds, 126–127
Refund transactions, 133–134
Register, *see* Point of service (POS) stations
Restitution, 155, 201–203
Retirement fund, 123
Reward programs, 83, 90–94, 126
Rim locks, 5
Risk management, 89, 259
Risk perception, 125–128
Robberies, 173–191
  alarm systems, 27–28, 176–180
  armed guards, 81–82
  armored car program, 190
  cash handling procedures, 180–186
    bank deposits, 181–185
    cash drops, 181
    cash on hand, 180
    checks and balances, 185–186
  closed circuit television, 174–176
  crisis management, 259–262
  employee awareness programs, 89–90
  incident reports, 218–219
  inside information, 179–180
  locking mechanisms and, 8, 10
  physical security, 173–180

police contact, 187–189, 190
POS station, 173–174
signage, 190, 191
"sleep-ins," 27–28
staffing, 189–190
terminology, 223
training issues, 186–189

S

Safety issues
employees and robberies, 173–191
liability, 163–166
Sales audits, 129–139
closed circuit television integrated system, 70
discount activity, 134–135
exception reports, 129–131
no sales, 135–136
petty cash and paid-outs, 138
price look-ups, 136–137
refund transactions, 133–134
summary reports, 139
underground currency, 137–138
voided transactions, 131–133
Scams, 193–199
Screening of employees, 119–120, 182, 211–212
Search and seizure of property, 168–170
Security consultants, 215
Security operations
apprehension criteria, 223–232
criminal trespass, 241–246
crisis management, 257–266, 259, 260, 264
incident reports, 217–221
law enforcement interaction, 247–255
legal issues, 164–166
procedural development, 215
prosecution criteria, 233–239
Security personnel
armed vs. unarmed, 81–82
vs. electronic access controls, 15
electronic article surveillance, 54, 56
financial issues, 19
legal issues, 171
management, 75–83
in robbery prevention, 186, 190
Self-service environment, 1–2
Service and maintenance agreements, for alarm systems, 39
Shipping/receiving
audit of procedures, 101
closed circuit television, 70
employee dishonesty, 124–126

Shoplifting
apprehension criteria, 223–232
civil recovery and civil demand, 201–204
closed circuit television in prevention, 65–67
criminal trespass, 243–246
electronic article surveillance, 49–50, 57–58
employee awareness programs, 89–90
employee interdiction, 113–115
guard force in prevention, 76
lock boxes and cables, 20–26
locked showcases, 20
opportunists vs. professionals, 107–115
self-service and, 19
Short-change scams, 193–195
Showcases
advantages and disadvantages, 20
keying schedule, 10–11
Signage, in robbery prevention, 190, 191
Sleight-of-hand con, 195–196
Staffing, gender issues, 189–190
Stalking, 213
Standard of reasonableness, 167–168
State agencies, 253
Stockrooms, audit, 103
Summary reports, 139
Surveillance, *see* Closed circuit television; Electronic article surveillance

T

Tagging, *see also* Electronic article surveillance
ink tag, 56, 60
innovations, 56, 59
magnetic, 57, 58
in music industry, 60
source, 60–61
Telephone lines, alarm systems and, 44
Television, *see* Closed circuit television
Temperature variance detectors, 44
Tennant associations, 253
Termination, 212
Theft, *see* Investigation and interview; Robberies; Shoplifting
Thumb-turn knob, 6–10
Till-tappers, 174
Tortious infliction of emotional distress, 167
Tortious interference with employment, 167
Torts, 166–167
Trainees, loss prevention awareness, 87–88
Training
in alarm system, 39
in electronic article surveillance, 55
employee theft, 89

external theft, 89–90
of guards, 81
inventory control, 88–89
in police contact, 187–189
risk management, 89
in robbery prevention, 186–191
safety, 164
shoplifting prevention, 115
Trespass, criminal, 241–246
Tubular locks, 5
Turnstile justice, 234

U

Undercover operatives, legal issues, 171
Underground currency, 137–138
Unemployment, 122–123
Unscheduled entry, alarm systems, 47

V

VCRs
advantages and disadvantages, 174–176
in closed circuit television, 71, 73

electronic access controls and, 17
Vehicles, 182
Victimization, 206
Violence in the workplace, 205–214
domestic problems and, 211
financial issues, 205
hiring practices, 212
job developments and, 207–211
physical security, 213
predicting, 207–212
psychological issues, 206–210
risks to employees, 206–207
security industry profile, 213
terminating employee, 212
threats, 213–214
Voided transactions, 131–133

W

Warehouse/distribution center
audit, 103–106
guard force, 82
Women, staffing issues, 189–190
Written statements, 150–160, 170